KT-364-241

The Best of
Plays and Players

1953 - 1968

Edited by
PETER ROBERTS

with photographs
from the archives of
ZOË DOMINIC

Methuen · London

BATH COLLEGE
OF
HIGHER EDUCATION
NE͟WTON PARK
LIBRARY

CLASS
No. 792·0942° Ro͟b͟

ACC
No. 0010 8879

A Methuen Dramabook

First published simultaneously in hardback and
paperback in Great Britain in 1988
by Methuen London Ltd
11 New Fetter Lane, London EC4P 4EE
and in the United States of America
by Methuen Inc 29 West 35th Street,
New York, NY 10001.
Copyright © 1987 Peter Roberts

Printed in Great Britain
by Richard Clay Ltd,
Bungay, Suffolk

British Library Cataloguing in Publication Data

The Best of plays and players. – (A Methuen
    dramabook).
    1953–1968
    1. Theatre – Great Britain – History –
    20th century
    I. Roberts, Peter
    792'.0941   PN2595

    ISBN 0-413-52960-6
    ISBN 0-413-52970-3 Pbk

CAUTION
This book is sold subject to the condition
that it shall not, by way of trade or otherwise,
be lent, resold, hired out, or otherwise circulated
without the publisher's prior consent in any form
of binding or cover other than that in which
it is published and without a similar condition
including this condition being imposed
on the subsequent purchaser.

Contents

Preface

Plays and Players, which made its first appearance in October 1953, was the brainchild of its publisher, Philip Dossë. He had started his own company – Hansom Books – to publish a series of seven monthly magazines on the arts; the first was *Dance and Dancers* which came into being in January 1950. Before that Philip Dossë had been working on a greyhound newspaper and it was always said of him that he began his arts empire with the ballet magazine because he had fallen in love with a dancer whose identity however remained a mystery.

Like Lilian Baylis, founder of the Old Vic Company, Philip Dossë was a cheeseparing eccentric with nothing to invest in his enterprise except a great deal of manic energy. That made him a difficult man to work for and an unlikely patron of the arts. Yet his magazines did undoubtedly make a valuable contribution to postwar British cultural life in the 30 years that he published them. The roll-call of his titles reads, in alphabetical order, *Art and Artists*, *Books and Bookmen*, *Dance and Dancers*, *Films and Filming*, *Music and Musicians*, *Plays and Players* and *Records and Recording*. Yet, in the 12 or so years that I worked for him in various short-lease basement premises in the Victoria area of London, I do not ever remember his saying that he had been to a theatre, cinema or concert or that he had read a book or listened to a recording.

What was there in it for him? Since he was unwilling to delegate – he would often even operate the company switchboard himself – he had neither the time nor the energy to enjoy the arts to which his magazines were devoted. He certainly did not do it for money. He could never afford to go on holiday, wore second-hand clothes, drove a very modest car, mostly used to distribute magazines, and lived in a council flat with his mother who was co-director of his publishing company without ever making an appearance in the office.

Outside his own subterranean business premises he was rather a shy man and did not therefore take advantage of the entrée to the arts cocktail circuit to which his position as an arts publisher entitled him. Undoubtedly his magazines gave his bachelor life a sense of busy purpose as well as some insight into the politics and the working of cultural life in the Britain of the period, if not to direct enjoyment of it. His journals also gave him some power. Although the salaries he paid his editors were as atrocious as their working conditions, getting out his magazines each month was an exciting and challenging occupation as well as one that could be a stepping-stone to better things. This meant he could indulge in playing one editor off against another, and in this hothouse atmosphere of intrigue and occasional backstabbing his staff all learned to dread the handwritten notes scribbled on scrap-paper demanding their presence in his office.

Apart from being journalistic jacks-of-all-trades – critic, gossip writer, sub-editor, proof reader, messenger and layout artist – Philip Dossë's editors had to deploy considerable skills in ensuring that their contributors were eventually paid their nominal fees. In this, timing was a matter of the utmost importance and it was helpful to take careful account of grapevine indications of the mood of the moment. The writers most unlikely to get paid were those from overseas who were least able to press their claims on the phone. Sometimes these hardworking commentators from far off would choose to holiday in London thinking to float their break on the accumulated Hansom Book fees only to receive on their apearance the smallest payment-on-account to get rid of them. After a few years as assistant editor and editor of *Plays and Players*, I learned to open London bank accounts for some of them and invent unexpected appearances so that their fees could never amount to such proportions that settlement would be a permanent impossibility.

After thirty years of penny-pinching endeavour the harsh economics of totally unsubsidized magazine publishing caught up with Philip Dossë in the summer of 1980 in the form of a personal overdraft so extended he could stretch it no further to pay either his editors and their contributors or his printers. He carried out a carefully planned suicide in the flat where his mother had recently predeceased him. The magazines he had built up over so many years of hard grind did not reappear until the autumn of 1982 when they were acquired by Brevet, a subsidiary of the Croydon (UK) Printing Company who printed them.

Before concentrating on *Plays and Players*, meanwhile thanking the various contributors for permission to reproduce their articles here, it would be appropriate to list the editors of the magazine in the thirty years covered by this anthology: Ronald Barker, October 1953 to October 1955; Frank Granville

Barker, November 1955 to April 1962; Peter Roberts, May 1962 to June 1972; Peter Buckley, July 1972 to January 1973; Peter Ansorge, February 1973 to January 1975; Michael Coveney, February 1975 to June 1978; Simon Jones, July 1978 to February 1979; Robin Bean, March 1979 to June 1980; Peter Roberts, October 1981 to October 1983.

When Ronald Barker produced the first issue in October 1953 – which incidentally sold for one shilling and sixpence (or 7½p) – the coronation of Elizabeth II had recently brought over the first major wave of sightseeing tourists whose increasing presence was to prove such an important factor in the prosperity of post-war British theatre. But at that time there was no Chichester Festival Theatre to welcome them and the Royal Shakespeare Company was still seven years off. The National Theatre Company did not come into being until ten years later and the National Theatre building on the South Bank was not opened until *Plays and Players* was already well over twenty years old. Instead there were starry summer seasons given by an ad hoc Shakespeare Memorial Theatre Company in Stratford, while in London the Old Vic under Michael Benthall was struggling with its five-year plan to present all 37 Shakespeare plays in the First Folio on an inadequate budget. In the conservative world of West End theatre dominated by H. M. Tennent's 'Binky' Beaumont, a recently demobilised Peter Saunders was trying to break into the management game and, finding the established impresarios keeping the best theatres to themselves, had opened *The Mousetrap* the year before at the tiny Ambassadors.

In 1953 the often cosy and parochial world of intimate revue, in which a rising star called Dora Bryan was making her mark, had not yet been shattered by the arrival (in 1960) of the satirically irreverent and politically-conscious *Beyond the Fringe*. In 1953 Sandy Wilson's *The Boy Friend* began the British theatre's slow process of recovery from the acute inferiority complex brought on by the ultra-professional and all-prevailing American musical. This complex was to be further eased in the 1960s and 1970s, first by Lionel Bart's (*Fings Aint Wot They Used T'Be*, *Oliver!*, *Lock Up Your Daughters*) and later by Andrew Lloyd Webber and Tim Rice (whether operating jointly or separately).

'Director's Theatre' – the in-phrase of the 1960s reflecting the achievements of giants like Joan Littlewood with her Theatre Workshop at Stratford East and Peter Brook with the newly-formed Royal Shakespeare Company – was to make itself felt towards the end of the magazine's first decade. It was, however, in the field of new writing that the biggest changes took place following the magazine's début. At the start of the 1950s writers like Noël Coward, Emlyn Williams and J. B. Priestley, all of whose best work had been done in the 1930s, were still names very much to be reckoned with, though their postwar work proved on the whole to be disappointing. T. S. Eliot with *The Cocktail Party* and *The Confidential Clerk* and Christopher Fry with *The Lady's Not For Burning* and *Venus Observed* had given rise to much excited speculation about a renaissance of poetic drama in the second Elizabethan era. But this new movement came to little as the new reign actually began. Rather, two years after the magazine started its long life, it was the founding of the English Stage Company at the Royal Court in 1956 under George Devine and its deliberate championship of new dramatic writing that led to something far more enduring. In Sloane Square a first generation of writers as diverse as John Osborne, John Arden and Arnold Wesker were to compete for interest with others being launched elsewhere like Harold Pinter, Brendan Behan and Shelagh Delaney. And they were to be followed in the 1960s and the 1970s by wave after wave of new arrivals including Edward Bond, Peter Nichols, David Hare, Howard Brenton, Tom Stoppard, Michael Frayn, Simon Gray, Peter Shaffer, Caryl Churchill and many others.

In the 1950s when *Plays and Players* first came into being the giants of the theatre had not been the writers but the actor knights and dames – Olivier, Guinness, Richardson, Gielgud and Redgrave; Ashcroft, Evans, Robson and Thorndike. Looking back over the three decades spanned by these two volumes it is fascinating to see how those leading players reacted – or did not react – to the new writing and how new generations of players came along to interpret the new dramatists. Olivier, before moving on to be founder director of the Chichester Festival Theatre and then the National Theatre Company at the Old Vic, enthusiastically embraced the New Wave by starring in Osborne's *The Entertainer* in 1957, whilst Gielgud retreated into Shakespeare anthology programmes and delayed coming to terms with the new writing until much later when he appeared – along with Richardson – in Storey's *Home* in 1970 and Pinter's *No Man's Land* in 1975. Ashcroft, as a leading player with the Royal Shakespeare Company, which under Peter Hall started doing new plays as well as classics, was also on the Council of Management of the English Stage Company and therefore put herself in the vanguard of new developments, in contrast to Robson who went into a premature retirement on the south coast. Fortunately the new waves of writers were matched by new waves of players, beneficiaries of the recently introduced local authority grants that placed a different sort of young hopeful at the drama academies, who destroyed the finishing school atmosphere at many of them: actors such as Tom Courtenay, Albert Finney and Joan Plowright. Some of the new players, like Vanessa Redgrave, Judi Dench and Ian McKellen, did much of their finest work in the classics, whilst others like Alan Bates tended to adhere to the long run system in the West End (albeit in plays by Pinter and Gray) rather than taking advantage of the improved working conditions offered by the repertoire system in the new ensembles.

Over the years all this activity has been reflected in *Plays and Players* in different ways by different editors. But I think it is fair to say that throughout the magazine has occupied the middle ground: it has never been a mainly pictorial record of the year in the (largely West End) theatre like *Theatre World*, which was incorporated with it in 1962, nor was it primarily a champion of the avant-garde like *Encore*, which it also took over in the 1960s. It certainly gave due prominence to the new writers and was fortunate to have on its panel of reviewers critics like Martin Esslin and John Russell Taylor who had both written invaluable guides to the new movements. But in so doing it reported widely also on the classics, the musicals and the staple fare of the West End. Nor did it neglect the regions as new theatres were built (and companies founded or extended) such as those in Nottingham, Exeter, Sheffield, Colchester and Birmingham. And the magazine played a useful role in providing a shop window for young critics – Michael Billington, Michael Coveney, Robert Cushman, Frank Marcus and Benedict Nightingale all reviewed regularly for *Plays and Players* before going on to be the critics of, respectively, the *Guardian*, *Financial Times*, *Observer*, *Sunday Telegraph* and *New Statesman*. Nor was theatre overseas neglected. *Plays and Players* has been fortunate to have some distinguished contributors in this section such as Robert Brustein in North America. In putting together this anthology, however, I have rarely drawn on these reports as I believe readers will chiefly want to recall what a British theatre magazine had to say about the British theatre. Otherwise I have tried to provide a fair reflection of the magazine's balance of interviews and reviews and regional contributions.

When I first took over the editorship in 1962 it had been the practice at the end of the year to write a light-hearted 'Credits and Discredits' summarising the year and to invite a single authority to write a critical résumé. I thought that it might be more interesting to invite the London theatre critics as a whole to vote for the performances and productions which had most impressed them during the previous twelve months and in the process to contribute thumbnail sketches indicating what had led them to make the choices that they did. Thus, after 1962, the 'Credits and Discredits' disappear from this anthology and are replaced by a summary of the London critics' poll each year. It would have been nice to be able to reproduce the whole of the critics' end-of-the-year comments but that idea had to be set aside in view of the space available.

Since the 'Credits and Discredits' and the summary of the critics' poll provide a brief annual summary of the theatrical highlights, I have not written another myself but have assembled a series of notes on each year which I hope will jog some memories of what was happening in the world as a whole and so enable the mix of reviews and interviews to be read in a global context rather than in a theatrical vacuum.

It has been an enjoyable experience tracing the original contributors, some of whom have dispersed far and wide. I would like to thank them for their co-operation and the publishers for their patience as these two volumes were slowly put together. I hope that they may be enjoyed partly as a tribute to the magazine's founder publisher, Philip Dossë, whose fearful energies provided a constant dynamo over so many years as his editors came and went.

Peter Roberts, 1987

List of Illustrations

Except where stated otherwise, all photos are by Zoë Dominic. The remaining photos are supplied by the Mander and Mitchenson Theatre Collection, though permission to reproduce them has been obtained from the original photographers where known.

68 Three of the best: Peggy Ashcroft as Miss Madrigal and Edith Evans as Mrs St Maugham in Enid Bagnold's *The Chalk Garden*, Haymarket, April 1956 (Photo: Angus McBean); John Clements and Laurence Harvey as the Absolutes, father and son, in Sheridan's *The Rivals*, Saville, February 1956 (photo: Houston Rogers); Peter Ustinov's *Romanoff and Juliet*, Piccadilly, May 1956 (photo: Denis de Marney)

70 A rehearsal break during Osborne's *The Entertainer* with Laurence Olivier as Archie Rice, Royal Court, April 1957.

81 Seen at The Royal Court: Geraldine McEwan as Frankie Adams in Carson McCullers's *The Member of the Wedding*, February 1957 (photo: Sport and General); George Devine and Joan Plowright in Eugène Ionesco's *The Chairs*, May 1957 (photo: David Sim); Peggy Ashcroft as Brecht's *Good Woman of Setzuan*, October 1956 (photo: Sport and General); Robert Helpmann as Georges de Valera in Sartre's *Nekrassov*, September 1957

82 Marcel Marceau

84 Paul Massie and Kim Stanley in Tennessee Williams's *Cat on a Hot Tin Roof*, Comedy, January 1958. (Photographer unknown)

87 Paul Rogers as Lord Claverton and Anna Massey as Monica in T. S. Eliot's *The Elder Statesman*, Edinburgh Festival, August 1958, then Cambridge Theatre, London, September 1958. (Photo: Scottish Tourist Board)

90 Actors of the year: Sam Wanamaker in his own production of Tennessee Williams's *The Rose Tattoo*, New Shakespeare Theatre, Liverpool, 1958; Paul Scofield in Wolf Mankowitz's *Expresso Bongo*, Saville, April 1958; Albert Finney (with Charles Laughton) in Jane Arden's *The Party*, New, May 1958

94 Three views of *A Taste of Honey* in rehearsal at Theatre Royal, Stratford, East London, May 1958: Frances Cuka (Josephine), Shelagh Delaney (author), Joan Littlewood (director), Murray McIvin (Geoff); Avis Bunnage (Helen), Cuka, Littlewood; Bunnage, Cuka

100 Ralph Richardson as Victor Rhodes in Graham Greene's *The Complaisant Lover*, Globe, June 1959; and with Phyllis Calvert as Mary Rhodes and Paul Scofield as Clive Root

108 Three talking points of 1959: Kenneth Williams with Fenella Fielding in the revue *Pieces of Eight*, Apollo, September (photographer unknown); J. G. Devlin, John Kelly, Pauline Flanagan, Etain O'Dell and Bill Keating in Sean O'Casey's *Cock-a-Doodle-Dandy*, Royal Court (photo: Guy Gravett); Ian Bannen as Musgrave with Freda Jackson as Mrs Hitchcock in John Arden's *Serjeant Musgrave's Dance*, Royal Court, October (photographer unknown)

119 Joan Plowright as Beatie Bryant, with, above, Gwen Nelson as her mother, in Arnold Wesker's *Roots*, Belgrade, Coventry, May 1959, then Royal Court, June 1959

122 Joan Plowright as Daisy and Laurence Olivier as Bérenger in Ionesco's *Rhinoceros*, Royal Court, April 1960, then Strand, July 1960

181 Glenda Jackson in the *The Theatre of Cruelty* season, as above

182 Experimental make-up for the *Theatre of Cruelty* season, as above

184 Nicol Williamson in rehearsal as Bill Maitland in John Osborne's *Inadmissible Evidence*, Royal Court, September 1964

184 *Inadmissible Evidence* (as above) in rehearsal with Sheila Allen as Liz, director Anthony Page, Nicol Williamson and author John Osborne

188 Two scenes from Edward Albee's *Who's Afraid of Virginia Woolf?*, Piccadilly, February 1964: Arthur Hill as George, Uta Hagen as Martha; Richard Easton as Nick, Uta Hagen, Arthur Hill and Beverlee McKinsey as Honey

192 Scene from Clifford Williams's production of Marlowe's *The Jew of Malta*, Royal Shakespeare Theatre, Stratford-upon-Avon, 1965

195 Eric Porter as Barabas in *The Jew of Malta*, as above

196 Michael Bryant as Teddy, Terence Rigby as Joey and Ian Holm as Lenny in Harold Pinter's *The Homecoming*, Aldwych, June 1965

200 George Devine as Baron von Epp and Ferdy Mayne as Kunz in John Osborne's *A Patriot for Me*, Royal Court, June 1965

201 Jill Bennett as Countess Sophia Delyanoff and Maximilian Schell as Redl in *A Patriot for Me*, as above

202 Michael Bryant as Lenny, Vivien Merchant as Ruth, Terence Rigby as Joey and Paul Rogers as Max in Peter Hall's production of Pinter's *The Homecoming*, Aldwych, June 1965

205 Three scenes from Edward Bond's *Saved*, Royal Court, November 1965: John Castle as Len, Barbara Ferris as Pam; Richard Butler at Harry, Barbara Ferris, Gwen Nelson as Mary; John Castle and Gwen Nelson

207 The baby-stoning in *Saved*, as above

214 Best actor and actress: Paul Scofield (Khlestakov) with director Peter Hall and Paul Rogers (The Mayor) in rehearsal for Gogol's *The Government Inspector*, Aldwych, January 1966; a portrait of Vanessa Redgrave

216 Wallas Eaton as Sir Jolly Jumble and Arthur Lowe as Sir Davy Dunce in Otway's *The Soldier's Fortune*, Royal Court, January 1967

217 Arthur Lowe with Maurice Roeves as Beaugard in *The Soldier's Fortune*, as above

223 Three views of Jerome Robbins's production of *Fiddler on the Roof* with Topol as Tevye and Miriam Karlin as Golde, Her Majesty's, February 1967

224 *Fiddler on the Roof*, as above

229/230 Two winning performances: Laurence Olivier as Edgar and with Robert Stephens as Kurt and Geraldine McEwan as Alice in Strindberg's *The Dance of Death*, Old Vic, February 1967; and, overleaf, Shepherd as Arnie with Eileen Atkins as Joan and Noel Dyson as Mrs Ellis in David's Storey's *The Restoration of Arnold Middleton*, Royal Court, July 1967

13

1953

The year that Plays and Players came into being was the year that Queen Mary and Stalin died . . . and the year that Britain's new monarch, Elizabeth II was crowned. It was also the year in which there was a royalist coup d'état *in Iran and the year in which Egypt became a Republic.*

In the field of the arts, the post-war ascendancy of America and France in the area of new dramatic writing was reflected in the interest in the new plays from Tennessee Williams (Camino Real) *and from Anouilh* (The Lark).

Leading ladies. Above: Eileen Herlie in
Venice Preserv'd. Above right: Claire Bloom.
Right: Pamela Brown (with John Gielgud and
Margaret Rutherford) in *The Way of the
World*

They are standing in the wings of the Theatre Royal of my imagination, the younger generation of actresses, the Misses Siddons. Their names are Eileen Herlie, Pamela Brown, Yvonne Mitchell, Claire Bloom, Dorothy Tutin, Joyce Redman, Margaret Leighton. They are the young aristocrats of acting. Each one a thoroughbred, born of greasepaint and footlight. Their combined eyelashes would stretch from the Tennent Productions' offices in Shaftesbury Avenue to the Shakespeare Memorial Theatre at Stratford-on-Avon – eyelashes made of steel coated with mascara, which is as well, since there are times when they have to hang on to a part with them – having first beaten the others to it, by them. And how fortunate we, the playgoers, can count ourselves, that not one of these eager, handsome, gifted creatures can dare allow herself to rest on her hard-fought, hard-won laurels: there's a sister close behind her.

First Eileen Herlie. and this is because although her work has all the attack, pace, weight, certainty of the star player – and though her entrances upon the scene are as electric, her exits from them as extinguishing – she does not play her personality instead of her parts, as so many of our high-powered Siddons Sisters are apt to do. Eileen Herlie is an actress. And though one may leave the theatre with the feeling that she has taken her rolling-pin to the character and worn it down before remoulding it – first boned her chicken, then inserted her gifts into it – it is the chicken and not Miss Herlie who emerges. Setting aside her unfortunate Medea, too young attempted, there are some most accomplished portraits in Miss Herlie's histrionic gallery of passionate ladies in parlous predicaments: her kindly, comely drunkard in *The Time of Your Life*, for instance, in which she compressed the heart-break and thc pathos of a wasted life into the compass of a thumbnail. The piteous majesty of her Andromache in *The Trojan Women*. The romantic, tragic, half-crazed young Queen in *The Eagle Has Two Heads*. Her righteous but impassioned Belvidera in *Venice Preserv'd*. All these parts owe everything to the actress in Miss Herlie; they have never been called upon to support the facade of her individual personality. Her characters are her step-children, not her progeny. One sometimes has the feeling that Miss Herlie has carved her characters from butter (her Paula Tanqueray, for instance) for there is a smoothness, a cut-and-come-againness, a generosity about them: they must be Danish butter, off the ration. Moreover, however desperate their plight, no matter to what lengths they have been driven, like Clarissa in the eighteenth century novel, they remain respectable though raped. But it is only in this over-all respectability, this ample generosity that they resemble one another. Miss Herlie acts her characters – she does not hold to them the mirror reflecting only another angle of herself. With Pamela Brown it is pre-eminently otherwise. Miss Brown with wit, inspiration, that voice of hers – part turtle-dove's roo-coo, part nutmeg grater – and the wide-eyed gaze, withal, of your conjuror astonishing himself at the diversity of the objects he produces from his sleeve, this prodigious Miss Brown, then, with a flotilla of minxes in full sail after her, fans spread and streamers out, and a shoal of foals for tender – comes to harbour escorting – just herself – her accomplished, decorative, exasperating self. For Miss Brown seems only to have

The Young Actresses

by Caryl Brahms

up her sleeve Miss Brown – her ace of aces. But what a self Miss Brown has! Her face has been carved in ivory by Epstein. Her hair is a sort of cinnamon seaweed seen through ink. She has that quality of mind that scintillates. And with all this, she has ability to throw a line with a flick of the voice as lethal as the tribesman's speeding knife. Highly artificial, beautifully controlled, her minxes, sphinxes, witches and so on, give me more pleasure than the combined performances of all her sisters' swans – which is most unfair since la Brown's art is nothing but a bag of tricks suspended on the high-wire of her wit. Give her another part and out they tumble from the baggage again, nicely calculated, beautifully deployed. The gods forfend that we should have Miss Brown act a character instead of her fascinating self – I don't suppose that – now – she would care to – or bear to – do it.

If ever there has been a danger of Miss Yvonne Mitchell's becoming the poor man's Pamela Brown, that time is past. Now her vivid dark-haired beauty takes counsel of her heart. She is the only actress who has made Cordelia credible to me, and oh, Callboy, have I seen a clutter of Cordelias in my time! And though it is the pace and spirit of her interpretations, the cataract of charm that she unleashes on to the stage, that have made her growing reputation, it is in her quieter moments that her work touches us to tears. Miss Mitchell was born to play Beatrice, but I look forward, some day, to seeing her play the monument scene in *Antony and Cleopatra.*

Of Miss Claire Bloom I always feel that she is a pond – an orphan pond – Miss Vivien Leigh's orphan pond. A very faithful pond in her reflection of her – I had almost written 'choreographer's' – producer's intentions – admirably quick to ripple at the very breath of his will. Orphaned by the plaintive solitude of her personality. And our next Viv Leigh. But let us not leave her docile beauty and her eager talents at this, for the former, God in his wisdom has given her; and she works ceaselessly to increase his dower of the latter. Miss Bloom is always a little better in a part than we had expected – that little lacking from what we would wish. And someone should take her into any High Street to see how women walk – with weight, purpose, but not with conscious grace.

The connoisseur of acting should see Miss Dorothy Tutin now, in *The Living Room* (the first play by Graham Greene and the first fruits of a new management, Donmar: which I am told is the soubriquet of Donald Albery and Margot Fonteyn). Miss Tutin should be seen at once because her chief quality is the most fragile of all – it is youth. She does not hurl an eyebrow, heave her faintly perceptible bosom, gaze wanly at the gallery or go through all the other antics of the craft but, instead, feels for the young girls she brings upon the stage, and thinks as they do. Is them, in fact. And this delicate essence is the very distillation of the core of acting. What she may ripen into is open to question – probably another Dulcie Gray, growing older gracefully. But for the next ten years at least this quiet actress will give the discerning playgoer infinite pleasure.

The Misses Margaret Leighton and Joyce Redman might be termed the good old troupers of the Siddons act. Fling them into any part and they can be counted on to emerge with all their guns still firing. Both are apt to turn a play into a hurly-burly. Both are frighteningly well-equipped for this purpose. They are a blest pair of sparking-plugs, able to ignite the most turgid of lines with the brilliance of the timing with which they apply the spark of their personality to their material. In addition, Miss Leighton, at least, has a heart under that Lancastrian crust of common sense.

So there they stand, the Siddons Sisters, in the wings of the Theatre Royal of our imagination; alert, palpitating and on tenter-eyelashes. And as we watch that lively, lovely, eager bevy we can only grieve, with Hazlitt, that 'of those whose business it is to imitate humanity in general, and who do it sometimes admirably, sometimes abominably, some record is due to the world; but the player's art is one that perishes with him, and leaves no traces of itself but in the faint descriptions of the pen'.

OCTOBER
1953

Comedy in 1953

by Richard Buckle

Comedy is a conspiracy between author and actor to make the spectator rejoice at the absurdity of his fellow men. The more perfectly they succeed, the harder it should be to apportion credit between them. The pleasure of comedy is to observe how certain characters react to certain situations; the essential of comic dialogue is that it should express and reveal character; and the great moments in comedy are when characters, reacting to a given situation, seem to expose their whole nature in a single line, or one word, or perhaps in a mere gesture. The perfection of comedy, ultimately, depends on the timing of the actors; and a playwright should be happy if his actor, by throwing away, or perhaps even leaving out, a brilliant line into which has been concentrated a whole lifetime of wisdom, can make the audience roar with laughter. So delicate and perverse a machine is comedy, constructed as it is to surprise by the expected, that the best way for an actor to put over his author's line may sometimes be not to say them at all. Ideally, I believe, the playwright should create vehicles for given actors: this is the way to ensure a maximum of comic effect. The comedy should be a collaboration between them. It will be seen that I take a less pretentious view of the dramatist's vocation than Bernard Shaw: but then, I also believe that ideally there should be no such thing as revivals. Comedies should be written in a day, for the actor of the day, to last no longer than that day.

It is quite by chance, and for reasons that have nothing to do with their excellence as comedies, that a few old pieces, like *Twelfth Night, The Way of the World, The School for Scandal* and *The Importance of Being Earnest* are still performed. I am sure there were dozens of contemporary comedies just as good in performance. Certainly the one thing a writer of comedies should never consider is whether his plays will be interesting after he is dead. If he did that, if there could be such a fool, I should think he would be lucky to get his plays performed in his lifetime. Posterity? It does not exist. We do not, though, as the reader will have observed, live in an ideal world. Accidents happen. Things go wrong. Father Time is sometimes hopeless at timing. Gielgud is born a hundred and fifty years later than Sheridan. People misunderstand their gifts. Traditions die out. Oscar Wilde writes *The Importance* for Hawtrey and because Hawtrey simply cannot fork out the fifty pounds which Oscar must have at once – how I sympathise! – sells the play to Alexander.

Two principal misfortunes, it seems to me, have befallen the English comic theatre since the war. The first is that audiences have acquired a taste for comedies which are not funny. These are called Family Plays. In a sense, of course, one could say *Hamlet*, *Ghosts* and the *Agamemnon* are family plays which are not funny: but the point about these family plays which have become such a popular feature of our post-war theatre is that they are meant to be comedies, yet only provide the mildest amusement. Social security, rationing and queues have perhaps induced a fear of immoderation in the British heart; and perhaps the Family Play in which a display of wit would seem out of place is a typical product of the century of the Common Man. The pleasure of comedy, of course, is to see ourselves: but a quintessence of ourselves, heightened in colour, sharper in outline, refined of insignificant peculiarities, more condensed in speech, larger, brighter, odder than life. These Family Plays reduce exaggeration to the smallest degree compatible with the putting of a play on a stage. Their heroines are not great flaunting Millamants and Bracknells, but mousy mothers from Maida Vale. Their dialogue is as flat and ordinary as cocoa can make it; and the worst that can happen at the end of their second acts is that an extra guest turns up for supper on Cook's night out and Mum has to open a tin of Batchelor's peas.

Arthur Watkyn's *For Better, For Worse*, which started at the Q, then moved triumphantly and at once to the Comedy, is a perfect example of the Family Play. Quite well written, produced and acted, it exploits quite adequately the baby face and voice of Geraldine McEwan, who plays the hard-up, newly wed heroine. The young couple with little or no money find a flat, furnish it with the help of understanding parents, have people to dinner, run into plumbing difficulties, start a baby (as far as I can remember) and end up with an extra two pounds a week. Now I believe it is possible to write a comedy in which nothing much happens, but I do prefer one pitched in a higher key. The Family Play is designed to produce not laughter but an occasional cosy chuckle.

The second sad thing about comedy in Britain today – and it may well have something to do with the kind of plays that are written – is that the great school of high comedy acting stemming from Charles Hawtrey is dying out. We still, it is true, have Ronald Squire, whose dry and apathetic charm was not quite sufficient to justify Tennents' revival of Lonsdale's *Aren't We All?* at the Haymarket. What an actor he is, and how I should have liked to see him in Lonsdale plays thirty years ago! Surely they cannot have seemed so crudely constructed, so elementary in character drawing, so feeble in wit, then. There is still the more positive charm of A.E. Matthews, master of throw-away comedy; but lately he has appeared only in films. Gladys Cooper has developed late in life into the great lady of high comedy, but since she brought her light touch to grace *Relative Values*, she has not been seen in another play. These are giants in finesse; and indeed we can boast that among the middle-aged and established we have some superb comedians.

After Edith Evans and Sybil Thorndike were to be seen no more in *Waters of the Moon* and Robert Morley retired from *The Little Hut*, I should say that Athene Seyler's Lady Hunstanton was the most accomplished performance in London. In the same play, *A Woman of No Importance*, Isabel Jeans fluted exquisitely on her one rococo note. I liked enormously the sly humour of Wilfred Hyde-White in Louis Verneuil's *Affairs of State*, which competes with Alan Melville's *Dear Charles* – an ingenious vehicle for the inimitable Yvonne Arnaud – and Roger MacDougall's *Escapade* for the title of the best comedy running in London. In the latter play, Nigel Patrick surprised me by showing extraordinary subtlety and gave me hope for the possibility of a revival of the kind of acting I admire. But who is there under thirty-five who can play a young Hawtrey part, a young du Maurier or A.E. Matthews part? The most promising candidate for this kind of role that I have been able to find is an American.

Hugh Herbert's *The Moon is Blue* was a play from America which I preferred to the more highly praised *Seven Year Itch*, and in fact thought nearly excellent, though spoilt by padding in the middle scenes; and it was notable for three performances. As the sophisticated innocent, Diana Lynn seemed to have a new line of her own; and Robert Flemyng, that admirable actor, badly miscast as the old roué, brought off his role with such a *tour de force* of technique that it was almost embarrassing. These two got all the notices, but it was Biff McGuire, as the quiet and gentlemanly young hero with a sense of humour, who pleased me most of all. His exit line, spoken to the 'professional virgin' whom he is leaving in his flat while he goes out to buy something for her to cook for their supper – 'I'll get some eggs and bacon while I'm about it' – was thrown away with such dead-pan, teasing charm. There is no young actor in London for whom I would rather write a comedy, and I vote him my second garland of the year.

And to whom does the first garland go? In this curious star-spangled year, when we have seen Coward in Shaw, Wolfit in Sheridan and Gielgud in Hammersmith; Richardson as a ghost (I didn't believe in that one) and Wynyard, lighting up a dull play with her beautiful profile, as Helen; Buchanan's return in not a bad farce; Wilde rewritten by Paul Dehn, but in vain; and at the Lyric, Hammersmith, a brothel scene in which an old man pretends to be a dog and has himself flogged by a tart: – in this curious busy year I have most enjoyed, most admired and most laughed at a septuagenarian actor-manager in a play written by himself. On the second occasion I went to see Sacha Guitry in *N'Ecoutez Pas, Messieurs* at the Winter Garden, I was sitting with A. E. Matthews, who has been on the stage since Guitry was born; and I watched him leaning forward in eager fascination throughout the evening, though he understands not a word of French. He said afterwards that Sacha Guitry had given him the best lesson in acting he ever had in his life. I too, with my shorter experience, thought that I had never seen a comedian like Guitry: and I am amused to hear my young intellectual friends from Paris – the capital of novelty – ridiculing his art. If you go on for ever in Paris you are finished: in London you are made.

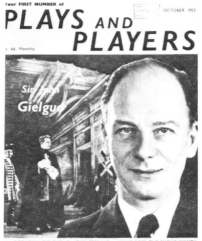

In his inflexions of voice and deftness of gesture Guitry seemed to embody the art of the old Italian comedians, refined by the subtlety of France. His play was a perfect vehicle for his perfect performance: in fact the production was an illustration of my ideal collaboration between actor and author. Four actors and a telephone – yet the situations were intensely theatrical and the dialogue was of a wit to stock Shaftesbury Avenue with jokes for a decade. Guitry's first act was a monologue on women and the theatre. In his second he had a brilliant scene witih Heather Thatcher, a loquacious Englishwoman who, thinking he understands English, tries to persuade him not to seduce her daughter but to take herself instead, and to whom he answers at random with nods, shakes of the head and inane smiles, interspersed with gestures of desperation towards the audience. A marvellous moment of comedy was shared by Guitry the playwright and producer, Guitry the actor and Jeanne-Fusier Gir, who played his talkative housekeeper in the great tradition of French comic maids. (Which reminds me I have made no mention of the visit of the Comédie Française to the St James's Theatre, or of their splendid *Tartuffe* with Ledoux). 'Has Monsieur never noticed my extraordinary memory for telephone numbers?' she said, if I remember the dialogue roughly. 'No'. 'Anjou 48-60, Balzac 12-79, Passy 93-11, Odéon 53-89 – '. Then, when Guitry interrupted her 'But whose are those numbers?' it was the rapidity with which she gave her indignant shrug, shooting out her hands and making a deprecating little French noise between 'Oooh!' and 'Aaah!' that seemed to me to reach the very heights of high comedy.

Happily, there are signs that the Family Play is on the wane. Who will now write a series of dazzling plays in which our great masters of the rare art of comedy can display their powers to the full and inspire a continuance of their tradition by the younger generation? We can be sure that when he does – whoever he is – his work will be dismissed as frothy, superficial nonsense by the more tea-sodden critics. But who cares about them?

NOVEMBER
1953

The Young Actors

by Caryl Brahms

Where are our future Gielguds, Oliviers, Redgraves, Wolfits? I made a list of the leading younger actors. I blinked. For the list read: Paul Scofield, Richard Burton, Denholm Elliott, Alan Badel, Paul Rogers, James Donald and Michael Gough. A self-effacing list. But where, with the exception of Paul Scofield, is the star personality in it? Where is the actor with the bright lights in his veins? And does this spirit of self-effacement, this passion for being a good team member, this aversion to anything twice as big as life, really make for acting anything like big enough for the theatre? Does it make for great acting, or great theatre-going?

If to be an actor is to enter another man's skin, to become flesh of his flesh, to think with his mind, to tread the earth with his weight, to breathe his very breath, then Paul Rogers is very nearly the greatest actor of his day; and Gielgud and Wolfit no actors. But acting is not only that combination of observation and conscientious photography that we call character-acting. There is in all great acting another, a more dangerous, a more exciting element – the extension of the actor's own vibrant personality and this is where your Gielguds, Oliviers, Wolfits fill the bill. A great actor's art is a mirror held perpetually in a flattering light. Like the mirror a great actor isolates the character he plays from the distraction of its background; lends the character his own importance: graces him with his own good looks; delivers his utterances with his own wit and pathos – with masterly timing. Your great actor, in fact, portrays his characters as they would like to think they are, say as angels straight from heaven, or creatures tortured in some hell of their own devising. In other words, your great actor must be twice as large as life and even louder. He is a chameleon, taking on the colour of every part he plays, but maintaining his own shape in all of them. That is what makes him a star. That is why his audiences look for his appearances on the scene. His entrances make the lights shine brighter, his exits lower them again. And if you conclude that a great actor is not necessarily a good actor, you may not be far off the mark.

Paul Scofield has this vibrant personality. It has made him a star. Richard Burton lacks star personality; he has to get by with his turned-down Hollywood contract instead. Burton is a better actor than Scofield; Scofield is a greater actor than Burton. Scofield is the John Gielgud of his age-group. Like Gielgud he leaves a benediction upon a well-written line. Like Gielgud, he is himself in every part he plays: himself, grown older, younger, in this or that predicament. Like Gielgud he has many mannerisms and does not disdain to deploy the tricks of his trade. (He who does is no great actor). But where the more experienced actor is graceful, Scofield is apt to gangle still. Experience is slowly bringing him a surer control of limb and voice. He is, however, his own worst enemy, in that he is as wilful as Wolfit, and no other living actor can quite afford to be as wilful as all that, unless he has Wolfit's inexhaustible gusto for the great adventure which, to him, is the theatre; his warm humanity; the sureness of his timing, swift as a rapier thrust; his noble voice.

I have said that Richard Burton is the better actor, the lesser luminary. He is more compact than Scofield, but less sunny; no taller than Olivier, but with something of his power and drive; lacking, as yet, Redgrave's faculty for becoming the very last person one would think he could possibly ever be. Burton has something of Robert Helpmann's strange, curdled quality (but without the contagious excitement of any performance that Helpmann gives); and he has a quiet but latent sense of humour. Burton is a leading man who has arrived too early at the signpost. Where does he go from the Old Vic? Will he advance to tread the road that Olivier took before him, or is he for the Waste Land? Time will tell.

Given more girth, Denholm Elliott might have been born to play Horatio. But he has a lean and hungry look and an acute sensitivity. So he will probably cover the gamut of neurotic but pleasant enough young men from the pitiful young man in *The Seagull* (the one nowhere near Sorrento) to *Hamlet*, who is the daddy of them all. Elliott could become this country's first exponent of Jean-Paul Sartre and Anouilh.

Your SECOND number of

PLAYS AND PLAYERS

NOVEMBER 1953

1s. 6d. Monthly

Vivien Leigh

Stories of VIVIEN LEIGH and MICHAEL REDGRAVE ● John Fernald on WHAT I SAW IN RUSSIA ● Richard Buckle on THE CONFIDENTIAL CLERK and THE DEVIL'S GENERAL 50 CASH PRIZES FOR READERS IN ENTRY-FREE CONTEST ● The Sleeping Prince

Alan Badel, the most original of the bunch, owes little of his highly individual art to the revered Elders of the theatre of today. He has a sardonic appearance, a genuinely whimsical bent, together with a sweetness of personality that suns it in his work enchantingly. He is, as it were, the very acid-drop of actors. His Ariel was the best I have ever seen, swift as fire and fine as flame. And his Romeo, though the complexity of Badel's own nature was too much felt in it, haunts me still with its quietist poetry.

I believe that Paul Rogers is about to be the actor that Cedric Hardwicke might have been. Rogers' Shylock was extraordinarily complex and unusually noble. He came from Spain and not from the Mile End Road. His clowns are lunatic. His villains calculating, crafty, ruthless. He has the greatest range of any in this group, even if he has not so far touched the heights. A Macbeth, someday, or the future Antony to Yvonne Mitchell's (future) Cleopatra.

James Donald is the most engaging actor on the list. Elegant, unpredictable, a stylist, lacking only the drive and direction of an unappeasable ambition and an appetite for every kind of part. And since your great actor is always a glutton and James Donald is not, he, alas, remains a fashionable actor.

And Michael Gough is a likely lad for a passionate political suicide, abdication, or walking-case of amnesia, any of which he would play with considerable panache. This pool may be a little too shallow to reflect more than the outer aspect of a hero-malgré-lui. Gough is the viola rather than the violin. But within the limitations of his natural scale he ranges easily from the passionate to the comic. I would like to see him bringing that intensity of emotion to a trivial high comedy of present day manners.

We must not blame our younger leading actors because they have not the technique, the experience, the authority and the skill of our established stars. We must remember that not so very long ago Gielgud, Olivier, Redgrave and Wolfit were, none of them, Forbes-Robertson.

1953

What I Saw in Russia

by John Fernald

To see half a score of Moscow and Provincial productions hardly qualifies one to generalise about the Russian Theatre. But on this evidence, its strength seems to lie not in its contemporary playwrights, directors or designers but in the wealth of its tradition, the dramatic literature of its quite recent past, the richness and profusion of its acting talent and the enthusiasm of an enormous public which fills every theatre everywhere seven nights a week with a matinée on Sundays. The settings I saw were not exciting and were often crudely lit, though the opera and ballet, traditionally magnificent, can challenge comparison anywhere in the world. I was occasionally surprised by what to me seemed a sort of casualness in the work of the directors, an apparent lack of feeling for nuances of tempo, for evocative grouping, for taking charge of a scene and sweeping it up to a climax. But the acting! That was a different story. I have never known such a high all round level of sheer acting talent as I saw everywhere around me in that short time.

I must pass over somewhat hastily the first night I spent in Moscow, for then I saw an Offenbach operetta, the badness of which was a complete mystery in the light of what was to come. The operetta was disillusion indeed; mediocre, realistic scenery straining to be vertical, strain, in fact everywhere, particularly among the chorus each of whom seemed to be saying 'This isn't me really,' just like English amateurs. By contrast, the leading man was full of confidence; he looked like Siegfried dressed up as Lord Fauntleroy and frequently had to make a hurried exit through the trapdoor. But apart from this the standard of plays presented seemed to be high. At the moment, there are at least three Shakespeare plays and four by Chekhov: Tolstoy, Gogol, Shaw, Dickens and Gorky dominate the playbills.

I saw *King Lear* by the Minsk company in Leningrad. Lear was acted by a great square man with a vibrant bass voice – physical attributes quite commonplace in Russia, magnificent for Shakespeare and only too rarely found here. I would say that his performance ranked with the best of our time. The Cordelia was even more exciting, an actress in her middle thirties far too old to the English way of thinking, but rich in personality and experience. I have always wanted to see Cordelia played not as a juvenile, sweet and soft and vulnerable, but as a woman elemental in the power of her love, every whit as strong in her goodness as her sisters are strong in evil. I found this at last in Leningrad, and I found there too, what I was to see everywhere else – a company with no 'tail,' where everyone seemed to have the same mastery.

Pygmalion was on when I returned to Moscow – a refreshing performance and most recognisably faithful to the author. All the laughs were in the right place and there was a delighted roar and applause for Eliza's famous exit line. Be it noted, Shaw's 'toff' characters were not exaggerated but played with observant realism and integrity. The word integrity comes constantly to mind when watching Russians acting. They do not yield to the temptation to overplay, which comes from thinking too much of what the audience *wants* and too little of what the character *is*. The restraint is due to the teaching of Stanislavsky which is at the very root of the Russian stage. His influence is not confined to the Moscow Art Theatre, but lives everywhere in the drama schools, in the big theatres of Moscow and Leningrad and in the provincial repertory companies. 'There is no other way but his,' said the director of the Lunarcharsky State Institute of Theatre.

To see Stanislavsky's way with Chekhov is to see this work at its finest. In 1938 Nemirovitch Danchenko, Stanislavsky's lifelong friend and partner and himself a director of equal stature, produced *The Three Sisters*. That production, with its original cast, is still running in Moscow today; and to say that it was the most overwhelmingly beautiful thing I have ever seen in the theatre is to admit that I cannot write well enough to express the extremes of my admiration. Here was everything I had ever wanted from a Chekhov production, a perfect blend of realism with theatrical effects such as only great acting, great direction and great writing can achieve. They do not say in Moscow 'Let's go and see *The Three Sisters*'; they say, 'Let's go and pay a visit to the three sisters'. And that is just how it is. Danchenko died in 1940 but his production lives on, and the Russian theatre being what it is,

DECEMBER 1953

PLAYS AND PLAYERS

1s. 6d. Monthly

Gladys Cooper

W. SOMERSET MAUGHAM on GLADYS COOPER ● RICHARD BUCKLE on THE SLEEPING PRINCE and ANTONY AND CLEOPATRA ● INFANT PRODIGIES BY V. C. CLINTON BADDELEY ● DOROTHY TUTIN by BARON ● WALDO LANCHESTER on PUPPETS CARYL BRAHMS on AMATEUR THEATRICALS ● Playguide ● Someone Waiting ● Kin

there is every reason to suppose that it will last at least another decade. Already the members of the cast are over fifteen years too old but in Russia this could not matter less. Chekhov's widow, now in her seventies, was playing Madam Ranevsky until five years ago and was still actively on the stage until last year.

In England the delicate balance of a Chekhov play often eludes us: we have been known to exploit the quirks and foibles of Chekhovian oddities to suit the exhibitionist desires of a particular actor, and to distil a meretricious 'atmosphere' from a mournful counterpoint of tears and barking dogs. But humour is the keynote of the Russian productions – humour and courage in the face of despair. The atmosphere is there in full measure but only as a foil to the optimism which they seek and find in all his plays except *Ivanov*. Significantly, *Ivanov* is seldom if ever performed. Optimism may seem to us an odd quality to find in Chekhov, but personally I have never doubted that it was there. And when I saw those three sisters as the soldiers marched away, with tears on their cheeks but indomitable courage in their eyes, I was quite sure that Chekhov would have said that this was so. He certainly would have been a happy man had he seen how widespread has become the style of acting which he loved. In *The Seagull* and *Uncle Vanya* and in the other plays I saw, the actors have mastered the art of appearing to speak almost in confidence and yet are distinctly heard at the back of the gallery. True, they are helped in this by two things. Most of their theatres are acoustically better than ours: they are not fan-shaped and designed to cram as many seats as possible into a restricted space, but have auditoriums small in proportion to the stage.

Russian audiences are quiet and attentive, finding it in no way necessary to smoke or eat during a performance, which may take as long as four hours. Indeed, Russian audiences are as exciting as Russian acting and as I finish these lines I have a memory of scores of teenagers in the Moscow Art Theatre crowding to the front of the stage at the fall of the curtain to toss roses to three middle-aged, rather plain, but very wonderful actresses.

Credits and Discredits of 1953

Congratulations of the Year: to Tennents for giving us six new plays and for their courage in reviving *Aren't We All?*; to the Old Vic for getting such a good press for *Hamlet*; to Michael Redgrave and Peggy Ashcroft for their Tony and Pat; to T. S. Eliot for another box-office success; to Sacha Guitry for the comedy performance of the year; to the Americans for taking a further long lease on Drury Lane; to Mogens Wieth for his superb performance in *A Doll's House*; to all those film stars who, in 1953, rediscovered the stage.

Mistakes of the Year: *Lucky Boy, Bruno and Sydney, The McRoary Whirl*.

Disappointments of the Year: *Wish You Were Here*, Burton's Hamlet; *Romeo and Juliet* on records.

Names we have missed: Beatrice Lillie, Hermione Gingold, Robert Helpmann.

Welcome back: Vivien Leigh, George Formby, Jack Buchanan, Flora Robson, Trevor Howard, Alec Clunes, Wilfrid Lawson.

Mogens Wieth with Mai Zetterling in *A Doll's House*, **Lyric Hammersmith**

Come Back Soon: Jean-Louis Barrault, Edwige Feuillère, Sacha Guitry, Jean Vilar.

Plays we should like to have missed: *Birthday Honours, The White Carnation, Macbeth* as done by Wolfit's cubs.

Expect a hearty welcome when you return: The Lunts, Robert Donat, Noël Coward.

Pull up your socks department: Arts Theatre Club.

Lost Causes of 1953: British musicals.

Kiss and make it up department: Frankie Howerd and Jack Payne.

Not good enough department: Very late and very intimate revues.

Names we shall miss in 1954: Godfrey Tearle, Ruggiero Ruggieri.

Bores of the year: Gilbert Harding and the Old Vic Facade.

The most boring controversy of the year: Did Marlowe write Shakespeare?

Please don't do it again: Paul Dehn rewriting Oscar Wilde; Martin Browne trying his hand at farce.

We weren't surprised, were you dept?; at the short run of *Anastasia, Blind Man's Buff, Four Winds*.

We were surprised at the long runs of: *Affairs of State; For Better for Worse; Love from Judy; Trial and Error*.

Good luck in 1954 to: Michael Benthall at the Old Vic.

Gamest trouper of the year: Donald Wolfit.

Gamest little trouper of the year: Anna Neagle.

Gamest: Eva Bartok.

Books we have liked: Harold Hobson's *Theatre* and *The French Theatre* and Michael Redgrave's *Actor's Ways and Means*.

Books we have loathed: *Cécile Sorel* and all those dreary one-act plays.

Overworked theme for 1953: adultery.

For the most unselfish performance: Eric Portman in *The Living Room*.

For upholding the tradition of the theatre: Sybil Thorndike.

For carrying an old show on young shoulders: Jean Carson.

Translation of the year: Emlyn Williams's Dickens.

Speed it up department: Christopher Fry.

Forgotten name of 1953: J.B. Priestley.

Cheers department: Agatha Christie for filling the Winter Garden without stars.

Bravest try of the year: Frances Day in management.

Our hopes for 1954: An extended London season by the Stratford company; to see *Tea and Sympathy* from New York and *Sud* from Paris in London; more new plays from new playwrights; more experimenting by the club theatres; knowing Mistinguett's age.

Michael Redgrave and Peggy Ashcroft as Antony and Cleopatra, Stratford-upon-Avon

1954

The year that Nasser assumed power in Egypt and Ho Chi Minh in North Vietnam was also the year that the US Senate censured McCarthyism. In Britain it was the year that Roger Bannister became the first man to run a mile in under four minutes. In the world of music, Britten produced The Turn of the Screw *and Walton* Troilus and Cressida. *In the theatre, Julian Slade unveiled the musical,* Salad Days *and John Van Druten the play* I Am a Camera. *A foretaste of changes soon to come was given with the publication of Kingsley Amis's novel,* Lucky Jim.

All at Sea

*A Day by the Sea at the
Haymarket reviewed
by Richard Buckle*

A play which provides good parts for such actors as Sybil Thorndike, Irene Worth, Megs Jenkins, John Gielgud, Ralph Richardson and Lewis Casson cannot be altogether devoid of merit, I suppose. One starts by assuming this in all humility. Yet what would Mr N. C. Hunter's *A Day by the Sea* be like without them? One feels a desolate lack of quality throughout. There is a fascination about the plotless play, in which human beings are represented as helpless flies caught in the spider's web of their own inefficacy. Because nothing really happens in such plays, because they seem to have no end, and because they are the antithesis of what we are accustomed to think of as dramatic, there is no reason why they cannot be well written and well constructed works of art. This we know from certain illustrious examples. (I avoid deliberately mentioning the name of a great playwright whom Mr Hunter seems never not to be mentioned in the same breath with!) Such works are the theatrical equivalent of certain *Etudes* by Chopin. Hunter's idea for this play is, in fact, rather a good idea, rather a pretty and poetical one.

**Lewis Casson and Sybil Thorndike in *A Day
by the Sea*, Haymarket**

A Day by the Sea – the title suggests the nature of the work – may be a decisive one in the lives of four people. What is said in the garden at the top of the Dorset cliffs, or what is said on the beach below, may give a happy turn to their four unsatisfactory existences. The necessary words are spoken in the course of a long summer afternoon, but, apparently, they are spoken too late. Everything must continue as before. I like all this very much; and I like the idea of the Regency Gothic house surrounded by rhododendrons, silent in the sunlight, and the picnic on the beach, and the kite caught on the cliff, and all the characters moving in a sort of melancholy dream.

Then, it cannot be denied that Hunter has the gift for creating characters – or rather the gift for writing parts which actors can turn into portraits of genuine characters, which is perhaps not quite the same thing. At any rate, we must allow him a share of credit for the fact that every personage in the play seemed real at the time and proved memorable afterwards. We remember particularly certain dialogues in which the main business of the play is transacted.

There is the talk between the kind, busy lady of the rhododendrons and her disappointed diplomat son about his childhood girl-friend who is recuperating from two unhappy marriages and whom it seems he ought to be nicer to; there is the account given to her hostess by this unlucky young woman of the mess she has made of her life; there is the proposal of the diplomat to this woman he might have made happy twenty years before. The sub-plot, if such it can be called, concerns the drunken doctor, who acts as companion to the aged brother of the lady of the house, and his attempted 'rescue' by the governess of the widow's children. The doctor's scenes with his charge, with the diplomat, who dislikes him, and with the governess are interesting. Hunter has certainly achieved something in the contrasting of these characters and in his orchestration of the scenes between them.

So far, it would seem, so good. Are not this attractive theme and these varied characters enough to satisfy us with the play? No, no, alas! they are not. In spite of the incomparable acting of the six principal players, and in spite of Sir John Gielgud's inspired direction, *A Day by the Sea* is profoundly unsatisfactory because of the barren and colourless nature of the author's mind. There is not a vestige of originality, not a spark of poetry – except the verses quoted by the doctor and the diplomat – not a witty line and not a luminous remark in the whole course of the play. An essential quality of the plotless play is poetical suggestiveness. Even the most commonplace remarks must be charged with universal significance. Let me give an imaginary example of an effect Mr Hunter's great predecessor might have achieved with meagre means. What is the dullest bit of dialogue we can think of?

VERA: Will you have some tea?

IRINA: *Tea*! *Exit*.

Dull, certainly out of context: but when we know that Irina is haunted by the uselessness of her genteel upper-middle-class existence, that her one longing, never to be satisfied, is to emancipate slaves, to succour the struggling populations of Asia and free them from their servitude on the plantations which make

Europeans rich, that tea-parties and tea-drinking are for her a symbol of the futile inactivity to which she is condemned, that her one and only door of escape has just been closed to her because her father has forbidden her to marry the specialist in tropical diseases whom she adored and with whom she would have travelled among the tea plantations of China, giving herself up to the good works for which her soul had always yearned – then, at the word 'tea' we share her vision of dreary spinsterhood, of thwarted philanthropy and of the bent and sweating millions whom she can never serve; and her exit has all the dramatic effectiveness of a tremendous *coup de théâtre*.

Hunter, far from turning the commonplace into poetry, tends to do rather the opposite. Take one example of the banality of his dialogue. He has brought together the overworked, idealistic diplomat and the besotted cynical doctor. They have an argument about the possibility of progress. Are men rising gradually above the level of the other animals, or will they remain for ever brutal, bloody and belligerent? This is a huge and thrilling question, besides being one which bears on the central theme of the play – Hope *versus* Apathy. Mr Hunter's characters speak schoolboy platitudes, and one's attention wanders. Their conversation is not very different from this:

DIPLOMAT: Surely you must admit we have made some advance in science, art, religion in the last two thousand years?

DOCTOR: No, not at all, old boy. Back just where we were.

DIPLOMAT: But people are gradually learning to hate war.

DOCTOR: Don't you believe it. Red in tooth and claw.

DIPLOMAT: Well, if not in our time, in our children's time, or our children's children's –

DOCTOR: That's what you idealists will always say. But believe me, you can't change human nature.

DIPLOMAT: You're a doctor. Look at our hospitals –

DOCTOR: All humbug. Red in tooth and claw. *etc., etc.*

I am not quite sure how skilfully the second two acts are put together, because Gielgud's direction will cover a mass of deficiencies: the first act is surprisingly bad, and the exposition as crude as can be imagined. This is the sort of thing that goes on between Sybil Thorndike and Irene Worth.

THORNDIKE: Delighted as I was to see my son John last night when he arrived back on leave from the Embassy in Paris where he has been First Secretary for so long that I am beginning to wonder whether he is ever going to be promoted, I do think he might have been politer to you, at dinner, considering that you haven't seen each other for twenty years and that you must have so much to talk about, although he appears to be a confirmed bachelor and you are a widow twice over with two children whose devoted Scottish governess is leaving tomorrow.

WORTH: Being rather conventional, he probably resents the scandal over the suicide of my second husband who was so much younger than myself; but I was delighted to see him again and to remember the happy times when we were children together after you invited me here because I was an orphan, which was of course long before your old brother gave up mountaineering and came to live with you, and you found him such a handful to look after that you took as a sort of permanent non-paying guest a penniless broken-down doctor, who drinks.

It will be gathered that I do not admire the play as such: its performance by the most incredibly star-studded cast in recent history leaves nothing to be desired. I do not know which of the actors is most accomplished.

Dame Sybil Thorndike is adorable as the harassed mother, struggling to keep her house and garden in order for a son who will not occupy them. She hits off the exact note; sympathetic, a little plaintive occasionally, but uncensorious. Gielgud has the hardest part and plays it in a masterly way. An office-working fish-out-of-water among the country people, reserved, fastidious, but with a devotion to his work, humanitarian but exasperated with individual human beings, he presents a nervous and pathetic figure. His bewilderment on learning the widow had loved him passionately when they were young, his mounting hope that it may not be too late to put things right, his disappointment, and his final burst of enthusiasm about gardening which brings the curtain down, but which we guess from the expression of fond doubt on Dame Sybil's face is doomed to be ephemeral, are all expressed with the most meticulous art. I recall, among innumerable felicities of intonation and timing, a moment in his conversation with the doctor mentioned above, when he opens his mouth to say something and closes it in quiet exasperation as the doctor's voice goes droning on. As the woman who will not marry him, Irene Worth is attractive in her disillusion. She has less to say than the other chief characters, and spends a lot of time sitting, knitting and looking. This she is very good at. Her roundish pussy-cat face is sometimes alight with humour, and sometimes clouded with tragic memories or premonitions. Her eyes can shine with pity.

Sir Lewis Casson looks wonderfully senile, sleeping in his garden chair; and whenever he wakes up to make a remark he scores heavily. The mottled and bloodshot doctor of Sir Ralph Richardson is a character of obvious appeal, so that one is tempted to pronounce his the best performance, when perhaps it is only the most striking. Megs Jenkins is so sweet and warm-hearted as the plain, lonely governess that it seems hard to believe he can refuse her, which he does most touchingly in one of the play's best scenes.

Direction is everything in a play of this kind, which can be made or marred by delicate undulations of mood and tempo. John Gielgud's subtlety is infinite: he misses no chance. If a number of people come away from *A Day by the Sea* thinking they have seen a masterpiece, which is not impossible, that will be due to him.

Philosophy Without Tears

The Burning Glass *at the Apollo*
reviewed by Richard Buckle

Charles Morgan's recipe for making plays would seem to be a sound, scientific and commercial one. There are, of course, many good methods of making effective plays, although there is no known method of writing a masterpiece. Mr Morgan's method is to take a sure-fire slap-up melodramatic plot connected with some vital topic of the day, blend it with a love interest, spice it with quotations from the easier poets, and smother it with dollops of middle-brow philosophy and eyewash.

When one is writing plays to a recipe for pleasing other people (even if one is pretending not to), rather than writing them to please oneself, which is the artist's way, one has to keep a sharp look-out for fluctuations of the market. In 1946 people may lap up the romantic excesses of melodrama; in 1950 they may want more pseudo-Shavian discussion. My guess is that in his latest play, *The Burning Glass*, Mr Morgan has slightly overdone the eyewash. Besides this, there is no star with a big name in his play – which is odd. Whether he has miscalculated or not, it is clear that no pains have been spared. There is something for all of us in *The Burning Glass*, and something for all the different people that make up each of us – for all, that is, except the pernickety, bright-eyed fanatic who cares only for pearls of great price. For the ordinary sensation-loving theatre-goer there are plotting, abductions, suspense and thrills. For the schoolboy there is a fantastic scientific invention – a huge-scale, fascinating toy. For the repressed spinster there is some talk of sex. Because everyone, almost without exception, secretly prefers to see rich, upper-class people on the stage in handsome surroundings, we are all relieved to observe a few titles and Prime Minister on the programme; and we feel cosy at the knowledge that the world-shaking events of the play will all take place against the gracious background of a country seat near the Channel.

Spinners of words in novel or play have learnt in the course of centuries that certain types of character hold a powerful appeal for great numbers of their public. I suppose sex is really at the back of it. The Eccentric Great Man is always irresistible, be he Shaw's Caesar or the Man Who Came to Dinner. His feminine counterpart is the witty-worldly-wise old lady who walks with a stick and 'still retains traces of her former beauty.' Then there is the Faithful Wife, who understands, condones and forgives the admirer who tries to seduce her – usually her husband's best friend – and holds long complacent discussions with her husband about him. She is a particularly disgusting type. The necessary pair to her, of course, is the It-is-a-far-far-better-thing character, the rakish cad who causes all the trouble – you can't help loving him – and who proves you right in thinking there was good in him all along by making, ten minutes before curtain call, the Supreme Sacrifice. All these Mr Morgan has managed to get into his play.

Finally, because Mr Morgan is a Welshman and therefore presumably descended from a griffin or dragon, there are the clouds of bardic hot air, the near-poetry, the philosophy-without-tears, the 'fine writing' and the talk of 'great matters,' all of which are designed to leave an audience of Book Society members – the best Type of Englishwomen – confused, mystified, intoxicated by the advantages of a college education, flattered at being 'made to think,' and, yes, *elevated*, they know not how or why.

Much the best and most honest part of Charles Morgan's play is the melodramatic plot: it is because this is cleverly planned that *The Burning Glass* is, after all, a good rather than bad play. We learn that Christopher Terriford, whose weather control research unit adjoins his country house, has come upon a method of concentrating light in such a way that it can burn up whole tracts of country. This 'burning glass', of which, in case of accidents, he entrusts half the formula to his wife and half to the village doctor, would render 'us' omnipotent in case of war. The scientist's mother has summoned the Prime Minister, an old flame of hers, to share this fearful knowledge; and he is expected to drop in at one in the morning. Terriford, however, doubts the advisability of telling even so great and disinterested a man his formula. Has not the time perhaps come at last to suppress the discoveries of science?

Terriford's junior partner drinks too much, talks too much, and is in love with Mrs T. He also has an unattractive and suspicious-looking friend – a foreigner – who calls for him in a white tie and encourages his bibulous and conversational excesses. Act II introduces the bearded Prime Minister, and there is much discussion of right and wrong. Terriford will not give up his secret, 'but will lend the use of it' only in case of war. From tomorrow onwards he must have continuous protection as elaborate as the Prime Minister's. After the great man has gone, the partner returns drunk with his shady escort and is got to bed. Terriford, summoned into the drive to help the foreigner start his car, is kidnapped.

By Act III our country house has become, unknown to the world, the centre of the world. The burning glass has been used to cook a tract of enemy territory and to turn a remote lake into a dust-bowl: but Terriford has not been returned. The American President keeps demanding to share the secret formula, but Mrs Terriford, despite the importunities of the Prime Minister and his titled secretary, will not give it up. She consents to help the partner set up the machine, and that is all. Zero hour approaches when the burning glass must be turned on the enemy capital, killing, perhaps, Terriford along with the rest. There has been no response or comment from the enemy. Have they perhaps discovered the secret? Suddenly Terriford staggers in.

Well, we have won this scorching cold war, but what of the future? Should Terriford withhold his knowledge from the world? Too late! His unstable partner, in the course of frying Eastern Europe, has memorised the whole formula. Luckily the cad realises he is untrustworthy and, since Mrs Terriford can never be his, decides to take poison. This he does on stage, while the little woman watches him pluckily in a mirror. The Prime Minister says a few well-chosen words, and the curtain falls on an atmosphere of hope for mankind.

An excellent plot, of which my only criticism is that I felt cheated of a big zero hour scene, with a running commentary on the devastation caused by the burning glass. Terriford's reappearance, I felt, should have been in the middle of such a scene. The outstanding performance was that of Laurence Naismith as the Prime Minister: speaking like Sir Winston, looking like Lord Salisbury, he was a splendid figure. As the mother, Dorothy Green was just right and manipulated her stick with quizzical

dignity. Faith Brook must be every 'best-type-of-Englishwoman's' idea of what she would like to be; and Michael Goodliffe made the qualms and scruples of the scientist seem decent and reasonable. The caddish partner of Michael Gough was a lively performance; and Robert Speaight's villain suggested admirably the insidious brilliance of the foreign Third Programme don.

I have nothing against Charles Morgan's recipe for writing commercial plays – after all, whoever wants to write an uncommercial play? – except the odour of sanctity and prefaces with which he surrounds them. He is so determined to be a great man of letters, a great humanist, a great gentleman. Greatness is usually a new, raw, unpalatable thing: and Mr Morgan is too smooth altogether. His love scene between the wife and the cad, however, strikes an ungentlemanly false note. When Mr Morgan makes Michael Gough say 'I want to go to bed with you. I want to press my naked body against yours' – or something of that kind – I feel as if a bishop has lifted his skirts in the middle of the Coronation.

1954

I am a Diary

I Am a Camera *at the New (Now the Albery)*
reviewed by Caryl Brahms

Christopher Isherwood – not the Isherwood who wrote that perceptive short story, *Sally Bowles*, in *Goodbye to Berlin*, but the Christopher Isherwood who is the suitably negative hero of the play which John van Druten has based on it – is a Camera. He tells us so in the opening lines of the play. Late-comers have only themselves to blame if they leave the theatre in a tizz about the title. A Camera, he insists, with its shutter open, quite passive; recording – not thinking. . . . Yet what comes out on the glossy is not a stage-play. Not a series of situations set in increasing tension. Not a pattern of people in the throes of a dilemma that is worked out, for better or worse, as the curtain falls. Far less is it some titanic conflict of values, eternally opposed, that tears our small, bright, temporary world asunder and purges us with pity as the imponderables clash. The finished print is none of these compact theatrical concepts – tidy, taut, impassioned as a poem.

It is a Diary – a day-to-day journal – a dramatised note-book of impressions – each woe treading on another's woes – each equal in importance, or unimportance, according to whether we are living them or merely looking back on them – until Fate, the dramatist, gives life a twist, and then we say 'Things like this don't happen to people like us!' 'I' – the Isherwood-van Druten 'I', that is – 'Am a Diary'. A journal kept by an English novelist in Germany, during the early 'thirties – the beginning of the end of the Years Between. The years when Hitler was an ever present atmosphere in the shadows of Berlin.

Christopher Isherwood writes in a room in Fraulein Schneider's flat. Outside, Jew-baiters brawl and prostitutes ply their trade. Inside, the chatty Schneiderchen mothers her boarders, and Christopher teaches English to Natalia, the daughter of a rich Jew who owns a Department Store. During one of these English sessions Fritz, a friend who has his way to make, calls on Christopher, bringing with him Sally Bowles – an unknown quantity. Unknown, of course, to Christopher. But we can recognise her at a glance for what she is: the Spirit of the Nineteen Thirties – a thoroughly nice West Kensington girl, gone gay and faintly native. Living for and in the minute with the singleness of purpose of a clam intent on keeping its shells closed. Living, moreover, on a diet of eggs beaten up in Worcester sauce. Existing from gin to gin. The two couples act and react on one another. Christopher and Sally form a friendly alliance against the world. The pages of the journal turn – now Sally finds she has started a baby – now she is convalescing after not having it. Now a rich American comes into their lives and for 'gin' read 'champagne'. Now he leaves them feeling suddenly deflated. At the end of the play Sally decides that she loves Christopher and tells him so as she closes his door for ever behind her. Christopher too. But I was not convinced.

Dorothy Tutin as Sally Bowles

It will not, then, be the dramatic content of the play that will draw playgoers to the New Theatre. They will, however, find some of the best acting to be seen on the West End stage today. In particular, the delicately achieved relationship between Christopher and Sally. We who have been about the highways and byways of the Theatre have long known Mr Michael Gwynn to be a sensitive and adroit player. Here he gives a performance of gangling and growing charm. His unerring sense of timing tells him just when to poise a sentence to draw a laugh – he seems never to have to sweat for it. His Christopher is a sensitive lad on an even keel – perhaps a little too hollow to move one to anything much stronger than a little gentle amusement; possibly – almost certainly – not meant to do more. He is an excellent foil to Miss Dorothy Tutin's spirited Sally.

Miss Tutin, that player with a gift of tears for those who are attuned to weep with her, now shows that she has also a great appetite for comedy. She somehow contrives to combine the satiric with the entirely credible. Sally Bowles looks like the two dimensional scribble of a cartoonist at his most inspired; she sounds like Tallulah Bankhead's daughter. The method is the same. And so, or very nearly so, is the voice – that kind of curdled cooing that could only come from a turtle-dove with laryngitis. And I, for one, can't wait for Christopher Fry to write a play for her.

And there are other excellent performances – Miss Marianne Deeming's Schneiderchen, as sweet as sugar icing, and with a relish for life that zings through the entire theatre, is not the least of them. And Renée Goddard's forthright, loyal, courageous, regulation Good Jewish Girl is excellently achieved in its attack and its integrity. And I do not wonder that both the London Library and the Times Book Club were out of copies of *Goodbye to Berlin* last week.

Why I Write in Verse

Christopher Fry had already written A Phoenix Too Frequent, The Lady's Not For Burning, The Firstborn, Venus Observed *and* A Sleep of Prisoners *when this article appeared.*

It is almost true to say that I write plays in verse to find out why I write plays in verse: or at least that I write plays in verse because that is how I write plays. I believe poetry to be as natural to us as one of our senses; that indeed it *is* one of our senses, and not something to which we are either temperamentally suited or unsuited. I mislead you if I seem to be saying that verse, or poetry, is a vague subject. Poetry is so exact that nothing can exactly define it except itself. It moves like an athlete over hurdles, to perform the most, most economically. In its purest form, change one syllable and the spirit has fled. . . . The pursuit of poetry, or the creation of its works, is an apprehension of truth beyond the power of rational thought. But it is not, therefore, irrational. To an all-seeing eye it is the reason itself. Or, in human terms, it is reason transfigured. These words – truth, apprehension, power, and so forth – are not much help to us, I know; if anything, the reverse. They are like the sparks flying up from the hoof-beats of a rapidly disappearing Pegasus.

Let me suppose myself, for the moment, to be a man to whom poetry seems unimportant and unattractive, I can easily imagine it. The outward face of the world has infinite variety; action of any kind, from the trivial to the heroic, can absorb our days and leave us gasping for time. A fairly full life can be lived collecting matchbox tops alone: not to mention botany, astronomy, gastronomy, psychology, geology, anatomy, discovery, mountaineering and pub-crawling – I could fill the evening with a list. There is no end to the prose possibilities, to the expression of this actual appearance of life. It is understandable that I should be impatient with a form of speech which is apparently foreign to the everyday: a distraction, an indulgence, if you, like, a dream of fair words. All would be well with my life of prose if there were not moments when action suddenly seems like a flame burning on the surface of a dark sea; when human behaviour dies upon itself for lack of nourishment outside its common experience; when the extreme diversity of life threatens to disintegrate altogether unless it can be unified in some place of the mind. For we cannot listen to poetry in quite the same way that we listen to prose. You cannot, for instance, try to translate it into prose in your mind as you, listen to it; or rather, you can – many people do – but what you are left with is not the experience of what was written. Poetry is the humility of language; it waits and is filled, and we can receive it only in the same spirit. But though language can be humble it can also be – and is, usually – so obstinate, so determined to set up difficulties, so opaque between the vision and the expression, that we have to be content too often with a very rough approximation to what we need and search after. . . .

There are many people to whom verse in the theatre is irritating, or boring, or distracting, or pretentious flight of fashion; and in certain moods I can pish and tush with the best of them. This point of view is not held so strongly about literature in general. It is not often said that there should be no such thing as poetry at all. . . . What reason is there for limiting the theatre to one form of communication? It is even believed that the prose play and the verse play are in opposition, or that the one precludes the other; there appears to be a kind of colour bar in the matter. Such rivalry is nonsense. Indeed, prose and verse existing side by side counter each other's dangers. If they pass altogether out of each other's reach they cease to be themselves, becoming on the one hand journalese, official cant, or any other string of sentences: and on the other a vagueness, an abstraction, a preciousness. This interplay of difference, one touching the hand of the other as it separates, like men and women dancing the Grand Chain, is what keeps each in its own state of grace. One explanation of our impatience with a verse play is that the spring of theatre is action, and any insistence upon words is felt to hang like heavy clothes on the body of an athlete. When we go to the theatre we go to be interested by a story of lives living out their conflicts in a concentration of time. We do not go to hear them discuss the matter; we go to see and hear them live it. But we know that words and actions are not unrelated. One illuminates the other: and the full significance of action can be explored only by words. If we compare the murder of Maria Marten in the Red Barn with the murder of Duncan in Macbeth's castle, we see that in each the physical action is roughly the same, but the significance of the action is entirely different. The one is merely done, the other is experienced, and the experience is in the words. What is more, the experience is the true nature of the action. The experience ultimately *is* the action. . . .

From the way I am going on you would think I was talking

about the Eleusinian Mysteries, not about a theatre in which you propose to spend an entertaining evening. It is the fault of the question: Why Verse? I should really write a play which would be so good that the question would never arise: a play which would please, not some of the people some of the time, but all of the people all of the time: which would be both the immediate appearance of things and the eternal nature of things, and both combined with such felicity that you would hardly know, in your enjoyment, whether you drank from 'Helicon's harmonious springs' or were the lady Mr Rattigan calls Aunt Edna. Poetry in the theatre is the action of listening. It is an unrolling exploration: following your nose; or it would be better to say following your ear, for sound itself, pure sound, has logic, as we know in music, and what does that logic accord to if not the universal discipline felt along the heart? What part this logic plays in our life here on the earth is beyond calculation. If it wakens harmony, modulation, and the resolving of discord in us, we are nearer to our proper natures. The general lines of the play, the shape of the story, the disposition of the characters, should point and implicate by their actions and their wider uses the texture of the poetry.

The large pattern of the action should have a meaning in itself, above and beyond the story: the kind of meaning which gives everlasting truth to myths and legend, and makes the fairy-story into a sober fact; a meaning not so conscious as a parable or so contrived as an allegory but, as it were, tracing a figure which the poetry can naturally and inevitably fill.

This is all very well, you may now say, this fine theory; but we have to put up with verse plays as they are, not as they ideally should be; it seems to us that a good deal of these plays could be written at least as well, and more honestly, in prose. . . . I have no answer to satisfy you if you believe that human nature, or human personality, is divided into two parts, of whatever proportion, the prosaic and the poetic. I think we live always with a foot in each camp, or rather that there is no moment when we can safely say that we belong entirely to one or the other. There is no moment when we can certainly say that even our apparently most insignificant actions have not a significance greatly beyond ourselves. It is this tension between two meanings which verse conveys, favouring sometimes one, sometimes the other. The prosaic or colloquial can be rhythmically just sufficiently charged to resolve into the implication of verse at a moment's notice, even half-way through a sentence, and back again, without disturbing the unity of the speech, in the way that the spirit and the flesh work in ourselves without noticeably sawing us in half. The writer's responsibility is to know when he can safely break free of this, and relax for contrast into the rhythms of prose. . . .

In *The Dark is Light Enough* there comes a moment when the situation reduces everyone to silence, when there seems no way of the scene going on without bringing the curtain down. And then the Countess begins to speak:

> How shall we manage, with time at a standstill?
> We can't go back to where nothing has been said;
> And no heart is served, caught in a moment
> Which has frozen. Since no words will set us free –

Not at least now, until we can persuade
Our thoughts to move –
Music would underground-us best,
As a tide in the dark comes to boats at anchor
And they begin to dance. My father told me
How he went late one night, a night
Of some Hungarian anxiety,
To the Golden Bull at Buda, and there he found
The President of your House of Deputies
Alone and dancing in his shirtsleeves
To the music of the band, himself
Put far away, bewitched completely
By the dance's custom; and so it went on,
While my father drank and talked with friends,
Three or four hours without a pause:
This weighty man of seventy, whose whole
Recognition of the world around
During those hours, was when occasion
He turned his eyes to the gipsy leader
And the music changed, out of a comprehension
As wordless as the music.
It was dancing that came up out of the earth
To take the old man's part against anxiety.

A comprehension as wordless as the music. It is this comprehension which poetry tries to speak: this revelation of discipline that comes up out of the earth, or is felt along the heart. It is this which verse has to offer. I hope, out of the goodness of your hearts, you will not hold any of this against me if, in five years time, you should find I am writing plays entirely in prose.

Credits and Discredits for 1954

Congratulations to: John Whiting for the best play, *Marching Song*, and for showing that he is the best of the younger dramatists; to Tennents for maintaining their high standard of production in a difficult year and keeping so many stars employed; to Sandy Wilson for the success of *The Boy Friend* in London and New York; to Terence Rattigan for returning to the top of his form; and to the Arts Theatre for doing its job properly.

Mistakes of the year: *A Midsummer Night's Dream* as produced by the Old Vic for export; Shakespeare on TV.

Disappointments of the Year: Ann Todd's Lady Macbeth; Ingrid Bergman's Joan of Arc and Cornelia Otis Skinner.

Names we have missed: Hermione Gingold, Robert Donat, Alec Clunes and Flora Robson.

Plays we should like to have missed: *After the Ball, The White Countess* and *The Manor of Northstead.*

Welcome Back: Beatrice Lillie, Evelyn Laye, Ruth Gordon, Eileen Herlie, Rex Harrison, Lilli Palmer, Mary Ellis, Zena Dare and Cathleen Nesbitt.

Come back soon: Sybil Thorndike, Carol Bruce, Jean-Louis Barrault, Edwige Feuillère, Googie Withers, Harold Lang, Sam Wanamaker, Sacha Guitry and Jean Vilar.

Pull up your socks: The Ralph Birch Organisation.

Lost cause of 1954: the standard of acting in Shakespearian plays.

Kiss and make up: The stage and TV.

Not Good Enough department: The Old Vic and TV plays.

The Dark is Light Enough, designed by Oliver Messel, with, centre, Edith Evans as the Countess

Lucky ones: Julian Slade and Valerie Hobson.

Unlucky one: Peter Ustinov.

Most boring controversy of the year: Commercial TV.

Please don't do it again: Noël Coward adapting someone else's play as a musical; Frith Banbury directing Shakespeare.

We weren't surprised at the short runs of: *No Sign of the Dove, After the Ball, Thirteen for Dinner, The Duenna* and *The Bombshell.*

We were surprised at the long runs of: *The Manor of Northstead* and *Relations are Best Apart.*

Good Luck in 1955 to: John Whiting.

Best performances of the year: Eric Portman, John Gielgud, Siobhan McKenna, Peggy Ashcroft, Dorothy Tutin, Gladys Cooper, Diana Wynyard and Margaret Leighton.

Best productions of the year: Peter Glenville's *Separate Tables* and Tyrone Guthrie's *The Matchmaker.*

Young players who have added to their laurels: Virginia McKenna, Michael Gwynn, Barbara Jefford, Tony Britton, Zena Walker, Penelope Mundy, Peter Wyngarde, Arthur Hill and Alec McCowen.

Bravest performance of the year: Robert Morley.

Success Story *(continued)*: Agatha Christie.

Bad performances of the year: Laurence Harvey as Romeo; Robert Flemyng as Forster in *Marching Song.*

Best set design: Oliver Messel's for *The Dark is Light Enough.*

Best musical: *The Boy Friend.*

Thanks to: Fred Carter, for introducing Leslie Bricusse to the West End.

Our hopes for 1955: Better plays, better acting, better productions.

1955

The year that Russia formally brought an end to its state of war with Germany and withdrew its troops from Austria was also the year that the Soviet Chairman Malenkov resigned to make way for Khrushchev and Bulganin. A general strike in Argentina forced Peron into exile.

In Britain, Churchill's resignation was followed by the prime ministership of Eden and a Conservative win at the General Election . . . Miller produced A View from the Bridge, *Tennessee Williams* Cat on a Hot Tin Roof *and Beckett* Waiting for Godot . . .

Theatre in the Round

by Stephen Joseph

Stephen Joseph, director son of publisher Michael Joseph and actress Hermione Gingold, was a post-war pioneer and champion of arena staging. The Alan Ayckbourn-directed Scarborough Theatre is named after him.

The arena theatre is a theatre in which the audience sit all round the stage – like a circus but, usually, smaller. Acting and production in the round have a special interest to us because scope is offered for certain kinds of experiment which our theatre at the moment, for various reasons, denies. The theatre with a proscenium arch or frame, evolved from the apron stage of the 18th-century which, in England, was the compromise between the Italian perspective stage, with its raked floor – still sometimes in evidence, and the open stage of the Elizabethans. The open stage, of course, is still a valid dramatic unit and, like the arena, has been used for many exciting productions in Europe and America.

The origins of present day interest in arena theatre were the circus productions of Reinhardt, the Realist Theatre in Moscow, and the American projects of Norman Bel Geddes and Robert Edmond Jones, all of which belong to the so-called new Movement of the '20s. In America the arena theatre has played a special role since plays in the round are presented to people all over the country who have never before seen live theatre.

Proscenium stage theatres are big buildings and for many years speculators have avoided this particular sort of investment; but the building necessary for a financially self-supporting theatre in the round can be as simple as a garage, a ballroom, an assembly hall, a gymnasium, a factory, a store and so on. Because of this there is a relatively flourishing arena theatre movement in America. There are also some buildings specially designed for the purpose such as the Penthouse Theatre at the University of Washington in Seattle, which I visited when I was in America and which does not look nearly as antiseptic as its photographs make out. The other arena theatre that I visited in Washington had recently been a garage.

Places have been built or adapted in Italy, France, Russia and even in England – though in England pathetically few. Jack Midgely, late drama adviser for Norfolk and now of Essex, deserves credit for trying to demonstrate the potentialities of arena theatre in this country with amateur actors in school halls, in gymnasia, in Women's Institutes and in Norfolk. John English's arena theatre is not an arena theatre. He does productions on an open stage and tries to make it as much like a proscenium arch theatre as possible. This, I think, is a pity. Some of our university companies have done plays in the round, but the possibilities of this method have not been fully explored, and some discussion is perhaps worthwhile.

Discussion is second best, of course, to going to an arena theatre and seeing a performance or two, but London has no arena theatre, and apart from an occasional festival production or amateur performance there is little enough to see. The reasons for this scarcity of arena production in England are, firstly, the licensing regulations. These were drawn up for timber-built, gas-lit theatres, with proscenium arches, and which demand a safety curtain, which can have no function in an arena theatre and, therefore, stops arena theatres being built. Secondly, the scarcity of suitable halls or building sites prevents clubs prepared to experiment with tuppence farthing from doing so. The absurdity of the licensing laws should be remembered when we are campaigning for the preservation of old theatre buildings, for here is one bad reason that new theatres are not going up.

So let me take you to an arena theatre in America. The first thing that may strike you is that there is no scenery. Oddly enough, almost every sort of play ever written has been done in the round without this particular difficulty causing much anxiety. The point is that scenery is only one of the jewels on the fingers of drama and, with some other trappings, can be laid aside with impunity; theatre in the round brings us face to face with the essentials of drama – good acting and good plays.

If you consider the way people are usually seated in a theatre you will see what I mean when I describe the auditorium as being on one side of the acting area. Think of the acting area as a rectangle, then open staging allows a three-sided auditorium and an arena stage a four-sided one – and if, for simplicity's sake you draw a diagram in squares to illustrate this you will arrive at the startling conclusion that, without going any farther back from the acting area, there is eight times as much space for seating the audience in an arena theatre than in a proscenium theatre. But I hasten to add that this is not quite the true state of affairs since the square does not represent any real auditorium. However, it is undoubtedly one of the outstanding advantages of arena staging that more people in the audience can see and hear the actors than in most ordinary theatres. This is not only a gain for the audience but for the actors as well – as we shall see in a moment. Although there need be no scenery, in the canvas and three-by-one sense, the arena theatre is not without visual appeal; the most important thing to see in the theatre is the actors acting; but visual aids may include masks, costumes and lighting which can be used when and how the play demands.

A lot of people cannot stomach the idea of a theatre devoid of red plush, gold cupids, house curtains and footlights. Personally, as an advocate of arena theatre, I do not wish to pull down historic buildings, Aunt Edna should be able to go where she pleases; but these particular things are not essential to drama, and some of their particular magic and charm can be replaced by another magic and charm in an arena theatre – its decor and lighting. The houselights fade into blackness, lights come up on the acting area and we cease to be aware of the rest of the audience in the sudden concentration of our attention on the actors who have taken possession of the stage. In an arena production the conventions that are most upset on stage and concern mostly the actor are the little textbook adages about facing front, kneeling on the down-stage knee, standing with the upstage foot slightly in front of the other, upstaging other actors and taking centre. You can see these ideas put into practice – and badly – by many of our most reputable performers in the West End. But there is no up and down stage in the arena; there is no need for a stage whisper – the truest of whispers will be heard. movement and grouping have a new importance. Above all, the arena theatre exposes insincere acting, at the close range from which the arena audience watches, a good actor can be crystal clear even when only his back is seen.

It follows also that many artists experienced in our vast proscenium theatres may come across very phoney in the round. The audience is near, the actor needs to be in earnest; this is all to the good with most modern – and some classical plays. Several people

who ought to know better have talked rubbish about the intimacy of the arena theatre; they have supposed that we claim it as an advantage of the arena theatre that the audience is so involved in the play that they no longer distinguish between actors and audience – which can be very embarrassing. Stories of gentlemen and others leaping onto the stage in defence of Desdemona or to finish off Macbeth tells us less about the power of a particular method of staging than about the occasional presence of morons or adults with child minds in audiences.

There must be separation between actors and audience in the adult, though not necessarily in children's, theatre; there are all sorts of ways of effecting this separation – putting the actors on a platform, putting them behind masks, in costume, seating the audience in formal rows (of fairly comfortable seats often enough), putting the actors in bright light and the audience in comparative dark, putting the actors behind a frame, making the actors speak set lines, move set moves and behave as if the audience were not there, giving them a vocabulary and syntax unlike that used in conversation.

Without going further, you will see that many of these established ways of separating actors and audience are available to the arena theatre. Intimacy in this case means simply that members of the audience are close enough to the stage to see and hear better than Aunt Edna's poorer friends usually can, with the result that actors can convey thoughts and feelings more convincingly, so that the entertainment is at once more exciting, and worth time and money.

The particular opportunities offered us by the arena theatre, then, include a style of acting freed from techniques of projecting over large physical distances, and substituting a particular integrity and intensity capable of transmitting thought and feeling in all directions. There is the chance of taking Antoine's dilemma to a happier conclusion – no need for us to remove the fourth wall at all. The whole business of theatre if it is an art implies convention; but I believe that the conventions of theatre in the round – at any rate as I have seen it in America – are more acceptable to filmgoers and TV viewers than the conventions so dear to proscenium theatre goers.

This means that with theatre in the round we may be able to win a larger audience back to live theatre. There are chances too of giving these audiences new plays – and if there is anything desperately needed in the theatre world it is an easier market for the beginning playwright. There are signs that the production of classic and foreign plays can be presented without the awful consideration of high production costs. Certainly these things are being done in America and on the Continent. Most important of all, there are possibilities in arena theatre for giving every sort of audience a new and exciting experience of drama, the oldest of the arts.

The British Theatre has always passed through recurring phases. Generally it has been the Actors' Theatre, giving way to the Playwrights' Theatre, or, in course of time, the same action in reverse. In the Between War years we had a predominantly Playwright's theatre, that is to say a theatre in which the interest was centred more upon the playwright than upon the actor. It was a period rich in fine writing. Shaw was still in his prime, and Galsworthy, Bennett, Bridie, Maugham, Priestley, and many others, were giving of their best.

At the end of the 1930s, change was in the air. Change always comes from the outskirts and perimeters, and then penetrates into the centre. It came in this case from the Old Vic – the Old Vic of Lilian Baylis, where, during the 1920s and 1930s, concurrently with the Playwright's Theatre of the time, a great school of classical acting was coming into being. In the forefront of this movement were John Gielgud, Sybil Thorndike, Edith Evans, Laurence Olivier, Ralph Richardson, Donald Wolfit, Peggy Ashcroft, and half a dozen others.

The influence of that group, as it began to assert itself, was profound. With the beginning of the war, playwriting was naturally at a discount, and the British theatre became predominantly an Actors' Theatre, a Star Actors' Theatre, which was rich, as ever before, in the portrayal of the classics. It found a ready-made audience in the former Old Vic devotees, who had now reached maturity. These constituted a comfortable, middle-class and middle-aged audience of considerable dimensions.

Trained in youth to the appreciation of the classics, this audience definitely knew what it wanted, and because the actors were able to satisfy that want in such rare excellence, it was able to impose its tastes upon its fellow playgoers. It is the audience and the actors, rather than the managers, who for the last 15 years have conditioned the fact that the London theatre has relied so largely on revivals – and upon foreign importations which lend themselves so greatly to performance in the grand manner. But in the meantime, the outskirts and the perimeters have once again been active. During the last 15 years, concurrently with the star system at the centre, there has been growing up a Provincial repertory system which has no parallel in the western world.

The number of permanent repertory companies has increased from about 20 before 1939 to about 80 today. This does not necessarily mean that the Provinces are seeing as much 'live' theatre as they did before the war, because it must be remembered that touring from London to the smaller towns has correspondingly declined. It does mean, however, that a resident company with a style and a standard of its own is attracting a larger audience than that which patronised the touring companies, and that a new standard of audience appreciation, based upon 'non-star' performances has, in the course of years, come into being.

There are, today, a large number of actors and actresses who are content to work only in repertory, though promotion to London is naturally always their ambition. Partly under official fostering, and partly by the nature of things, a ladder system has been evolved whereby artists who have received initial training in the smaller companies can ascend to the larger companies. In this way the repertory movement has become a homogeneous whole.

New Stars for Old

An optimistic mid-1950s assessment of the growing ascendancy of the company over the star player from Charles Landstone associate Drama Director at CEMA and the Arts Council 1942-1952.

Edwige Feuillère in LA DAME AUX CAMELIAS

Its keynote is a performance which stresses the company as an entity and not as individual performers. The perimeter theatre has thus quite spontaneously and unconsciously been building up the antidote to the star system. After 15 years the influence of this new repertory audience is beginning to be felt in the metropolitan theatre, for it must be remembered that the West End, after the first few weeks of a run, depends upon the Provincial visitors for continuance. In the last 18 months there have been four significant happenings.

In 1953, the Players' Theatre in London produced a musical play, *The Boy Friend*, a burlesque of the 1920s. The cast, all good actors and actresses, were not in the star rank. The play attracted immediate attention, but the management of the Players' refused to allow a transfer to the West End until all the original cast were available. It was eventually produced at Wyndhams' early in 1954 and, as all the world knows, this team of unknowns has achieved a startling success. The accent is on the word 'team'.

In August of the same year came the fairy-tale triumph of *Salad Days* at the Vaudeville. For four years with the Bristol Old Vic Company, Denis Carey had been building up a team spirit. The individual members of the company might change, though a nucleus remained with him throughout. *Salad Days* was the third musical play presented at Bristol which had been written by Julian Slade and Dorothy Reynolds. The strength of these three plays lay in the fact that the authors were members of the company and that the parts were actually written to fit in with the known characteristics of each individual artist. There is no need to expand on the phenomenal success this company of little-known actors has achieved in London.

In February of this year *Sailor, Beware!* came to the Strand Theatre from repertory. André Van Gyseghem had produced it at Worthing, but was not available at the time of the West End production, so the task was entrusted to Laurence Gilliam, the Director of the Repertory Company.

There is one part in the play which calls for an outstanding performance. Many a star would have grasped at it. The management very wisely decided to retain the repertory actress, Peggy Mount, who had played the part at Worthing, together with most of the supporting company. It is rumoured that, because they had no star, they were refused Provincial dates, and had the greatest difficulty in finding a London theatre. The owners of the Strand Theatre can be glad today that they decided to part from convention.

The fourth and last example is *Serious Charge*, which opened at the Garrick Theatre. It is true that, although this was again a repertory play, the original cast was strengthened by two or three very good London artists of reputation, though I do not think that any of them would claim to be stars. Nevertheless, most of the company came direct from repertory, and the leading part was played by Patrick McGoohan, a product of Sheffield and Coventry, who had never before appeared on the West End stage except in very minor roles. Again, the answer can claim to be success, although the play did not have a very long run.

These four productions, coming one on top of the other, cannot be merely accidental. I, personally, am convinced that future historians of the theatre will attach great significance to them. They are the sign that, once more, the pattern of British theatrical taste is undergoing a change. The 15-year role of the Star Actors' Theatre is beginning to fade out, and the long patient work, often drudgery, of the repertory movement is to have its reward in a theatre wherein the company, as a unit, will be the star attraction.

With the first performance of *Titus Andronicus* at the Memorial Theatre, Stratford-upon-Avon, Peter Brook has launched his latest sensation in the theatre, himself designing the production, composing the music and directing the play. Many years ago, when Brook first read *Titus Andronicus*, it was his ambition to produce it with an all-Negro cast. He saw the play as possessing primitive, barbaric energy, in which all the murder, killing and revenge had a natural place. Then, later, when he returned to the script, he realised that Shakespeare had modelled his early work on the Roman writer Seneca and not on contemporary Elizabethan work. With this in mind to guide him – for Brook's idea of a director is that he should be a narrator, helping to clarify and explain the ideas of the dramatist in concrete terms before an audience – he set about making notes which he could put before Leslie Hurry, the designer. Unfortunately Hurry then found that he would be unable to undertake the work because of other commitments. Brook was bewildered at this stroke of fate. To whom should he turn? Wakhevitch, Dalí or Messel? While he was looking through his own rough sketches he came across one composed of three large columns, and decided to have it made up as a model to see how it would look. When he saw the result a few days later he knew that he would tackle the designing of the production himself. I asked him if he thought it a good idea for a director to design his own productions.

'I can do it about once in every five years,' he replied. 'And then only at a place like Stratford where I can rely upon the people who are going to carry out my work. During the last week of production the responsibility becomes so staggering that there can be few last-minute changes. To design your own production has one enormous advantage. In the normal course of events you choose your designer to bring an added decorative quality to the play. Now that designer, being an artist, will naturally feel certain moments that he wants to highlight, and these are sure to be different from those which the producer has planned. Therefore, if I design the sets, I know that the highlights of production and of decoration will be identical.'

While he was talking, this short, rather stocky young man was using his hands to emphasise his points as though playing the keyboard of the grand piano which lay open before him. He seemed quite unable to contain the energy which was surging through him. Even his hair seemed to be standing on end. 'As to finding a consistent style of acting,' he went on, 'it is downright impossible. Shakespeare wrote on two different levels. One was realistic, the other was when he lifted his characters out of naturalism and made them as formal as anything Racine ever

OCTOBER
1955

Brook and *Titus Andronicus*

Plays and Players' first editor, Ronald Barker, interviewing Peter Brook

created. It is the producer's job to unite these two styles and not to stifle one at the other's expense, or else the play will become unbalanced and blurred. I like to keep the parts as clear and vivid as the colours I use for the costumes.'

I asked him about his views on the music. 'Ah – there I have very definite ideas. I believe that in the concert hall the audience listen with both their ears, concentrating on the music they are hearing, and which most are sufficiently knowledgable to appreciate. In the theatre, on the other hand, music is only important in creating atmosphere and underlining mood. Because of this I have called my own particular brand "quarter-ear-music". In *Titus* the problem was tricky, because most of this kind of music is typically modern and I wanted a barbaric sound. So I did it myself. I can best explain my method by giving an example. The first scene in *Titus Andronicus* is all plot. Then in the next we are immediately transported to the hunting scene. To obtain the fresh open-air effect, I could have plunged from the darkness of the first setting to a blue cyclorama. Actually, I used a rather wonderful, bright, unearthly green. For the music, I had a fanfare played on the horn and trumpet and recorded at normal speed. Then the speed was increased so that the dexterity of the playing sounded inhuman, and the result was then put through an echo chamber so that I got an unearthly, brilliant sound to match the green.'

'And you feel that this kind of music is right for *Titus*?'

'The audience is so busy taking in the story, watching the stage and all that is happening, that melody and counterpoint would have been ineffectual. Only texture, rhythm and timbre are important. That is why the zither music for the film, *The Third Man* was so successful – the same thing applies in the theatre.'

'And how has it all come about?' I asked. 'Are you satisfied?'

'All I can say is that it came out as I wanted. Laurence Olivier, Vivien Leigh and Tony Quayle were most patient and helpful. I owe everything to their performances. The show is theirs, not mine.' (Only a few days before, the three actors had said the same thing about their director). 'But working at Stratford,' he went on, 'is such an invigorating experience. Reg Sayle paints the scenery with such loving care, taking infinite pains to get the colours and texture exactly right, while Keegan Smith cuts his costumes with just the right theatrical extravagance. Nothing is too much trouble for them to get the right effect. All very satisfying to a director, specially when he does so many of the jobs himself.'

Peter Brook's production of *Titus Andronicus* with, left, Laurence Olivier in the title role

Credits and Discredits for 1955

Congratulations to: Laurence Olivier for reminding us what a fine Shakespearean actor he is and rocketing the prestige of the Stratford Memorial Theatre to new heights; Sandy Wilson for following up *The Boy Friend*, his first success, with another, *The Buccaneer*, in different style; Peter Hall and the Arts Theatre for presenting three-quarters of the year's best plays.

Mistakes of the year: casting Vivien Leigh as Viola in *Twelfth Night* and putting on *Romance in Candlelight*.

Pleasant surprises of the year: Eva Bartok's sensitive performance in *The Lovers*, and the popular success of *Waiting for Godot*.

Disappointments of the year: Wendy Hiller and Margaret Rawlings as the Merry Wives of Windsor.

Names we have missed: Alec Guinness, Robert Donat, Noël Coward, Richard Burton and Patricia Jessel.

Names we are glad to have missed: Anna Neagle and Richard Attenborough.

Forgotten name of 1955: Peter Ustinov.

52

Plays we should like to have missed: *Into Thin Air, The Sun of York* and *It's Different for Men*.

Welcome back: Binnie Hale, Joan Greenwood, Gordon Harker and Dirk Bogarde.

Come back soon: Orson Welles, Sybil Thorndike, Googie Withers, Ralph Richardson and Edwige Feuillère.

Pull up your socks: Laurier Lister.

Lost cause of 1955: British dramatists.

Not good enough department: Supporting players in *The Queen and the Rebels* and *Tiger at the Gates*.

Bores of the year: Anna Massey and Ruby Murray.

Dreariest controversy of the year: the costumes in *King Lear*.

Linguist of the year: Yvonne Arnaud.

Definition of the year: 'Television drama is just repertory in an iron-lung.'

We weren't surprised at the short runs of: *The Tender Trap* and *The Diary of a Nobody*.

We were surprised at the long runs of: *The Bad Seed, Lucky Strike* and *The Shadow of Doubt*.

Three Arts Theatre productions under Peter Hall's regime.
Left: *Listen to the Wind*
Centre: *The Burnt Flower Bed* by Ugo Betti
Right: *Mourning Becomes Electra* by Eugene O'Neill

Good luck in 1956 to: Denis Cannan, author of *Misery Me!*, and Peter Greenwell, composer of *Twenty Minutes South*.

Best performances of the year: Laurence Olivier in *Titus Andronicus*, Michael Redgrave in *Tiger at the Gates*, John Gielgud and Peggy Ashcroft in *Much Ado About Nothing*, Alfred Drake in *Kismet*, Nigel Patrick in *The Remarkable Mr Pennypacker*, Peggy Mount in *Sailor, Beware!* and Irene Worth in *The Queen and the Rebels*

Best productions of the year: Peter Brook's *Titus Andronicus*, Douglas Seale's *Henry IV* and Peter Hall's *South* and *Summertime*.

Bravest performance of the year: Max Wall in *Pyama Game*.

Bad performances of the year: Ronald Shiner in *My Three Angels* and Leslie French in *The Sun of York*.

Success story (*continued for the third year*): Agatha Christie.

Young players who have added to their laurels: Denholm Elliott, Denis Quilley, John Neville, Paul Daneman, Zena Walker, Clare Austin, Patrick McGoohan and Alec McCowen.

Impersonation of the year: Emlyn Williams as Dylan Thomas.

Our hopes for 1956: to see a good play by a British author, and to see Emlyn Williams as Emlyn Williams.

1956

The year of Nasser's seizure of the Suez Canal and the Suez crisis was also the year that Russia invaded Hungary and, on a lighter note, Prince Rainier III of Monaco married Grace Kelly.

In Britain, Macmillan introduced Premium Savings Bonds as well as the MOT and parking meters. Motorists also suffered the reintroduction of petrol rationing. Colin Wilson produced the study, The Outsider. *Anouilh in France unveiled his new play,* Poor Bitos. *But Britain's coming pre-eminence in new dramatic writing was signalled with the appearance of Osborne's* Look Back In Anger *and Brendan Behan's* The Quare Fellow.

1956

Pace Without Poetry

Caryl Brahms reviews Peter Brook's production of Hamlet.

Paul Scofield as the Prince

The Scofield-Brook-Tennent – and shall I couple Moscow? – *Hamlet* has come to the Charing Cross Road, following hard on its embassage of honour to Russia. The seasoned playgoer calling to mind the many lovingly prepared productions of the last 30 years of this, the best-loved tragedy in the treasury of the theatre, may well wonder how it was that the honour fell to this particular presentation – one that missed magic by a short wand.

Before discussing its shortcomings let us proceed to its vigorous virtues. First, then, Wakhevitch has designed for it an all-purpose set which is both simple and impressive, and which greatly helps the producer's bent for speed. Through this set, which looks like a militant stone beehive, the action whirls, swirls, beats and buzzes, as racing thoughts in a fevered mind. This *Hamlet* is a piece of living, livid theatre in which action – or rather activity – comes first, and poetry last. In it Paul Scofield, whom we have watched grow up, not only in another production of this play, but in many parts on many stages, comes definitely to maturity. The playgoer may not agree with his reading at all points, but such is its depth and dignity that it compels him to respect it. We have then, on the credit side, a swiftly moving, strongly contemporary production, framing a distinguished and adult performance.

Yet in these very virtues lie its shortcomings, since pace has outdistanced poetry; decisive acting has banished indecision. And lacking his agony, Denmark is indeed without its mixed-up Prince. If speed is Mr Brook's presiding genius, it is also his besetting daemon. We can be sure that he cares passionately for the fell clutch of circumstance that impels people to behave according to its dictation – above all, Mr Brook is an inspired puppet-master. Is he as deeply concerned with the hearts of his characters as with their outward response to the lash of the whip – as fascinated by the thing they feel as he is by the moves he invents for them to make? We have still to be convinced.

Like Rossini's opera *The Barber of Seville, Hamlet* the play has become so weighed down with a Gothic load of preconceived ideas, made-over business, echoes of half-remembered intonations, the ghosts of lines spoken in the past which stalk the present so that, sorely as both would be missed, the greatest service we could do these works would be to ban them from our stage for the next 10 years and then re-study them, so freeing them of the prejudice, not only in the minds of player and producer, but in our own minds, too. Who knows but that the result might be a Hamlet, not as our psychoanalysts and dons set him before us, but in the far more simple way that Shakespeare thought of him in the mind's eye of a working dramatist.

My guess is that the author saw a young man in the throes of the triple shock of the sudden death of his beloved father, the sudden remarriage of his still beautiful mother and the sudden suspicion that his stepfather had killed his father. His natural aversion to becoming the instrument of vengeance at war with the impulse in him to avenge, results in some of the most universally loved and touchingly muddled poetry that man has known. It is my belief that the drama and poetry of *Hamlet* is just as simple and as compelling as this. The most courageous thing that a producer of *Hamlet* can do is to give us, not his new reading of the play, but the play that Shakespeare wrote.

Mr Brook is a brave man. Other excursions in other fields have proved this point. What a pity that he has more love for the chessboard and the strong light that falls across it than for the people in the play – for the things that they do rather than the words they say. What a chance this was to return unobtrusively to Shakespeare! But the way of genius is not to be unobtrusive, and that Mr Brook is an inspired director is not in question. He has gone as far as producer may in ridding the play of 30 years of overtones but in the process, coarseness has crept in – in part due to casting, never this producer's strongest point – and partly because of a certain inhumanity which years and the world will no doubt rectify.

And now to the observed of all observers – to the Hamlet. With this interpretation Mr Scofield has left his salad days behind – too far behind, perhaps. Gone is the coltish amble, the strangulated voice, endearingly halfway between a coo and a croak, the over-frequent recourse to an unhouseled soul whose counsels once appeared to be kept in the general direction of the gallery. This Hamlet is precisely and decisively placed, stylishly enacted, beautifully spoken. His movements are purposeful and swift, his frenzies carefully considered. He leaves the playgoer in no doubt that, in his own good time, he would have dealt faithfully, lethally and in cold blood with Claudius. The sanest, least petulant of a long line of sable princes, he still brought what poetry there was to a prosaic production.

Mary Ure, the Ophelia, who made so pleasing an impression in *Time Remembered*, was so completely miscast that it will be quite some time before one playgoer, at least, will be able to forget her, and Diana Wynyard, following an approach undreamt of by dons and psychiatrists, clearly decided that old Hamlet had married beneath him, and went to heroic lengths to thrust home this point.

There remain three performances of unusual persuasiveness. Alec Clunes has found for us a Claudius as smooth and worldly as a practised after-dinner speaker, as plausible as a north-country politician, as perfectly placed as a figure on the apex of a pyramid of acrobats at the moment of Tar-rah! As with the best kind of con-man, it was hard to believe this man to be a villain. He is the murderous usurper only nor'-nor'-west: blows the wind in another direction, and we have the country gentleman turned king – as much at home with hawk and handsaw as with an Ambassador from a foreign power. But Claudius is a character who caught the busy actor-dramatist napping. Does he not declare 'There's such divinity doth hedge a king that treason can but peep to what it will,' who is the very man who treacherously killed his king? But take it for all in all, we have not looked upon the like of the Clunes-Claudius before, either for grace or loneliness or technical excellence.

Ernest Thesiger's foolish, fond old Polonius, though not the most comical, is certainly the most touching I have seen – simple, guileless, old. And the silent-footed non-smoking ghost of John Phillips, friendly not fuming, made young Hamlet's filial affection the more believable. Less admirable are the most unfunny of grave-diggers and the least martial Fortinbras that ever stalked stage.

Why, then, of all the excellent and moving productions of

SHIRL CONWAY in PLAIN AND FANCY

Hamlet that this country has boasted and that this very management, not to mention the Old Vic, and Stratford-on-Avon, has presented, was it this strongly dramatic, but miscast and unpoetic production that had to get to Moscow?

Give Us A Chance!

Composer Vivian Ellis who enjoyed a big post-war success with Bless the Bride *(and whose 1920s musical* Mr Cinders *enjoyed a long running revival in the 1980s) defends the English musical.*

The main difference between the American and English Musical lies in the two countries' attitudes towards light music. In America, light music, or show music, is taken seriously. It is seriously reviewed. In England this is not the case. The late Sir Charles Cochran told me that Sir Thomas Beecham could see no difference between Jerome Kern's music and any other light music – which surely shows that even Sir Thomas is not infallible. Everything else stems from this. American light music is part of the American way of living. It is taken seriously, and treated seriously. Singers, orchestras, performances in general, all have to conform to a higher standard.

In my autobiography, *I'm on a See-Saw*, I wrote that a song is 'as good as it is sung'. This is no exaggeration. A poor score, well put over by an American company, or even an American producer, sounds wonderful to our ears. Yet we have the singers here. I attended with Cochran, 17 auditions in New York for an American leading man – and there were, in my opinion, just as good artists here. It is the same with productions. Remember, we only see America's tried successes, not the flops – and when they're bad, they're as bad, if not worse, than ours. The majority of critics, dance bands, and gramophone companies seem unaware of this. Each new American Musical is acclaimed as a masterpiece – *before it opens*. Let an English Musical try and get as much advance publicity in the press! Let an English show tune try and get a recording. I had to wait one year to get *This Is My Lovely Day* from *Bless The Bride* played on the big British dance bands. Most English Musicals can't afford to wait so long. Nobody would play my *I'm on a See-Saw* from a show called *Jill Darling* at the Saville Theatre in 1935 – until Chappells put it out in America, and it went on the hit parade. You cannot make a hit, but unless you give a tune a hearing, it might just as well stay in the composer's bottom drawer.

The American Musical starts off in this country with one great advantage. It has already been performed and tightened up. Its music has filtered through, on records, and in broadcasts, long before it arrives. Not that I am against this. I only suggest it might be equally beneficial to an English Musical. I can say this without prejudice, for I am in no way a disappointed composer. Far from it. You cannot dictate to the BBC, or anyone else, what or what not to perform. A far better way to fight American Musicals would be, instead of emulating them as so many English composers do, to establish an English style of composition, suitable to this country, with an accent on *melody*, of which most English composers seem to be afraid. This was the secret of the late Ivor

Novello's success. Another way is to raise the standard of popular music, instead of lowering it. At no period since the pre-Gilbert and Sullivan operas has popular music sunk to such a low ebb. For the last 10 years, nothing new has been said in American popular music. The 1914-18 war threw up a crop of wonderful composers, Jerome Kern, George Gershwin, Vincent Youmans, Cole Porter, and Richard Rodgers. (I do not include Irving Berlin, who is the greatest American songwriter, because a songwriter is a different thing from a composer.) Of those five composers only Cole Porter and Richard Rodgers remain.

The rest has been repetition, living on the great American myth. For it is largely a myth. The Americans are tremendous workers: they are also the world's greatest salesmen. Consequently, the American Musical is louder, cruder, slicker, often more pretentious, but usually more efficient than the British Musical in presentation. But we have compensating qualities. The British Musical has often more wit, taste, and charm. Take Sandy Wilson's *The Boy Friend*, for instance. There it was, at the Players Theatre, standing out a mile. I myself sent a West End manager to see it, but would he do it? No. Even after it was to be produced on Broadway, rival American managers said, in my presence, that it hadn't a dog's chance. In the theatre, nobody knows anything, and so anybody who knows something is a genius. The people who control the big theatres, which a musical show needs, are quite incapable of creating a show for themselves, so have to fall back on Broadway successes. They are supported by their clientele, of course: England today is the 49th State, aping American taste in crew cuts, jeans, and crooners who 'send them'. And what does America send us? Touring companies of their Broadway hits, which we lap up. France and Italy are more individualistic. The American musical and film haven't yet conquered them. They make their own, just as they make their own drinks.

Lately, I see signs of the tide starting to turn. One or two managers, with tremendous courage, and no theatres, like the late Sir Charles Cochran, and now Peter Saunders who put on *The Water Gipsies*, are prepared to lay out thousands of pounds on an unknown quantity. Both these crusaders share one attribute – a genuine love of the theatre. One day the British musical public may arouse itself from its apathy. The war gave us *Oklahoma!* and *Annie Get Your Gun*, but in my opinion they have not been equalled since. But as the public support them the supply will continue. Every country gets the Government – and the musical – it deserves. We are no exception. We have the writers, we have the artists and producers, but we need people who will *assemble* them together. Where would Gilbert and Sullivan have been without D'Oyly Carte, Paul Rubens and Lionel Monckton without George Edwards, or even A. P. Herbert and myself without Cochran? These managers knew, and others will one day know, there are other ways of making money than paying 12½ per cent for the privilege of reproducing an American show, however good. But first you must have the big theatres, owned by managers who can read and understand a play, and a score, as easily as a balance sheet. Supposing nobody created anything new in America, what would they do with the Coliseum and Drury Lane? Shall I tell you? They would revive an old American musical.

Waiting For God Knows What

by Peter Bull

Life for those who earned their living on the stage at the turn of the century must have been full of excitement, glamour and, above all, admiration. So far as I can discover it consisted mainly of having passionate letters written to you by famous playwrights or having champagne drunk out of your little bootees. This state of bliss obviously could not last, and now we, the buskers of the fifties, find ourselves tasting the reaction in no uncertain way. For it seems to me that we are back in the days of the eighteenth century, when things were thrown at you both on and off the stage and you were lucky to escape with your life if you had a shot at a role that was slightly outside your range. This was all very brutally brought to my notice during the rationing period, when my whole existence depended on the TV programme on which I was appearing. It is now an established fact that owners, viewers, part-owners, hirers of sets, their relations, friends and daily help regard their seeing of you occasionally on a small screen in a private or public house as a perfectly legitimate excuse to accost you in the open-air or on public transport. Having done this they proceed to revile you, bore the pants off you, hit you, or in rare cases – praise you. The pleasure of their praise, however, is usually offset by the blank look they give you after they have asked your name. I myself was lucky to escape starvation after the war, as the large grocery store which I patronise suddenly took to patronising me – 'That wasn't a bad little play you were in last night. You took quite a good part; . . .' 'Bloody awful yesterday;' 'What's going to happen next week to you and Anne Crawford?' – But a few weeks later back I was as old Mum Hubbard owing to an unwise decision to play in a piece about Pontius Pilate – written, rather surprisingly, by the author of *Worm's Eye View*.

Then there came the great ordeal of the Criterion theatre, where for some months I have been acting in an entertainment (?) called *Waiting For Godot*. This stimulating but nerve-racking experience forced me into a kind of *B——ss and Ma——n existence, with the important difference that I had no Iron Curtain behind which to hide. The iron or safety curtain was only lowered once during the evening at the Criterion, when none of us were on the stage. I used to wish every night that it would stick, as although I faced one or two tricky situations during the war, they were nothing compared to the nightly ordeal of facing the customers of Samuel Beckett's play. Mark you, as my mother would say, they soon stopped mass demonstrations, and only earthy cries of 'Rubbish', 'It's a disgrace', 'Take it off', 'Disgusting!' and 'What do you think you are doing?' come wafting over the footlights. In the early days of the run the noise of people slamming seats and crashing through the exit doors was disturbing, but this, too, was only a passing phase. But it is not very pleasant at the supposedly revered age of 43, after a long and undistinguished career in the theatre, to hear a lady in the front row say in a bell-like voice: 'I do wish the fat one would go.' I could not believe my ears and hurriedly looked round at my fellow artists, none of whom have ever looked thinner. But no, it was obviously with me that she was displeased, and it was difficult to know how to hit back. Luckily Timothy Bateson, who played my slave and to whom I am deeply attached both in life and on the stage (by a rope), leapt to my assistance and on our exit made as if to land on the lady's lap. The direct result of this was that neither the lady nor her party of 12 were there for the second act. Thinking it over, I was stirred to compassion, as I think she had made the grave error of supposing that *Intimacy at 8.30*, our gay predecessor at the Criterion, was still being played there and had imagined that a jolly, sexy evening was going to be had by all.

Peter Bull, with whip, as Pozzo in the first London production of *Waiting for Godot*

One always had to count the house twice during the evening, as those left when the Anthem was played bore no relation to those who started out to enjoy themselves at the beginning of the play. During Motor Show week, I remember, the exodus could not have been quicker if a fire had broken out in the stalls bar. I felt particularly sorry for the lady who turned to a friend of mine in the first interval and asked 'What do you make of it?' My chum, who is nothing if not guarded, suggested it made a change from all those ice shows, to which the lady replied, 'It's my last night in London and they said I *had* to see this.' She then burst into floods of tears. My friend comforted her by packing her off to the second house of the revue round the corner, featuring Benny Hill. But of course not everybody felt this way: a lot of people thought it was absolutely wonderful, a great treat, gloriously funny, noble, or 'just like life'. I thought *them* splendid too, because it meant that I was paid for several months longer than I'd ever hoped. But even they could be alarming, because they either sat spellbound in respectful silence or laughed their heads off in such a sinister way that the actors used to think they'd forgotten to adjust their costumes. It was the worst when they came round to the dressing-room after the play to tell us what it all meant. It was far too late for that anyhow, and it was disconcerting to hear that the character I'd been portraying for months represented Fascism, Communism, Lord Beaverbrook, Hollywood, James Joyce or, rather surprisingly, Humpty-Dumpty.

'It will be a conversational necessity for many years to have seen *Waiting For Godot*', proclaimed the posters and theatre lists – and woe betide those who did not take the plunge. I hear that husbands are being divorced because they wouldn't take their wives to see the damned thing. Invitations to grand parties are now only issued to those whose conversational powers enable them to discuss the play *ad infinitum*. It is a necessary qualification, I gather, to have seen at least three-quarters of the play – which, I fear, would exclude a good many of my friends, including Robert Morley. He is extremely worried by the whole thing, and rings me up periodically to issue a *pronunciamento*. 'I have been brooding in my bath for the last hour and have come to the conclusion that the success of *Waiting For Godot* means the end of the theatre as we know it.' Then he rings smartly off before I can reply. He came for half of the same performance as Boris Karloff, who stayed the course and is now asked out everywhere, and I was much touched by his loyalty. He would have stayed, he said, for the second act, but as he understood I was dumb throughout he saw no point in such masochism. I have not dared tell him that I was blind in the last act and acted my head off.

But even apart from financial considerations, the advantages of appearing in the play far outweighed the disadvantages. I do suggest that the gallantry of both actors and audience should be recognised, however, and a special medal presented to both parties by somebody like Johnnie Ray, himself an expert on stamina. I should like something to show the visitors should I be unlucky enough to end up in the same kind of hospital as the gentleman who played my part in another capital of Europe. And in order to lessen my apprehension of the future I have asked my manager, Donald Albery, to let me do *Noddy in Toyland* next Christmas.

* Burgess *and* Maclean, *British diplomats who defected to the Soviet Union in 1951.*

Helena Hughes and Mary Ure in the premiére production of _Look Back in Anger_, Royal Court

John Osborne, in _Look Back in Anger_, has certainly succeeded, if he has done little else, in putting on to the stage one of the most irritatingly boorish, verbose and bitter young men that ever exasperated an audience. This long, exacting and dominating part has something of virtuosity in the writing, as if the author had tried to cram into it all that he ever suffered, felt and kept bottled up in his young life.

It is evidently intended to be a fierce protest of youth against a world which it finds only frustrating and futile. But so concerned does Mr Osborne seem with being his own mouthpiece that characterisation and a convincing actuality of background go almost by the board. One cannot believe that this Jimmy Porter works in a sweet-store business in the Midlands and lives in a squalid one-room flat in the Midlands with an incredibly submissive wife who irons his shirt on Sunday evenings while he selfishly insists on listening to Vaughan Williams on the radio.

This is a stagy, conventional, unauthentic conception of the reality of working people; the man is merely an intellectual Bloomsbury exhibitionist, pouring out words by the hundred – smart, wise-cracking, cynical, brutal, self-centred, childish, sen-

Look Back in Anger

by Anthony Merryn

sual. The author has tried to make him likeable as well, but if his claim is that such uninhibited mixtures exist in real life, that hardly justifies the compelling of a long-suffering audience to meet them in the theatre as well.

Even so, there is an undeniable quality in the writing, a creative, poetic, witty use of words that might serve better for a non-naturalistic theme. What it lacks is character-drawing, economy and subtlety. The story itself does not amount to much. The wife at last leaves this flaying barrage to go home to her father, a contrastingly inarticulate colonel who regrets better days in India. The husband immediately sets up in her place a touring actress who kisses him within a few seconds of slapping his face. The wife returns, announcing wretchedly that she has lost the baby she was carrying, the actress departs, and the two are left to live unhappily ever after.

All this is told with some skill and tension, but any underlying significance is lost by the total absence of social and economic background, which is not made up for by shadowy harkings back to parents and defeatist comments on life, as if the characters were watching it instead of living it.

Kenneth Haigh showed a remarkable fluency and stamina in the leading role, and the urge to get up on the stage and strangle him at least showed that there was some kind of compelling life in his performance. Mary Ure put a certain drooping gentleness into the part of the inexplicable wife, and Helena Hughes made something of a contrast with the RADA tones of the actress. Alan Bates did what he could with uncharacterised writing in the part of the young friend in the next flat, an alleged Welsh worker of modest intellect, who scuffles on the floor with Mr Porter and makes love to his wife while he looks on; and John Welsh's colonel sounded the quiet grey note of correct British restraint.

1956

Sugar-Coated Satirist

by Frank Granville Barker

'The roots of the theatre lie in all-in wrestling. . . .' Whatever I might have expected to hear from Peter Ustinov, it was certainly not a statement of this kind. A few minutes earlier, as I sat in a restful, tastefully panelled room of his Chelsea home, I had wondered how I should start asking this Stormy Petrel of the English theatre for his views on drama and how he writes his own plays, but I had not bargained for this. And as I looked at his bearded but boyish face, taking account of his habitually twinkling eyes, I wondered for a moment whether he was pulling my leg. After all, he *has* taken part in some pretty crazy radio programmes. . . .

But I was soon reassured. When it comes to matters of the theatre, Peter Ustinov is serious enough. Not in a pompous way, for he has always been the avowed enemy of whatever is pretentious or consciously highbrow: his is the seriousness of someone who loves the theatre and writes for it as a perfectly accomplished craftsman who knows all its possibilities and limitations. It is not always easy for us to understand him, for he has a warmer, more fluid temperament than we British playgoers. His whole imagination, like his sense of humour, often carries him beyond the frontiers of our more down-to-earth taste. And he is often the most serious when he appears to be flippant, which allows him to spring continual surprises on us.

He started by telling me that, unlike most actor-dramatists, he never writes parts for himself or any other actor. The play is the thing, not the people who take part in it. Nor is he able to write plays about nothing in particular: he must have a definite theme, even though it may be a slight one. 'You ask me,' he went on, 'why I am so often attracted to satire. I think it is because I am naturally drawn towards comedy in the first place, and because I also need a theme. Comic situations and characters are not enough in themselves; they must express ideas, too. The obvious outcome of these two considerations is satire.'

His style lends itself to this purpose admirably. Believing that we are through with naturalism in theatre – for the moment at least – he favours a certain artificiality. And the texture of a play, more than its form, is what primarily interests him. His perpetual striving to achieve delicacy in the texture of his comedies has given them an elegant, thoroughly civilised quality. His current London success, for example, *Romanoff and Juliet*, has this unusual artificial air, emphasised in this case by a formal ending in a style reminiscent of the eighteenth century. The play is completely symmetrical – a fact that we tend to overlook only because the writing has such speed and feathery lightness. It is so consummately constructed that its structure is taken for granted. 'I am certain', he explained, 'that audiences are quite happy to accept conventions in the theatre. They do not demand naturalism. I have always felt this since I played with Edith Evans in *The Rivals* to an audience of soldiers during the war. This comedy, which makes no attempts to be realistic, made a tremendous impact on our audience, who even found that the 'asides' brought them into direct contact with the characters on the stage.

Ustinov thinks there has been too much insistence on realism, and too much striving on the part of dramatists to be 'profound'. He blames this on the popular conception that serious drama is more valid than comedy, pointing to the French, who forget that their greatest man of the theatre, Molière, was a wholly comic writer. 'What people do not realise', he went on, 'is that a play that is not in itself profound may have a profound effect on the audience, who are made to do the thinking themselves. I try always to wrap my ideas up in a comedy, a deliberately light play, so that the sugar comes off the pill afterwards – when the audience are on their way home in the bus. A play should be pure enjoyment at the time of seeing it: it can always be thought about later.' Just as so many modern plays lack lightness of touch, so our modern productions lack spontaneity. Ustinov has no time for the Stanislavsky practice of rehearsing a play for three months. He wants the players to speak the lines as though they have just thought up the remarks themselves. In comedy, particularly, this spontaneity is essential. Which brought us to those all-in wrestlers. 'Wrestling', Ustinov told me, 'is excellent theatre. Each wrestler has a definite character, is extremely funny, and at least appears to be performing without having had a rehearsal. Often the result of a fight has been thoroughly planned beforehand, but it has every appearance of spontaneity. When I was watching wrestling

in Hollywood some time ago, a large, sad-faced man came up to me and told me he liked my films. He went on to tell me he had watched the careers of many film stars, and had seen them rocket to fame and then pass into obscurity. Then he promised that if ever I was out of work as an actor he would make me a front-line 'heavy.' Seeing my blank expression, Ustinov went on to explain that wrestling has its straight men and its 'heavies', just as there are straight and character actors. Usually matches are engineered so that the straight man wins, but occasionally, to tease the public, the winner has to be a 'heavy'.

This is an illuminating comment on Ustinov as an actor, for he is ideal as a lumbering bear of a man with an absurdly soft heart – the type of person for whom we feel sorry all the time, even though he is sure to outwit all the straight characters at the end. And it explains much of his attitude to the writing of comedy. But he took great care to explain to me that this is only the way he feels at the moment. Continually experimenting, and possessing an exceptionally open mind, he is always liable to change his style. He is, too, convinced that our English theatre lacks the element of surprise: we always know what we are in for as soon as the curtain rises on the scene. So there is a good chance that he will surprise us all one day by writing an entirely different kind of play from the one we expect from him.

1956

Too Much Shakespeare?

by Peter Hall

Four years before he created the Royal Shakespeare Company in 1960, Peter Hall, fresh from running the Arts Theatre as a 'pocket-sized National Theatre' defended the post-war popularity of Shakespeare then under attack from J. B. Priestley

Shakespeare is the greatest blackleg in the business: we are asked to compete with a dramatist who starts with every advantage of prestige, who is sound culture personified, who can demand audiences of school children to eke out the matinees, and who does not even ask for a royalty for his services.

J. B. Priestley – *Encore*, Summer 1956.

In the last seven years, I have seen a major production of every play of Shakespeare's. This is a remarkable situation – never before has there been such a boom in the Bard. Apart from West End revivals and performances by repertory theatres, the Old Vic and the Memorial Theatre at Stratford spend all their energies on Shakespeare. He has never enjoyed such popularity before. The commercial theatre is thought to consist of plays jostling to get near Shaftesbury Avenue, played in quiet sets with quieter actors. But the sound and the fury, the passion and the splendour of Shakespeare are probably earning more money than the most popular hit with the starriest cast. This popularity is a symptom of new demand made by contemporary audiences. Ever since Irving was knighted and Shaw set about making the theatre intellectual enough to delight William Morris, it has grown progressively more polite and banal: when it is serious, it is ascetic, when it is popular, it is tame. The new popularity of Shakespeare is, I hope, an indication that this enervating process is nearing its end. So before we support the cry against too much Shakespeare, let us examine how far this new taste is a sign of the times.

Since the war, there has been a definite return to the theatre theatrical. The fact that audiences have wanted more colour, zest and excitement has led them on the one hand to the Ballet, and on the other to revivals of Shakespearean plays. For only in these plays can they find the old basic enjoyment of the drama, the huge emotions and heroic themes which are the stuff of the theatre. I believe that our conventional fourth wall realistic drama can no longer provide this excitement. The idea that a play is basically a room from which the omnipotent dramatist has cut away a wall to enable us to peep at an intimate 'slice of life' is only 80 or 90 years old. Ever since Chekhov and Ibsen, almost every dramatist has assumed that this realistic convention is the normal way of expressing a dramatic truth. That the convention is very new and does not necessarily possess perpetual validity is forgotten. Shakespeare's audience did not demand solid scenery – they did not wish to be embarrassed interlopers in a private room, but hearty participators in theatrical splendour. A lack of unity of time and place did not make them feel uneasy – they accepted the drama as it was given to them: with a unity of theme, certainly, but in all else fluid and fluent.

I do not wish to decry the original power of the fourth wall drama. A dramatic convention depends on the audience willingly

accepting the dramatist's premise – 'let's pretend' he says 'that this stage is a room' – or 'that this wooden platform is the field of Agincourt'. But there comes a time when the convention by which a play is presented is no longer an active admission of 'Let's pretend' by the audience, but the passive acceptance of something customary and stale. The first audiences at an Ibsen play were dramatically affected when one of the characters turned up a lamp. This realism was new to them. To see a character going though the realistic motions of living *in a room*, was as exciting as the spectacle of a real railway train running across the stage at Drury Lane to a later generation. When the lamp was turned up, there was indeed a 'lightening' in the emotional predicament of the character. Now it takes a scholar to show us this symbolism, and it would certainly need a heavily stylised presentation to make its effect on a contemporary audience. Every play they see has a housemaid whose main function is to turn on the lights and pummel the cushions. Neither of these actions gives them an emotional shock.

Mr J. B. Priestley has expended a deal of energy lately on criticising the Shakespearean boom. He accuses Shakespeare of killing the contemporary drama; audiences, it seems flock to Shakespeare and not to modern plays. I believe that sooner or later an audience gets what it needs, and if it prefers the Shakespearean to contemporary drama, the fault, I think, lies not with Shakespeare, our managements or our audiences, but with our modern dramatists. It is not true that all over the country there are drawers stuffed with neglected masterworks, and that the dramatists are the victims of stars and managements who stubbornly stick to Shakespeare. I doubt if there could be better opportunities than are offered at the present to new or old dramatic talent. Commercial managements are much more adventurous than they are given credit for, and there is keen competition for a new work of genuine originality. And if they fail, there are repertory and Art theatres only too ready to try out a play. The Arts Council Drama Panel fans with commendable desperation every spark of talent that might blaze into play. No, there is no lack of encouragement or opportunity. The fault is with contemporary dramatists who for the most part have forgotten what the theatre can do and who are out of step with the tastes of the present.

There are too many plays written according to a very old-fashioned text book. Characters speak not in a dramatic speech growing out of the situation in which they find themselves, but in a flat conventional speech heard not in Surbiton or Wigan but in the mausoleum of the West End stage. Too many plays are written as if we were still paddling happily blindfolded in the uneasy waters of the 1930s. Life for everybody has changed radically since the war, but Rule One in the would-be-dramatist's companion insists that popular plays must be written as if the war had never happened. Rule Two informs him that only characters who earn over £2,000 a year are truly worthy of his attention. The working class can only be used as comic relief or objects of ridicule in the most mechanical forms of farce. In a special appendix he will find patterns of working-class speech for the stage (charwomen, maids, plumbers, etc.). These are designed to remove all warmth, sympathy and humanity from the characters and extract the maximum comic effect with the minimum effort.

Is it any wonder that the sensitive theatregoer turns away from this narrow territory and supports Shakespeare, who is not only our greatest dramatist, but the most stimulating, humane and universal of poets? Plain realism can be better obtained from the film, but true drama, the spontaneous participation in the resolution of a crisis, is felt at its keenest in the theatre. And in our day, most frequently in the Shakespearean theatre.

It was encouraging that last year the four events which aroused the most interest were *Moby Dick, Waiting for Godot, Titus Andronicus* and the *Chinese Opera*. Is not this a sign that the public are eager for a new dramatic language? Recently a new play, *Look Back in Anger*, was presented at the Royal Court Theatre. While this is not original in form or presentation, it speaks a truly contemporary language and is expressing a truly contemporary theme. And it has won nothing but praise and support.

One hesitates to use the adjective 'Shakespearean' as a term of praise – for it is almost as rubbed in usage as 'nice'. But this article begs that the modern drama should become more *Shakespearean*. We cannot return to blank verse drama, nor should we expect the coming of a second Shakespeare. (When we scream at the dearth of new plays, we should remind ourselves what a rare wonder the good dramatist is. A decade that produces 10 really fine plays is fortunate.) It is rather that we should treat the stage not as an apology for a film set, but as a platform which confesses no limitations and no bounds in expressing individual and unique emotions, arising from contemporary problems.

In its largeness of scope the theatre has no equal. CinemaScope may be able to show our eyes the loneliness and wastes of the Sahara desert. But a man on a bare stage speaking the words of a dramatist can tell us more about the loneliness of the human heart in the desert. Our new theatre should, like Shakespeare, know no bounds of period, time, place or class.

So at the moment I am glad that we have 'too much Shakespeare'. It is undoubtedly a pity that our only two established theatres are devoted to nothing *but* Shakespeare. It is also a disgrace that this worship of the Bard seems to still our national conscience so that it persistently refuses to admit the need for a modern National Theatre with a permanent company and a repertoire drawn from the world's drama. With Shakespeare, we are becoming like the man who refused the present of a book: 'No, thank you,' he said, 'I have one already'. Stratford and the Old Vic busily playing Shakespeare blind our eyes to larger needs.

But all the same, I am far from suggesting that we should have less Shakespeare. I believe that an audience's taste can be stimulated, educated and improved, but only on the *right* food. The theatre will continue to shrink while its audiences are given warmed up fare that is dull to the palate. It is evident that Shakespeare is much to their tastes. It is up to our dramatists to concoct a new dish for our times.

Credits and Discredits For 1956

Congratulations to: George Devine and the English Stage Company for their courage in trying out a repertory of new British plays; John Clements for reminding us that Shakespeare isn't the only dramatist whose plays are worth reviving; Covent Garden for giving us in Ulanova's Juliet and Ramon Vinay's Otello the best Shakespearean performances of the year.

Mistakes of the year: neglecting the Shaw Centenary; failing to reduce Entertainments Tax in the theatre; putting on *Wild Grows the Heather*.

Disappointments of the year: the Stratford-on-Avon season and Drury Lane musicals.

Romance of the year: Laurence Harvey and Margaret Leighton.

Names we have missed: Michael Redgrave, Laurence Olivier and Hermione Gingold.

Forgotten name of 1956: Anna Neagle.

Plays we should like to have missed: *To My Love, A River Breeze* and *Towards Zero*.

Welcome back: Peter Ustinov.

Come back soon: Siobhan McKenna, Geraldine Page, Jean Vilar and Maria Casarès, and the Berliner Ensemble.

Lost cause of 1956: British musicals.

Pull up your socks: American musicals.

Not good enough department: the jokes in new English comedies.

Better than ever department: Peter Daubeney's international season at the Palace.

Bore of the year: the Lord Chamberlain.

Damp squib of the year: Calvin Hoffman opening the Walsingham Tomb.

Rebel of the year: John Osborne.

Best productions of the year: Tyrone Guthrie's *Troilus and Cressida;* Peter Glenville's *Hotel Paradiso;* John Clements's *The Rivals;* Peter Hall's *The Waltz of the Toreadors;* Peter Brook's *A View from the Bridge*.

Best performances of the year: Alec Guinness in *Hotel Paradiso*. Edith Evans and Peggy Ashcroft in *The Chalk Garden;* Hugh Griffith in *The Waltz of the Toreadors;* Michael Hordern in *The Doctor's Dilemma;* Paul Scofield in *The Power and the Glory*.

Three of the best. Left: Peggy Ashcroft and Edith Evans in *The Chalk Garden*. Top right: John Clements and Laurence Harvey in *The Rivals*. Bottom: Peter Ustinov's *Romanoff and Juliet*

Young actress of the year: Perlita Neilson.

Get well soon: Dorothy Tutin.

1957

The year that the Suez Canal was reopened and Eden resigned – to be succeeded as Prime Minister by Harold Macmillan – saw some liberalising influences – the Homicide Act abolishing the Death Penalty and also the Wolfenden Report on Homosexuality and Prostitution. As race riots in the USA made Little Rock and Arkansas household names, the Treaty of Rome saw the appearance of the Common Market which then involved six nations – France, Italy, West Germany, Belgium, Holland and Luxembourg. In the year in which Britain exploded its first hydrogen bomb on Christmas Island, Beckett produced Endgame *and Osborne* The Entertainer.

Knight at the Music-Hall

Unlike his contemporaries Gielgud and Richardson, Olivier was quick and eager to be identified with the new writing of the late 1950s and in this interview with Frank Granville Barker he talks of the appeal of Archie Rice in Osborne's The Entertainer *which transferred from the Royal Court to the Palace in the West End.*

Laurence Olivier in a rehearsal break of *The Entertainer*

Audiences at the Palace Theatre may be divided in their opinions of *The Entertainer*: many people are deeply moved by it, others chiefly amused, and some considerably shocked. But on one point all are agreed. Sir Laurence Olivier's performance as Archie Rice, a music-hall comedian whose world is tumbling about his ears, is one of the most exciting experiences our present-day English theatre has given us. The firm conviction and warm compassion he has brought to this role – at a time when we can still recall the majestic power of his Titus and Macbeth – proves that he is himself the complete entertainer. Many people, myself among them, were surprised that an actor whom we immediately associate with Shakespearean roles should fit so perfectly into the part of a seedy, and in many respects despicable, variety artist. At first sight it does seem a strange transformation, but after discussing the play and the role of Archie Rice with Sir Laurence himself it soon becomes clear why his performance is so shatteringly true to life and sympathetic.

Sir Laurence today may well seem a person far removed from the earthiness and honest-to-goodness vulgarity of Number Two variety dates and the dingy lodging houses in which none-too-successful comedians and contortionists pass their days. But he was not always a West End star, and he spent a lot of time with such people when he started his career. 'I started very young', he reminded me, 'and very low down'. During his early touring days, and while at Birmingham for two years, he shared digs with many music-hall artists, developing the strongest affection and respect for them. He agrees wholeheartedly with John Osborne that when the music-hall dies a great and valuable part of English life will die with it. Olivier has always wanted to do a song and dance routine on the stage. 'You've probably seen me at midnight

matinées', he said, 'and so you'll realise that I've always had this urge towards greater versatility'. He has always been aware of the close bond between the variety artist and the 'legit.' actor, and he has been impressed, even touched, by the astonishingly respectful attitude music-hall artists adopt towards the work of straight actors.

'I've seen them peer at us from the wings in wonder', he told me, 'as fascinated by our skill as *we* are fascinated by the skill of acrobats, ventriloquists and comics. It seems to mystify them just as much as a conjuror always mystifies me, even though all our tricks of acting are as much a part of their performances as they are of ours.'

When he asked John Osborne to write a play for him, Sir Laurence had no idea what the subject would be. 'Afterwards, however', he told me, 'I realised that Osborne *had* dropped me a hint. For he told me that you learn a great deal about public opinion from the music-hall. In politics, for instance, a comedian's patter can tell you far more than a newspaper. The temper of public feeling can be judged pretty accurately from a comedian's jokes about a political party or a foreign country: when he gets a gale of hearty laughter he is reflecting public opinion, but when he provokes only a few scattered laughs he is out of step.'

Osborne sent him the first act of *The Entertainer* as soon as he'd finished it, and this was enough to make Sir Laurence accept the part of Archie. He felt an immediate interest in the character – an interest that has deepened with time.

I asked Sir Laurence whether he had found this a difficult role, and if it had needed special study of music-hall personalities. 'The role came easily', he replied, 'partly because it was so well drawn in the play, and partly because I felt I knew Archie so well. As a professional actor, of course, the whole atmosphere of the play was already a part of me. I *did* go to quite a few variety shows while I was working on the part, but I didn't build up the character on any particular comedian I've ever seen. There may be odd touches of actual people I've seen, but nothing more.'

On the question of the decline of the music-hall, Sir Laurence has quite a lot of say. He feels that there are so many forms of entertainment to choose from nowadays, and such a feverish craze for novelty for novelty's sake, that any simple, fundamental form of art such as music-hall is bound to suffer. It is not like the very early days, when a whole town or village would go wild with excitement when they heard the news that 'the players' had arrived. 'The microphone too', he told me, 'has seriously damaged the whole atmosphere of the music-hall. It has the audience positively pinned back in their seats, practically deafened by all the noise. And it acts as a shield to the artist, who almost seems to be hiding behind it. There used to be such gallantry in the music-hall – the gallantry of the lone figure on the stage set against the whole audience, making them lean forward in their seats in their excitement and anticipation. Only occasionally today does this gallantry show itself: when the artist leaves his protecting microphone for a few moments. Then the old challenge reappears briefly, and the audience sit forward again. But it's only momentary.' He told me how he used to admire Robey, who needed no mechanical aids to project his voice and his personality through

the biggest theatre. When Robey spoke from the stage his consonants used to strike against the back of the pit like bullets. Music-hall stars of his calibre had the tremendous energy that is such an essential part of the theatre.

Archie Rice in *The Entertainer* may be no Robey, but for Sir Laurence he stands for a great deal of the vanishing glory that was the music-hall. And Archie has got into Sir Laurence's system.

'He's an insidious sort of fellow', he explained. 'I'll admit now that I'm going to have a terrific job to get Archie Rice out of my system. Except for Shakespearean roles, which are too completely different to be affected by him, any parts I play from now on will be coloured by Archie unless I'm very careful. He's really taken a hold on me.'

I felt I could add to that final remark. For surely the creation that is Archie Rice – Laurence Olivier will be just as difficult to forget for the audiences at the Palace Theatre.

1957

The Art of the Dramatist

John Whiting (1917–1963) precursor of the new wave of writers with, especially, his Saint's Day *(1951) and* Marching Song *(1954) on his experience of playwriting.*

My own experience of playwriting – and I can vouch for no other – falls into two parts. The first was a period of some six years during which four plays – *A Penny for a Song*, *Saint's Day*, *Marching Song* and *The Gates of Summer* – were written and staged. The second has been a period of three years during which I have not written for the theatre but have come to certain conclusions on the subject of writing plays which may be of interest and which I am tentatively beginning to put into practice. Let me tell you of the practical experience of the first, and relate it to the reasoning of the second.

The subject of plays, what to write about: we are so often directed in this matter nowadays. 'Look at that! Isn't it iniquitous! Why don't you write about it?' Or it may be: 'Aren't you angry about this? You should put it in a play.' Then we dramatists are always being urged to 'get down to real life', and that means that plays should be about 'life' and about 'people': about sociological life and working-class people. I find it difficult to accept this as a point of departure, and I think you will see why when I tell you how I have come to write plays. I have written a play from remembering a gratuitous act of cruelty which I committed when I was a child. I have written another from a sudden moment of understanding on seeing a man's face during a war trial. He wasn't working class: he was a soldier, and he was a *person*. Then I have written a comedy for no better reason – and *is there a better reason?* – than to make a friend laugh.

The 'things given' are a starting point. Many, of course, are rejected. Perhaps they are unsuitable for plays – or perhaps they bore me and I can't stand the thought of spending nearly a year of my life dealing with them. Sometimes an incident, a theme, will go out of my mind. I shall forget it completely. And this is very important. I forget things, almost unconsciously put them aside. But they come back – at moments of personal crisis, moments which have nothing to do with the work. They may come back on a day when I feel I wouldn't care if I never wrote another word or saw another play. Yet that can be the very moment which begins the play. All dramatic works have a point around which action is formed. It need not be a moment of 'theatre', of effect – in fact it should *not* be. It may never be apparent to audiences, and it may never be discovered in hundreds of years by scholars. It may never even be known to the actors – though if they're good ones they'll smell it out. This dramatic point is the 'thing given', the first idea which I've mentioned, translated into the play. It may now be a line of dialogue, or a silence, or a moment of action. It is not necessarily the ultimate point of the play. It forms the point of departure for the writer: he may work towards it, or he may work away from it. This point, of which the writer is most aware, is the germ of the structure of the play.

Theatre time is elastic. A play can be written which covers thousands of years – it has been written (Shaw's *Back to Methuselah*) – or it can be contained in a few hours. The placing of the crucial incident is the first step in the physical structure of the play. Now the play will begin to be seen. And the action will begin to be seen against some kind of background. It may, depending on the play – it should never depend on the whim of the producer – be a real place, a room, a garden, what we call a naturalistic setting. I find, as yet, that I'm unable to use the stage as a platform – merely a place. In my opinion, however, this is a perfectly valid usage.

I would like to approach the theatre in future with great austerity. I am a little sad about this, because I have a strong inclination towards the *baroque* theatre. And on the pure level of enjoyment I love the theatre at its silliest – Lehar, and that sort of thing. But all that is part of the museum now. When I say austere I don't mean bare stages with actors chanting hieratic drama. I mean, rather, a greater sense of truth – not naturalism, but the sense of truth that makes plays of apparent fantasy such as *Fin de Partie* or *The Chairs* more moving and more truthful than the examples of neo-realism and social significance that we get offered in the English theatre. Even so, I can think of no pure examples of this in the theatre anywhere. But there are two in the cinema, both films by the same man. Bresson's *Diary of a Country Priest* and *A Man Escaped* state the facts of a situation, they are made against the dramatic line, they avoid the moment of theatre – and by doing so they become intensively exciting.

So the play has a place and a time. All plays concern themselves with men and women – or at least with human behaviour, even if only in reflection. (I am thinking here of those rare plays with a cast of insects, animals or gods. And even Wagner found it impossible to depersonalise the characters in *The Ring* when it came to the practical job of writing.) It is wrong, however, to believe that the characters of a play *are* the play, that they make up the play. It is an easy mistake to make, because the people in a play are the most easily and immediately comprehensible factor. But in fact the play is formed by circumstances reacting on character. Plays are not, or *should not* be, just about very interesting people. In the past, before beginning to write a play the characters have always presented themselves to me. I mean that I have never had to *search* for people to act out the play. I have a title and a list of characters before a word of the play is

written, and as yet I have never had to add to or subtract from them. They have arrived just like a well-mannered cast on the morning of the first rehearsal. There is something called 'taking people from life'. This has always mystified me. Where else *can* you take them from? You can take ideas from art, but not people. They have been observed, sometimes subconsciously, sometimes at a distance, sometimes closely, and without any real intention of using them as material for a play. (I don't think anyone ever goes round with a notebook – like a birdwatcher!)

So: there is the theme; there is the place; and there are the people. The writing can begin. I don't think I'm being over-sensitive when I say that this act, this decision to begin, is as disgusting and horrible as committing a murder. In one's mind there is the pure ideal – the perfect crime, as you might say. Yet from the moment you pick up your pen you know that you're not going to get away with it. At best, you can hope to have a very good try. Everything has been planned: you know where everyone will be at any one time, and you are fairly sure what they will say at any given situation. But very little happens as you've planned it. The characters, in taking on life, take on initiative too. When you're young and just beginning to write, this can be very exciting. This spontaneous action appears to be the very fount of inspiration, and it can, I admit, produce those moments of 'theatre' that I now deplore. But it does not produce good plays. A play must have structure, or, like anything else, it would not exist at all. What is often misunderstood, however, is that dramatic structure is not something that can be discussed and elevated on its own. The structure of a play is composed of the elements of the play itself: the spoken word, the story, and the action of that story. And there is no one way of doing it: every structure will depend on the diversity of these elements.

I have said that the spoken word is one of the elements that forms the dramatic structure. In the theatre it is also the main factor in forming the characters. It is very difficult to see a point where the play can dispense with language, for if it does it changes its identity and becomes mime or ballet. Language must be considered an indispensable part of drama. Probably the true art of the dramatist is this art of the spoken word. And it is the most difficult problem facing the dramatist today. With the spoken word the dramatist forms his characters and his play, and so communicates with his audience. This presents a tremendous problem in this country, where society is divided into classes by types of language more surely than by any other thing. I don't mean just by accents: I mean by vocabulary and usage. It might be said that we in England today are a polyglot nation. I now believe that all language for the theatre should be taken from life. It is no longer possible to invent. This means that my concern cannot only be for the highly articulate man using words with care and for effect, but also for the idiot mumblings of the half-wit who lives down the lane. What people are, and what people do: showing this seems to me the absolute function of the play now. The dramatist must represent this without ornamentation, must leave the poetry out of the words, must rigidly refuse all which is for effect. Perhaps you think that this would make a dull play. Then may I ask you this? Are you more deeply touched, moved and amused by happenings in life or in the theatre? Surely in everyday life. Yet the incidents in life rarely contain literary poetry, and God is the clumsiest stage manager ever when it comes to the telling effect.

Theatre Workshop operates at the ancient and attractive if rather roughly treated Theatre Royal, Angel Lane, Stratford, E. 15. Currently it presents *Macbeth* in modern, to outmoded, clothes, or loosely – very loosely – Austerity to Edwardian garb. It has just returned from Switzerland, where it was booed, and Moscow, where it was more warmly greeted.

Candidly, I found the production rather insistently old-fashioned with its Expressionist technique of which the high bare platform, on or under which much of the action takes place, was the symbol. Its starkly exposed back-stage brick wall and clickerty-clack electrical system was visually all there was for our delight. But did not Mr Peter Godfrey give the London playgoer as strong an intimation that significance is all, at the old Gate Theatre in the early thirties? Further endorsement is surely pretty old hat?

What the production lacked in novelty, however, the programme supplied, and this fascinated me. I noted, for instance, that 'in accordance with modern theatre practice, National Anthems will only be played in the presence of Royalty or Heads of State'. I was not, then, unduly surprised that we were subsequently sent a little coldly away for the reason that Royalty was not present – the overall impression being that the occasions when Royalty visits this particular playhouse must be rare if not non existent. For myself I regard the loss of the National Anthem as a definite minus; for I quite like to beg a blessing on my monarch and my country – to play my part in a rather gracious Grace after snacks, feasts or banquets. But, I exhorted myself, we fought a major war so that, among other, and in our view necessary, freedoms, Theatre Workshop might opt out of God Savers when it so chooses.

Nevertheless, I resolutely, stubbornly and, in the words of Miss Ruby Murray, softlee – softlee murmured the words under my breath as I made my way towards the final friendly mingle around the bar. Miss Joan Littlewood, in the Producer's programme note, had given me a hard pill to swallow. No sea-green incorruptible anxiety-allayer, hers. And here the reader must forgive me if I break off this closely-knit argument of mine to ponder what difference it might have made had the Witches given the Macbeths a blood-red confidence capsule their sleep t'incarnadine (What! In our Chymysts?) and to recommend this line of speculation to the attention of Professor L. C. Knight who, I see, is to address a Sunday meeting of the club on the subject of 'How Many Children Had Lady Macbeth?'

Is a puzzlement, as they say in Siam.

I myself have always gone to Shakespeare for, among other things, the indefinable poetry of the years and centuries – for time's miracle of incrustation upon a work of art, which we call Patina. Miss Littlewood's pill is intended to do away with Patina.

Taking the Mickey out of *Macbeth*

Caryl Brahms reviews Macbeth *at Theatre Workshop*

'When we play our classics in our People's theatre', she writes, 'we try to wipe away the dust of three hundred years'. She gives us fair warning that she is in a mood to 'strip off the poetical'.

Did Miss Littlewood succeed? Did she take the curse off Shakespeare? She certainly did her best to take the Mickey out of the Macbeths. She brought home her meaning with the buzz and whine of Bombers. She mixed her World Wars and dressed her cast in some pretty peculiar uniforms with not a kilt among the clan. She has the quaintest idea of Royalty relaxing, and sent Macbeth strolling about his Palace in a golden crown, attended by an Edwardian parlour-maid in cap and apron and 'afternoon black', with starched streamers flying. Her Murderers were fit for funeral parlours. As to the text, she cut and she rationalised.

It would be a little less than true and more than unkind to pretend that, with her great instinct for technical effect and her burning purpose, which was to strip the piece of poetry and insert, instead, psychiatry, Miss Littlewood failed to make an impact all the time. I was, for instance, far more terrified of her invisible Banquo at the Feast, than ever of any action in a green Lime. And her Witches, three figments of Macbeth's imagination, haunted his court like the ghost of Hamlet's father most effectively. I did not miss the cauldron scene, with its moaning revenants, and indeed, quite took to the gist of the matter being played out in the Macbeth's bed-chamber between the chieftain and the Lady, with Macbeth muttering everybody's lines in his fevered sleep.

But I was conscious all the time of the great incongruity of all those soldiers out of *Journey's End* speaking Shakespeare's lines. And worse, I felt, were the clumsy attempts to make these mean something quite different from the author's purpose. Here was the sin against the dead, indeed. I am not going to pretend that it is only at Theatre Workshop that we find producers perpetually attempting to twist old sentences to new meanings. But to my mind it is both distasteful and dishonest.

Mr Lonnie Donnegan, in another sphere, has been in The Top Ten for some weeks now, with a pop-song about 'Putting on the agony, putting on the style'; and Theatre Workshop, in putting the agony on Macbeth after their own style, have nearly succeeded in getting Shakespeare into the Bottom Ten. Nearly, but not quite. For do what you will to Will, his poetry keeps breaking through and in his poetry, his understanding, his humanity and his heart.

How fared the actors? Lady Macbeth (Miss Eileen Kennelly) emerged almost unscathed. Determined as a Deb's Mum, smooth as a Colchester Oyster, pent up as a racing-car in neutral and older in experience than the nudes at the Folies Bergère; and wearing full, long, sweeping, timeless skirts that helped her characterisation, she wanted only experience to take her place in plays of situation. I would like to see her in *No Room at the Inn*, for instance, or *The Turn of the Screw*. Macbeth (Mr Glynn Edwards) did his best to atone for what he lacked in grandeur, by his grasp and intelligence. But your villain has more need of grandeur than your King; and your King needs an actor with a resounding voice: and your Macbeth is both; and this Macbeth had neither.

The evening was rounded off with the most unfunny Porter who ever grumbled his way from Castle to Keep. Because Shakespeare in modern dress is not, in any case, my dish, I am clearly not the best conceivable taster. So go, dear reader, and judge it for yourself, if you live nearer to Stratford-upon-Avon, or Stratford, Connecticut, or Stratford, Ontario.

It is more than half a century since an English poet wrote of 'the all-recording, all-effacing Files, the obliterating, automatic Files'. Critics should keep these lines in mind. It is so easy to speak of 'the best play for a quarter of a century', 'the best dialogue of our time', and so forth; to scatter the columns unwisely with 'great', 'wonderful', and the major epithets. When we look back at 1957, and then think ahead to those files of 50 years on – assuming, of course, that the world survives 1984 – it is hard to choose the enduring events. I doubt whether any new play we have seen, from home or abroad, will flash at once into the mind of my successor in 2007. But I suggest that one performance will, Sir Laurence Olivier's in *The Entertainer*: the memory of his acting may carry the play with it, just as we think of *The Bells* for the sake of Irving. The piece itself, by John Osborne, is a tedious affair about a music-hall comedian and his family. Its merit is that it allows Olivier to give a performance for which we do seek the major epithets. He is here a fifth-rate little man from hack revue, who says that he is 'dead inside', but who suffers damnably. We are permitted to see him both at home and upon the stage of the cheap theatre; and it is astonishing to watch Olivier's transformation into the nudging flash-Harry of a man with the extraordinarily observed voice. It is a voice that reminds one of cheap paint cracking and blistering from some rough deal board. The enunciation, with its racked vowels and the careful gentility that suddenly roughens into a loose-lipped coarseness of tone, is managed with uncommon art; but more cunning still is Olivier's emphasis on the wrong words, the way in which he pursues any stray pronoun and preposition and hammers them into place like rivets into a table too rotten to hold them. He shows, too, how he can express emotion in silence. In this play there is a minute of heartbreak that is entirely the actor's. We are grateful to such artists as Brenda de Banzie and George Relph, but the night rests upon Olivier's X-raying of a failure.

There is another full-length portrait of a failure in *Flowering Cherry* at the Haymarket, among the best home-bred discoveries of the year. Robert Bolt, a new name in the West End, is the dramatist. He presents a self-deceiving dreamer, a man who, with life crumbling about him, holds to his escapist vision of retreat to a fruit-farm in Somerset – as well as reminding himself constantly of a childhood in the West that has become a triumphant legend. With this in the past, and the golden apples of the future ready to pick at any moment, there is no time for the present: the present in which he is a vain, cowardly man in a London suburb, a husband and father who has lost the respect of either despairing wife or shifty children. Thanks to Sir Ralph Richardson, the man

The Best Plays and Players of 1957

by J. C. Trewin

can win our grudging sympathy at times, but he forfeits it at the last when, offered by his wife the realisation of his dream, he rejects it. He is too cowardly to venture. His wife's patience snaps. The play should have ended with her departure: it was a pity to force home the resemblance to Miller's *Death of a Salesman*, with Richardson's final collapse and death among the rising of a symbolic orchard. Until then, at the Haymarket, it is a play of quality, with Celia Johnson most poignant, in her restrained way, as the wife. The husband, Jim Cherry, comes to us clearly in Richardson's performance that captures the man's self-conscious anxiety, bred of a life of deceit.

A much quieter portrait, Paul Scofield's in *A Dead Secret*, will also keep the imagination. Rodney Ackland's period-piece – the year is 1911 – derives, in outline, from one of the most notorious poisoning cases of the century. It came to us in an intricate exercise in theatrical craftsmanship, heightened by Frith Banbury's use of the multiple set of that 'Willesden Park' house, with Scofield at its core. It was one of the actor's uncanny transformations, though he did no more, it seemed, than put on a moustache and turn his voice to a sombre, Midland-accented rasp. Scofield has the gift of thinking himself into a part. He never merely externalises. His Dyson from *A Dead Secret* still weights the memory: the arrogant man ruined by insensate greed. The best of the other British plays in London was possibly Priestley's *The Glass Cage*, though nobody would call it a major work. Still, the message ('There's too much hate') was something pleasantly unusual in the contemporary theatre. On the lighter stage, Jack Popplewell's *Dear Delinquent* was amusing, old-fashioned blarney, and Lesley Storm's *Roar Like a Dove* proved to be a cheerful fertility rite.

Some of the more important British plays remained outside the West End. In *The Hidden King*, which I have already discussed at length in PLAYS AND PLAYERS, Jonathan Griffin – with the tautly sensitive acting of Robert Eddison and the eloquence of Robert Speaight to aid him – wrote one of the major chronicle plays in the current theatre. (I do not hesitate to say this to searchers in the files during 2007.) John Hall, with two unusually-conceived pieces (one done by the Birmingham Repertory, another by Bristol Old Vic) arrived as an author with something to say, and the means of expressing it. And if I must take one more play from the provinces, I choose R. C. Sherriff's *The Telescope*, an acute study in psychology. The scene is the East End Dockland, and the principal characters are an idealistic parson and a youth who is very much of his period, a child of chaos unable to see a pattern in life.

As usual, much work came from abroad. I choose first a visitor from the Commonwealth, *Summer of the Seventeenth Doll*, the first important native Australian play, written in a fashion direct and forcible. It holds the feeling of that sad period when we know a delight must cease: the wistfulness of change-and-decay. France sent fewer good plays than normally (we ought at once to forget such silliness as *The Balcony*, an affair as feeble as its production). But there were useful nights: *Restless Heart* – not an apt title for *La Sauvage* – in which Mai Zetterling, more moving facially than vocally, took some of our hearts as a girl who could not find happiness. We were glad that Sir Donald Wolfit gave a showing to Montherlant, stronger in the Renaissance passion of *Malatesta*. And probably the most-regarded French play of the year was *The Chairs* by Eugene Ionesco, the Rumanian-Parisian writer who used his extravaganza (two old people at the top of a tower, marshalling an unseen company of phantoms) to enlarge upon the themes of emptiness, frustration, and despair. From America we had the under-valued *Tea and Sympathy*, with a lucid performance by Tim Seely; Tennessee Williams's clouded phantasmagoria of *Camino Real*, directed with spirit by Peter Hall; and Carson McCullers's own version of her study in loneliness, *Member of the Wedding*, an unusual summoning of mood, though the play could not match the book which begins with the sentence, 'This was the summer when for a long time she had not been a member'. Bertice Reading gave a very warm and touching performance of the Negress-cook; and it is Miss Reading again that I remember from William Faulkner's *Requiem for a Nun*, an almost sepulchrally portentous drama that I feel must be an acquired taste. For me it was a night potentially impressive but over-produced. Ruth Ford was too frigid in the confessional, but again Miss Reading, as the Negress condemned, offered a performance of a singular rapt beauty. Two plays of European origin were *The Public Prosecutor*, an excitingly-contrived piece of theatre (Kitty Black's translation from the Austrian Hochwaelder) that hardly delighted critics for whom 'theatrical' seems to be what one of my least-favourite plays calls 'a dirty word'; and *Man of Distinction*, a comedy, 30 years old, from the German of Hasenclever. This should not have been dug up, though at least we were glad of Denis Carey's ingenious production – here is a director – and for the grace and fun of the dancing Moira Shearer.

Classical revivals brought four or five splendid performances. A Stratford-upon-Avon season, otherwise matter-of-course, offered Sir John Gielgud's majestic enunciation in a typically adventurous Peter Brook idea of *The Tempest*, done later at Drury Lane; Alec Clunes's Faulconbridge, bold yet relaxed; and Dame Peggy Ashcroft's Rosalind, still the spirit of Arden. Stratford had originally fathered *Titus Andronicus*, the Brook production of two years ago, which had a wildly successful London season at the Stoll, Olivier turning the unremarked 'I am the sea' into one of the great utterances of the actor's theatre. The Old Vic, most gallantly and vigorously, continues its full Shakespearean cycle. (One theatre at least in Shakespeare's own capital city should always have the plays on show.) The performance of the year was John Neville's Hamlet in an unobtrusive Ruritanian-court production. Neville cannot be denigrated as a 'gallery idol': he is an actor of most delicate talent, and in this revival he is responsive to every emotion: a far truer Hamlet than his predecessor's at the Old Vic had been. During the Vic year we had, among much else, a cunning Byron-and-Snodgrass *Two Gentlemen of Verona*; a *Measure For Measure* in which Neville and Barbara Jefford agonised with strong emotional truth as Angelo and Isabella; and another Douglas Seale revival of the fierce mediaeval tournament of *Henry the Sixth* (Parts Two and Three, with a snatch of Part One.) In the provinces, Albert Finney, of the Birmingham Repertory Theatre – this was another Seale production – was unfaltering as a Henry

the Fifth, in the very May-morn of his youth, who took his cue from the line, spoken into the daybreak before Agincourt, 'The day, my friends, and all things stay for *me*'. Mark Finney's name for the future. From abroad we had Edwige Feuillère in the expert artificiality of *La Parisienne* and as a small-scale *Phèdre*.

On the lighter stage I think first of Michael Flanders and Donald Swann. Since January they have conducted their two-man revue at the Fortune, an 'after-dinner farrago' that someone – and I concur – describes as a success 'almost majestic'. A musical *Zuleika* would not have worried Max, though the heroine herself needed better casting; the serenely simple *Free as Air* (Savoy), with the freshness of *Let the grass grow*, won the other side of the Strand for the *Salad Days* partnership, Dorothy Reynolds and Julian Slade; and *Bells Are Ringing* (Coliseum) introduced the cheerful red-head, Janet Blair.

The year had its unhappy tidings as well as its good things. References to 'the bird' in the text of *The Crystal Heart* added to the disaster of a noisy musical-play première at which Gladys Cooper returned to London. And I give dishonourable mention to such events, on their various levels, as an eccentric satire, *The Making of Moo; Royal Suite*, among the tattiest comedies for a long time; and a modern-dress *Macbeth*, an effort – so its director proclaimed – 'to strip off the poetical interpretation which the nineteenth-century sentimentalists put upon these plays'. Never mind. All said, a year that has presented Olivier, Gielgud, Richardson, and Scofield in their finest form, introduced such a new dramatist as Robert Bolt, and offered as many rewarding nights as we have had in a fairly full programme, cannot be called a loss. I am sure that some things at least from 1957 will emerge from the 'daily deepening drift' of another age's file-room.

Congratulations to: George Devine and the Royal Court Theatre for continuing to encourage new serious dramatists and for discovering John Osborne; Sam Wanamaker for his enterprise in creating a lively theatre centre at Liverpool; Theatre Workshop for bringing a real concrete-mixer on to the stage in *You Won't Always Be on Top*.

Dramatist of the year: Eugene Ionesco, whose *The Chairs* and *Ademée* have shocked and delighted us.

Credits and Discredits for 1957

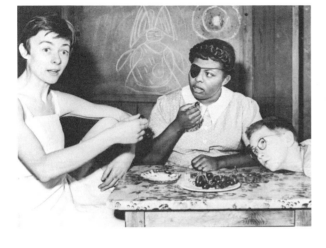

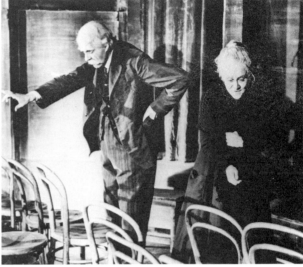

Seen at Court. Clockwise from above: Geraldine McEwan in *The Member of The Wedding* by Carson McCullers; Eugène Ionesco's *The Chairs* with George Devine and Joan Plowright; Peggy Ashcroft as Brecht's *Good Woman of Setzuan*; Robert Helpmann in Sartre's *Nekrassov*

Best performances of the year: Paul Scofield in *A Dead Secret;* Laurence Olivier and Brenda de Banzie in *The Entertainer;* John Gielgud, in face of an incredibly noisy production, in *The Tempest;* Joan Plowright in *The Chairs;* John Neville in *Hamlet*; Ralph Richardson in *Flowering Cherry;* Peggy Ashcroft in *As You Like It;* Alec Clunes in *King John;* Joan Heal in *Grab Me a Gondola;* and Vivien Leigh in the House of Lords.*

Best plays of the year: Ray Lawler's *Summer of the Seventeenth Doll* and Rodney Ackland's *A Dead Secret.*

Best productions of the year: Peter Hall's *Camino Real* and Douglas Seale's *Henry VI.*

Young actress of the year: Joan Plowright.

Come back soon: Marcel Marceau, Siobhan McKenna, Victor Borge.

Welcome back: Ralph Richardson in *Flowering Cherry* and Dorothy Tutin in *The Entertainer.*

Neglected dramatist: John Whiting, none of whose plays has been seen in London for three years.

Lost cause of 1957: English dramatists – no plays by T. S. Eliot, Christopher Fry, Charles Morgan or John Whiting.

Names we have missed: Michael Redgrave, Eric Portman, Alec Guinness.

Forgotten names of 1957: Hermione Gingold and Hermione Baddeley.

Worst productions of the year: *The Balcony* and *The Glass Cage.*

Disappointment of the year: the plays chosen for the Edinburgh Festival.

Bores of the year: the 'Method' and all those people who keep telling us how wonderful *My Fair Lady* is going to be.

Pull up your socks department: the Arts Theatre Club.

Damp squibs of the year: *Tea and Sympathy* and the Royal Variety Performance.

Not good enough department: American musicals – and British ones too.

Mistakes of the year: allowing the St James's Theatre to be demolished; and *Royal Suite, The Crystal Heart* and *Zuleika.*

Plays we should like to have missed: *Oh! My Papa!, All Kinds of Men, Meet Me by Moonlight, Man of Distinction.*

Not so fresh department: *The Egg.*

Shipwreck of the year: *The Tempest.*

Marcel Marceau

* *Vivien Leigh had created a sensation by protesting in the House of Lords at the impending demolition of the historic St James's Theatre.*

1958

The year that de Gaulle became President of France was also the year that Khrushchev consolidated his power in Russia with the dismissal of Bulganin. In Italy 1958 was the year in which the popular John XXIII succeeded Pope Pius XII. Rivalry between Russia and the USA in outer space was reflected in the launch by Russia of Sputnik III and by the USA of its series of Explorer and Pioneer rockets.

In Britain the year that Charles became Prince of Wales, saw the beginning of television series like Panorama *and* Your Life in Their Hands *underlining the growing popularity of the small screen with the consequent accelerating decline of the cinema.*

In America Bernstein's West Side Story *confirmed that in the late 1950s the USA was still pre-eminent in the field of the musical whilst the debut in Britain of Peter Shaffer with his new play* Five Finger Exercise *added a new name to the roll-call of British dramatists who were to win world-wide fame.*

Controversial Cat

Richard Buckle reviews Cat on a Hot Tin Roof *at the Comedy*

Cat on a Hot Tin Roof is about Maggie's efforts to get her estranged husband Brick back into bed with her. There are several good reasons why Brick should sleep with Maggie and why we want him to. First, Maggie is in love with Brick; then if they have a child it will make his old parents happy, and enable Big Daddy to leave his rich plantations away from Brick's detestable but fertile elder brother; and finally our sense of what is right and beautiful in human life makes us demand that the young couple should beget young. There is, however, one reason why Brick will not sleep with his wife; and his point of view becomes clearer in the course of Tennessee Williams's enthralling play. The play is a battle, with the wills of parents and wife ranged against that of the young man whose strength lies in the fact that he does not care for love or life or property any more. Brick drinks because he is afraid to face in himself an emotion which once seemed noble but which now fills him with shame. Brick's problem is that he loved his friend Skipper more than men usually love their best friends.

Paul Massie and Kim Stanley in the London première of Tennessee Williams's banned play *Cat on a Hot Tin Roof*

He and Skipper used to play football together, and once, when Brick was away sick, Maggie accused Skipper of being in love with her husband. To prove he was not queer, Skipper then went to bed with Maggie, and because this was not a success, Skipper began to believe he was 'abnormal'. He took to drink, made a declaration of love to Brick on the telephone, which Brick hung up on, then died. So it is Maggie's problem against Brick's problem, fertility against barrenness, life against death. There is a second plot, if such it can be called. Big Daddy, Brick's father who adores him, is Maggie's ally in the battle for life and the continuity of his race, but he himself is under sentence of death by cancer. The action takes place on the night of Big Daddy's sixty-fifth birthday, himself and his wife believing for the first two acts that he has been given a clean bill by the doctors, the rest of the family knowing that Big Mama must soon be told her husband has not long to live. So Big Daddy has his problem too, which for a time seems to take precedence of Maggie's and Brick's.

The art of the tragic dramatist is to open the shutter at the critical moment when his characters are forced to reveal their truth, when situations loom vast and inescapable as lorries from a fog. Impossible to deny the skill of Mr Williams in the way he chooses to confront us with his characters in their tragic dilemma. The play unfolds on the battleground of this Southern bedroom with its mouldering splendours and its tall windows open on the sound of crickets and wippoorwills in the breathless night; and as a theatrical experience it is superior to anything we have seen for a long time. The Southern habit of repeating phrases in conversation gives an incantatory strength to the dialogue which helps the drama to work its curious spell – and these repetitions are something entirely different from O'Neill's rambling reiterations in *The Iceman Cometh*. While O'Neill's characters seem to involve themselves in talk as a desperate means of postponing action, the dialogue of *Cat* carries the action forward in spurts like the fuse in a fire-cracker. It has the ring of inevitability, and yet there is no passage you could select and say, 'This is a gem of wit or poetry'. Mr Williams has rightly renounced the purple patches which, in *Camino Real* and other works, he failed, in my opinion, to bring off. There is no 'fine writing' in the play, just as there are no new or original ideas: for Tennessee Williams is neither a poet nor a prophet. But he is a masterly maker of plays, and this is the basic virtue. He can prolong a scene beyond what most dramatists would dare, too intent upon telling his story in his own way to care about safety or rules, yet so true is his instinct and so sure his craft that he is nearly always successful.

The play reads well, and it acts better, but from now on I shall find it hard to imagine it without Kim Stanley in the role of Maggie. Her performance in this most difficult part is a triumph of subtlety and vitality. Her first act duel with Brick is almost a monologue, and it is wonderful to watch her, obsessed by the sole idea of becoming his wife again, going at him with her drill of nervous energy, charged by love and will power, only to retreat and crumble miserably before the laconic implacability of his replies – then reviving, gathering strength and persuasiveness, rallying, as if inspired, to her vocational task again. During these bouts Miss Stanley's face changes from a mask of feminine charm

to the battered hopeless face of an older woman, and, as the noble impulse stirs her, changes back to beauty. The way she switches from catty defensiveness in brushes with her brother-in-law and his wife to a consoling warmth with which to envelop the moaning Big Mama is magical too. She does interesting things with her hands to her hair and clothes, and wears throughout, despite the 'unladylike' role she is called on to fill, an irresistible air of good breeding, which seems the more delightful for being surprising – a quality one expects less from glamorous American stars than from our more subdued English actresses, though few young English actresses I know can back such elegance with such power and fire. Leo McKern made a real man of the lusty, swashbuckling Big Daddy; but Paul Massie as Brick, lacking the personality and magnetism to carry off this stone-wall part and stripped of lines, was somewhat colourless, though he looked well in pyjamas. Bee Duffell's Big Mama was often touching, like a bouncing wounded bird, though I wondered why she was got up as a madam in a brothel.

Critics after the opening night complained of a lack of pace in Peter Hall's production, but by the time I saw it I did not find much amiss in this respect. The distant fireworks, and the incursions of odious children, which punctuate the tense action, might perhaps have been more poetically or more subtly arranged; but Leslie Hurry's set had a kind of murky opalescent atmosphere of doom. Few playwrights of our time have seized so greedily as Tennessee Williams on every resource of the producer's craft in the modern theatre – lighting, music, stage effects and noises off – to help him create the atmosphere of his plays.

There are two odd things about *Cat on a Hot Tin Roof*. The first, which I noticed on previously reading it, is apparent lack of unity. The first act is all Maggie's. In the second act, Maggie is inconspicuous, and Big Daddy takes over. In his 'talk' with the drinking Brick, the father begins by trying to make Brick face the fact of his (perhaps) fundamental homosexuality and to forgive himself as Big Daddy – who has knocked about the world a bit – understands and forgives him. It ends with a discussion of lies and the unwillingness of men to face the truth; and Brick, forced reluctantly to look into his own heart, retaliates by telling his father the doctor's true verdict, sending him offstage condemned to death. In the last act Big Daddy is invisible, and Maggie has to fight her brother-in-law and his wife over the inheritance, before being left alone with Brick to resume and win her private battle. So that is one odd thing: our attention is directed first to Maggie, then to Big Daddy, then back again, and we sometimes wonder who the hero is. The second odd thing is that, although the whole play may be regarded as a softening up process of Brick, in his determination not to sleep with Maggie, she ultimately achieves her aim (if that is what happens after the curtain goes down) by a trick. She removes all his bottles of liquor, and makes it impossible for him to get a drink – as he has one leg in a splint and cannot move without his crutch – until he has gone to bed with her. These oddities might be called defects in a work which was less gloriously successful than the one in question, but if a playwright can get away with a play like *Cat on a Hot Tin Roof*, who cares about rules or anything else?

The Elder Statesman comes to London with the reputation of having been the most pre-booked play of the Edinburgh Festival. It presents the passionate playgoer with an inescapable question. Is there a place, outside the English Stage Company, for the Theatre of the Poet – that there is great need for the poet in the theatre is not in question – and it is just my luck to find myself cast as The Oracle without The Answer Pat. The problem does not lie with the dramatist with the eye to see, the ear to hear, and the heart to feel, whose insight can turn people into poems – muddled, maybe, but poignant and glorious poems – so that their predicaments rise with them into the realms of high tragedy or highly comical tragedy according to the genre in which they are conceived. For to these writers a dramatic situation generates an incandescence which sets the stage alight with the tensions of people in opposition to one another or to fate, and what they do and say and feel in their moment of truth will be common to all mankind. The Theatre then is perhaps above all places the province of the poet whose vision passes into the characters he creates and is so deeply integrated that he speaks to us only with their voices and through them.

But the Theatre of the Poet is something very different. For here it is the Poet himself who speaks to us, not, as it were in the words of his characters, but in despite of characterisation. Here it is the word and its arrangement in the phrase that is important and the people in the play are nothing but the author's loudspeakers; necessary nuisances to be bundled on and off as summarily as

The People in the Play

Caryl Brahms reviews The Elder Statesman *at the Cambridge*

Paul Rogers and Anna Massey in T. S. Eliot's play *The Elder Statesman*

Nannie's anger, falling upon a nursery offender. And in passing we must not forget that the poet, treading the tightrope of his sentences with his obsession for finding the perfect word and setting it in the perfect place, is a greater show-off than any over-excited child high on his own spirits, in every sense, 'above himself'.

Let me try to show myself what I mean by citing some plays.

Sean O'Casey's *Juno and the Paycock* is the perfect example of the work of the poet in the Theatre. It has its own rich, lilting cadences; its laughter and its tears. No two people speak alike in it yet all speak with the accent and authority of truth. And as with all real tragedy we are aware that in its beginning lies the inescapable seed of its end.

Christopher Fry's *The Dark is Light Enough* is the equally perfect example of a play for the Theatre of the Poet. Here the people in the play speak with the gathered wisdom of their author and their personalities are expressed in their motives rather than in their words.

Of course there should and must be a stage for both naturalistic and poetic drama since no art can breathe and live and grow that sets itself within firm boundaries; and since, moreover, poetry is pervasive and slips into the most unlikely phrases spoken from the human heart there will always be a place for the poet who writes plays.

And yet the thought cannot entirely be banished from the mind that some poets – and I cannot say too clearly that Mr Fry is not among them; repeat not – would be more happily heard from the page than from the stage. But, you will be wanting to say, *The Elder Statesman* is not by Sean O'Casey; neither is it by Christopher Fry, but by T. S. Eliot, the Dean of the Theatre of the Poet.

What a predicament this sets for the honest theatrical analyst. A poet, author of a line of distinguished and successful plays (not one of which I have liked with an unqualified judgment), and, moreover, seventy years of age and therefore unlikely to alter the trend of his stage pieces – and why should he – has written a play I did not enjoy. Am I biased, unfair, carping, rather rude and in any case wrong? Probably. I put the point to my secretary. 'Um,' she said, 'difficult. I suppose you can't just write "I hated it, Caryl Brahms" and leave it at that'. Sensible girl, my secretary. But where the playgoer can discuss a play without even signing the sentiment, it is my job to show just cause for condemnation.

Why, then, did I, who so greatly love my Fry and my O'Casey, and somewhere in between, my Ionesco and my Godot; why did I hate *The Elder Statesman?* Not for its matter. For if I said anything at all it was 'love one another'. The advice is admirable if not new and heaven knows the world could ponder worse.

No, it was the stilted manner of the delivery of the message that maddened me; the way that it was always the writer, never the people in the play – or almost never – who appeared to be addressing us or one another; the cursory working-out of the plot, the obscurity of purpose and the lack of any communicated conviction.

Yet Mr Eliot is a fine, illuminating and convincing poet on the page – here is no writing-down, no literary slumming. And if I cannot understand a thought in one of Mr Eliot's poems it is not because it has been stated without care and passion, but simply that my mind is not in a sufficient state of grace to receive it. But back to the play, even though by now it must be evident that I would by-pass it and arrive with a deep breath of thankfulness straightway at the acting, if I could.

Lord Claverton, in his youth, ran over a man and did not stop but sped away uncomplicated. And, almost as an afterthought, he made a companion of a poor young man and taught him the ways of luxury. Then left him to fend for himself. When we meet him, Claverton is expecting death and is troubled lest his children should make the same mistakes he made at their age. On paper, and if I have read the play right, it seems to have a reasonably general application. It is the action that puzzled me, and I think it may be puzzling the cast.

Why did Federico Gomez, who has made a success but not a good thing of his life, find himself friendless and go through the grimaces of a moral blackmailer in the old red barn? And then the daughter, 'Father, I would gladly die for you'. You don't speak like that to members of your family – if you did they'd send for the doctor and tell you not to be 'affected'. That the son showed signs of taking up with his father's two torturers, his former friend and his former love, was more or less routine in this kind of situation. And if I go on any longer I shall find myself pointing out that Shakespeare had three words for that – stale, flat and unprofitable.

There are, however, two performances of feeling and accomplishment in the play. Mr Paul Rogers as Lord Claverton remains stylish and elegantly withdrawn and brings to arid lines an excitement in the timing of their delivery, like the thrust of a piston – exact, express, undeviating. And Mr Alec McCowen made me forget that the wastrel son was speaking lines. His first burst of passionate rebellion is a small *tour-de-force* that only a fine actor could accomplish – and many of us have known for some time now that in Mr McCowen we have a fine actor.

Miss Anna Massey, the devoted daughter, has learned a lot of lines and does her best to speak them. But I would have said that perky realism is her thing and that she is more the drawing-room comedy's Pamela Brown, with her own way of getting laughs and sharing her amusement than, shall we say, Mrs Siddon's daughter playing it down. Miss Eileen Peel, the early love, knew perfectly what she was doing and did it rather well and Mr William Squire made me suspect that he was as foxed as I was by his South American jetsam and so had taken refuge in his highly unlikely hair-style and the odd actor's trick.

Mr Hutchinson Scott designed two pretty but again rather puzzling decorations rather than two scenes, the colour of toffee and pampas grass and as to Mr E. Martin Browne's production . . . There is a kind of producer who can take a bunch of amateurs and make them act like professionals. Mr Browne has taken a cast of professionals and very nearly turned them into amateurs. But perhaps if one read the play unhampered by the stiff-jointed and old fashioned production one might find some reason for seeing it.

Credits and Discredits for 1958

Congratulations to: Dame Sybil Thorndike and Sir Lewis Casson, who have just celebrated their golden wedding, for their tireless and brilliant work for the English theatre at home and abroad; Joan Littlewood and her Theatre Workshop Company for their enterprise in presenting Shelagh Delaney's *A Taste of Honey* and Brendan Behan's *The Hostage*; Peter Hall on his appointment as Director of Productions at Stratford-on-Avon; and the Lord Chamberlain for lifting another corner of the censorship curtain.

Black marks to: Peter Sellers for allowing himself to become bored after only three months in his first West End role.

Success story of the year: Sam Wanamaker at the New Shakespeare Theatre, Liverpool.

Hostess of the year: Bea Lillie serving tea to all those matinée ladies at the Adelphi.

Welcome to: new dramatists Peter Shaffer (*Five Finger Exercise*), Bernard Kops (*The Hamlet of Stepney Green*), Beverly Cross (*One More River*), Shelagh Delaney (*A Taste of Honey*), N.F. Simpson (*The Hole* and *A Resounding Tinkle*) and John Mortimer (*The Dock Brief* and *What Shall We Tell Caroline?*)

Bores of the year: Samuel Beckett and his dust-bins; and *The Mousetrap*.

Actors of the year. Left Sam Wanamaker in *The Rose Tattoo*. Above: Paul Scofield in *Expresso Bongo*. Below: Albert Finney (with Charles Laughton) in *The Party*

Best productions of the year: Peter Wood's *Mary Stuart*, Douglas Seale's *Much Ado About Nothing*, Sir John Gielgud's *Five Finger Exercise*, and Peter Hall's *Twelfth Night*.

Best performances of the year: Googie Withers in *Much Ado About Nothing*; Michael Redgrave in *Hamlet* and *A Touch of the Sun*; Rex Harrison and Julie Andrews in *My Fair Lady*; Paul Scofield in *Expresso Bongo*; Irene Worth and Catherine Lacey in *Mary Stuart*; Beatrix Lehmann in *Garden District*.

Young actor of the year: Albert Finney in *The Party*.

Mistakes of the year: *Verdict, Pot Luck, Roseland, Beth* and *The Velvet Shotgun*.

Damp squibs of the year: *Cat on a Hot Tin Roof* and *Auntie Mame*.

Event of the year: the visit of the Moscow Art Theatre.

Welcome back: Bea Lillie, Florence Desmond and Charles Laughton.

Names we have missed: Sir Laurence Olivier, Alec Guinness, Eric Portman and John Whiting.

Rackets of the year: those thousands of black-market tickets for *My Fair Lady*; and theatre programmes at a shilling each.

1959

The year in which Fidel Castro seized power in Cuba was also the year that Cyprus became a Republic under President Makarios. 1959 saw Pope John XXIII in a search for church unity call the first Vatican Council in nearly 90 years. Riots in Leopoldville signalled the start of civil war in the Congo. In the same year Russia and the USA made rival moon probes with the Soviet Lunik series and the American Pioneer IV.

The morale of the British cinema in decline in the post-war years was boosted with the appearance of the film Room at the Top *whilst the new movement in the British theatre showed its continued vitality with the appearance of Behan's* The Hostage, *Shelagh Delaney's* A Taste of Honey *and Wesker's* Roots. *London had a new theatre – in the City – with the opening of Bernard Miles's* Mermaid.

Singapore to Sloane Square

Just before he began his 13 year collaboration with Keith Waterhouse in 1960 that resulted in a string of plays including Billy Liar *and* Say Who You Are, *Willis Hall found himself being hailed by Kenneth Tynan for 'the most moving production of the 1958 Edinburgh Festival' with his anti-war* The Long and the Short and the Tall *which came to the Royal Court in 1959. As a newcomer he explained his background and enthusiasm for the new climate of writing in the theatre in this interview with Frank Granville Barker.*

So many unkind things have been said about television by people connected with the theatre that it comes as a pleasant surprise to hear it defended by one of our most promising new playwrights. Willis Hall, author of that fine play *The Long and the Short and the Tall* at London's Royal Court Theatre, has found his work for radio and television of great value in his development as a writer, and he is not ashamed to say so. This 29-year-old author's road to the West End has been an unusual one, his progress having been steady and without sensational leaps forward. He first started writing while on military service in Malaya, and has followed a logical course of radio scripts, television plays, plays for repertory, the 'fringe' of the Edinburgh Festival, and finally the London heart of our English theatre.

With no literary or theatrical background Willis Hall dabbled at an early age in articles for newspapers in his native Leeds. Then, finding himself in Singapore, he began writing children's plays for Radio Malaya. This work presented something of a problem, for his radio audience was made up of Chinese children who knew only 'about 50 words of English', but it must have constituted a rigorously useful training. Throughout his last 18 months' service in Malaya he wrote several scripts each week, and he also made his first contact with the live theatre – as set designer for the Singapore Little Theatre.

He returned to England in 1953, and a year later started his professional career as a writer. For the first two years he wrote exclusively for radio, then in 1956 he launched out into the television field. For the BBC he has written many plays, children's scripts, and several features. One of his greatest successes is *The Royal Astrologers*, which began as a series featuring the same characters in one episode after another.

Under his exclusive contract with BBC Television Willis Hall has written a variety of plays, ranging from North Country comedy to a present-day setting of Greek tragedy. The latter was *Afternoon for Antigone*, in which Creon was transformed into the owner of a large ready-to-wear clothing factory. It was originally broadcast as a radio play with Donald Wolfit in the lead, and when televised it had Esmond Knight as Creon and Gwen Watford as Antigone. Last November saw the televising of *Airmail for Cyprus*, and this month *The Larford Lad*, a play about boxing, will be seen. Later this year the Television Playwright series will present his *Poet and Pheasant*, which has already been broadcast as a radio play and seen on several repertory stages, and *Last Day in Dreamland*, set in an amusement arcade. Willis Hall will be able to draw on personal experience here, for he once worked in an amusement arcade for several months. He still has six more plays to write under his contract, and he has been asked to write a farce for the Whitehall Theatre team's television series.

The live theatre first claimed his attention in 1957, his first attempt being a children's play written in that year but too late for the Christmas season. This was *The Royal Astrologers*, recently staged at Birmingham. His next play was *Poet and Pheasant*, a North Country comedy given its première at Watford last year and afterwards given other repertory productions at York and by several Harry Hanson companies. His third, and most important play was *The Long and the Short and the Tall*, originally given at last year's Edinburgh Festival under the title of *Disciplines of War* by the Oxford Theatre Group. Three days after this amateur première it was presented by the Nottingham repertory company – with equal success. At Edinburgh the play was widely acclaimed, Kenneth Tynan hailing it as 'the most moving production of the Festival'. *The Long and the Short and the Tall* was bought by Oscar Lewenstein and Wolf Mankowitz, who are presenting it at the Royal Court in association with the English Stage Company. Greeted as the 'best anti-war play since *Journey's End*' and a skilful and sensitive study of real people in an all too real and tragic situation, it has given Willis Hall an impressive launching into the arena of the British theatre.

He is now far from being an angry young man – as, indeed, he always has been. Though from a professional point of view he is equally happy writing for either stage or television, he derives more personal enjoyment from seeing his plays in the theatre. And he is fortunate in that he has 'arrived' at a time when our theatre has just awakened to the need for, and value of, plays about real people in real situations. Not so long ago no English playwright would have dared to present ordinary people on the stage in a serious play: working-class characters were employed only for comic relief, and they were written about in a patronising way that was thoroughly objectionable.

Now, however, we have a flourishing group of young writers who are peopling our stages with characters drawn from ordinary walks of life and are proving, like Willis Hall, that the vital stuff of fine drama is to be found in their lives. On this point he himself has taken a firm stand. He is determined to write always about the sort of characters met in real life, even when writing for children or when creating a play with a fantasy setting. This is also why he finds himself frequently drawing on personal experiences for his characters, though he does not do so for his plots.

He is very happy with the state of the theatre since this change took place two or three years ago. In addition to this strengthening of the London scene he is gratified to see that repertory companies in the provinces are showing themselves more and more ready to consider the work of new playwrights instead of waiting for West End plays to be released to them. The repertory movement, in fact, is at last showing signs of becoming what Miss Horniman tried to make of it, a part of our British theatre with a healthy, vigorous life of its own quite independent of changing West End tastes. He is also pleased to find so many fine actors eager to take part in this revitalising of the stage.

After the successful opening of his first West End production, Willis Hall returned to his home in Nottingham to continue his writing. He does this in the unromantic but practical atmosphere of an office, where he works steadily each day from nine until six, having recently formed himself into a limited company.

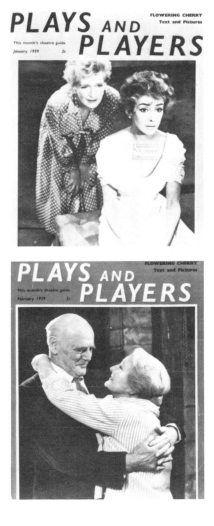

A Taste of Honey in rehearsal. Above: Frances Cuka (Jo), Shelagh Delaney (author), Joan Littlewood (director), Murray Melvin (Geoff). Below left: Avis Bunnage (Helen), Frances Cuka, Joan Littlewood. Below right: Avis Bunnage, Frances Cuka

Writing of the opening of 'Mr Beerbohm Tree's' new theatre – Her Majesty's – and incidentally this was a financial undertaking that nearly ruined Mr Beerbohm Tree, Shaw says: 'When you enter it you do not feel that you have walked into a Tottenham Court Road shop window – you feel that you are in a place where high scenes are to be enacted and dignified things to be done.' To each theatre its play, then; and to step out of Charing Cross Road into Wyndham's is instantly to be coaxed into the right frame of mind for the matinée performance of some 'winsome' comedy. It seems exquisitely reasonable that *The Boy Friend* should have run there within the aura of its cream and pale blue Dresden china charm till Dresden china doomsday. But now that *A Taste of Honey* has replaced *The Boy Friend* with The Girl Friend – 1958 model – she proves to be a very different dish – strong and sensible as Lancashire hot-pot (and just about as romantic). So that the first task the play must – and does – accomplish is to overwhelm the pale tint of prettiness with its own garish colour. Its next task is to break down the polite playgoer's prejudices – prejudices arising first from the gush of publicity that is tugging the play in its wake – a first play by a girl of 20 who, not being gormless, looked and listened while she earned her keep by ushering at a cinema and as a factory hand, and so equipped herself not so much with a conscious philosophy as with a God-given acceptance of what she heard and saw.

It had also to live down the legend of left-wing polemic, coming as it did, from Theatre Workshop in Stratford E. And finally it had to rise above being the play without a star in a theatre built to enshrine a star. And so it will be seen that this brave, brash, lively and at times quite lovely piece will have to fight the charm of its theatre and the attitude of its audience if it is to carry them with it.

The story of the play is as stark as a slag heap. Jo, an adolescent and neurotic girl, the child of her mother's encounter – 'It was one afternoon' – with a retarded youth – 'he had strange eyes – you've got them, too' – is left alone in sleazy digs at Christmas time, while her mother, clearly no better than she should be, gets wed and is off to a new life. Jo, in love with her own adolescence, with the age she is living in ('I'm a contemporary . . . I really live at the same time as myself, don't I?'), has an affair. Her lover is a coloured man, a sailor, 'He came in with Christmas and went out with the New Year.' While she is waiting for the child of this dark union, Geoff, a young art student, makes his home with her. Geoff is at that stage where he is weighing the make-do of adolescent homosexuality against the instinct of the normal male. He feels that Jo, about to be a mother, may be the answer to it all. But she looks on him as an elder sister. Close to her time, her mother returns, the marriage having broken up. She chases Geoff away; but on learning that her future grand-child is likely to have a darker skin than those of her neighbours goes off to drown her sorrows in gin. When Jo's labour pains begin she is alone. 'The dream's gone. The baby's real enough. That's life.'

Not, you will say, a pretty play. But a play which shines with the beauty of truth. A play which flashes with the grim wit that salty people pull out against themselves as mother and daughter claw verbally at one another. A play not to be missed – even while

Salad Days in Darkest Salford

Caryl Brahms reviews A Taste of Honey *at Wyndham's and* Fings Ain't Wot They Used T'Be *at Stratford East*

you hate it. A play to be respected. A contemporary play dug out of the present minute, like its daffy heroine and the life that goes on all around her. How much does the deftness, technical daring, visual beauty and general expertise of this play owe to its producer? We are not likely to learn the answer.

Miss Joan Littlewood is an animator of great gusto and imagination. She can take a bare stage and fill it with beauty. Light falls upon the scene and suddenly it lives. Miss Delaney is to be congratulated on her good luck in sending her first play to the right place at the right time. Nor does the young author's luck stop there. For in Miss Frances Cuka she has a leading lady of unusual interest. Miss Cuka is one of the weird sisters who could act a skyful of stars off the stage before you can say stir-the-cauldron. Her Jo is a bit shapeless, but then so is adolescence. And there is no touch of poetry, no needle of irony, that she does not command. We have already seen her as a dismembered head in a dust-bin, in Sloane Square, doing her best to be another Joan Plowright. In *A Taste of Honey* she is another Frances Cuka. And that is much more satisfactory.

Avis Bunnage, once again, allies brain and heart and bash and pace until she wins us over to her brassy, brash-tongued Helen by sheer assault. Mr Clifton Jones as the coloured boy, is pliant and pleasing and youthful and lithe and what in other, more experienced hands could have been offensive, became, instead, reasonably idyllic. As Geoff, Mr Murray Melvin is quietly believable.

Any playgoer who lacks the stomach for this important first play deprives himself of a rich and significant experience.

New geese being swans to the final glittering feather I have been an admirer of Miss Joan Littlewood's work too short a time to admit that there could be the slightest flaw in it. None the less I have to allow that fings ain't, y'know. Its title is a fair summing up of the current production of Theatre Workshop. But why? The play is lively if purposeless. The scene, which is a Soho gaming club, conscientiously teems with the entrances and exits of a cast of character actors devotedly doing their nut. The staging is Littlewood utility.

The play is punctuated with songs (if punctuation means stopped by) thrown into what ought to be the action like currants into dough and seemingly without much more premeditation. Perhaps the measure of the piece is that the best number, *G'night Dearie*, was better put over in Mr Lionel Bart's *Wally Pone*, by a bunch of amateurs at Unity. Miss Shelagh Delaney, almost, one might swear, by way of apologia, comes popping out of a two-line part in the last act, having herself a strange little interlude.

The author has a quick enough ear for dialogue but he must dig his foundations a bit deeper and so enable himself to build his edifice to the point. There were of course some good things in the picture of Soho cellarage. I shall try to call some of them to mind.

Most effective must have been Mr James Booth's Tosher; a jumpy, gabbing gent who sends out girls. With less opportunity but with steadfastness of vision, Miss Eileen Kennelly, last seen (by me) as Lady Macbeth, gives a performance in the round of

Lilly Smith, a faithful char. We laughed at Miss Carmel Cryan's Betty and with Miss Ann Beach's Rosey. But I did not believe that either of them walked the streets other than those painted on the old-time comedian's backcloths in touring revues. Mr Glynn Edwards anchored this rudderless gas-inflated air-ship to the crazy earth off Old Compton Street with his technically assured boss of the speiller.

The play was by Mr Frank Norman with songs by Mr Lionel Bart and set by Mr John Bury. And Mr Peter Wildeblood, widely known to be with Soho musical, can breathe again. I wish I could have liked it better. I wish I could have liked it period.

However it was amusing to find young Chelsea patronising the show and fascinating to watch Miss Shelagh Delaney out front (ah! ah!) waiting her turn to be served in the Coffee Bar and wearing that much-publicised raincoat. One could not but reflect how much more modestly a theatre-workshop deb. comports herself than her sister-under-the-squeal at Queen Charlotte's Ball.

MAY

1959

The Producer and the Mermaid

Shortly before Bernard Miles's Mermaid Theatre opened on Puddle Dock on 28 May 1959 with his production of Lock Up Your Daughters! *Peter Coe, the Mermaid's first resident director gave this interview to Plays and Players.*

Experiment is in the air at Puddle Dock. Out on the brink of Blackfriars the Mermaid is nearing completion and when Bernard Miles's Thames-side theatre throws open its plate-glass doors to the public on the 28th of the month an ideal will be within the grasp of Peter Coe, the Mermaid's first resident producer. A young director with fixed and controversial ideas on the growth of the theatre, Coe brings to this project in the City something more than the necessary number of years in provincial repertory. Tall, bearded and fine-eyed, he has all the outward appearance of a theatre fanatic but his infectious enthusiasm is firmly grounded on wide experience.

At 29 he has a succession of worthwhile productions behind him. After training at LAMDA he spent three and a half years as an actor, returned to the school as lecturer and producer and after two years launched out into the provinces. At the Arts Theatre, Ipswich, Val May had left for Nottingham and the commercial repertory was not a success. Peter Coe planned an exciting reversal of policy and out of his season came such productions as *Moby Dick, Henry IV, The Italian Straw Hat* and *The Waltz of the Toreadors.* Coe continued to gain experience at the Castle, Farnham, Carlisle's Her Majesty's and the Theatre Royal, Lincoln. At the Queen's Theatre, Hornchurch, another reportory of modern classics found Bernard Miles in the audience, watching *The Glass Menagerie* and describing it later as 'one of the most sensitive and imaginative productions that I've yet seen'.

But Peter Coe has not been totally confined to provincial audiences. The British Council invited him to produce *The Importance of Being Earnest* in Geneva and for George Devine he directed Charles Robinson's *The Correspondence Course*, the first of the Royal Court's 'productions without decor'. He has recently returned from a two-month visit to India where he produced *A Midsummer Night's Dream* with an all-Indian cast.

So much for Peter Coe's experience. So much for what Bernard Miles saw on the surface when he invited him to join the Mermaid.

But Coe brings more than competent direction. He brings ideas and ideals which he hopes will make the Mermaid not only a new theatre but the starting point for a completely new concept of drama in this country.

'My ideal,' says Coe, 'has always been to work on an open stage, moving from situation to situation without the restrictions of a proscenium set.' At the Mermaid he has that ideal, for there is no break between players and audience; the 48 foot platform stage blends the acting area with the audience and a 20 foot revolve enables scenes to flow unbroken into each other.

'This idea of a proscenium setting,' says Coe, 'has become so fixed in people's minds in this country that it now becomes automatic for a designer to give a backing to a window or to cut out the fourth wall of the set, not from necessity but purely from habit. The backing or the fourth wall may or may not be necessary. The tragedy is that these things are not even considered.' The wide acting area of the Mermaid stage will not only provide a freer atmosphere in the productions but will add a personal touch by bringing the audience into the spirit of the play. They will be actively concerned rather than being merely passive lookers-on. Peter Coe believes that this is only one of several aspects of the Eastern Theatre which are influencing ideas in this country. These aspects, he thinks, are already present to a certain extent and will eventually provide an entirely new dramatic style, although not necessarily in the original Eastern form. 'Perhaps that is the secret of our strong theatrical tradition,' he explains. 'We take years to assimilate a new form or idea but when it does appear it is very cunningly shaped into something of our own making.' With tremendous enthusiasm and first-hand knowledge he goes on to talk about performances in the Eastern theatre.

'The man in the audience really takes part in the play he's watching. He discusses the performance with his neighbour and when a player disappoints or pleases him he shouts out and tells him so. In this way the theatres are very noisy but the audience are personally involved with what they are watching and the theatre is much more alive. In the same way the Eastern actor spends much more time speaking to the audience. Over here actors are still concerned with pretending that no one is watching them but the habit is growing of bringing the audience into the play; of taking them into the actor's confidence.'

This Eastern influence, which he feels is gradually making itself felt through the plays of Brecht and his followers, is also responsible for the increase in the singer-actor, a phenomenon surprisingly difficult to find in the English theatre, who will, thinks Coe, become increasingly important.

'When a Kabuki actor stops acting,' explains the Mermaid producer, 'he starts to sing. When he stops singing he begins to dance. We are already seeing the first of these changes in the large number of plays with music now being produced. The second step may come eventually.

'I don't mean,' he adds, 'that all future actors will have to become acrobats but the blending of acting, singing and dancing is a thing of the future.'

The Mermaid's future programme shows vision and variety. There are old faithfuls (*Journey's End, Great Expectations* and

Treasure Island), there are classics ancient and modern (*Antigone*, Brecht's *Galileo* and *Les Justes* by Camus) and there are exciting proposed productions of Marc Connelly's *The Green Pastures* and the Wakefield Cycle of Mystery Plays. Peter Coe sums up this production policy as 'a theatre for Everyman.'

'We are not limiting the Mermaid to a certain style of plays,' he insists. 'At present there is this West End policy of associating the Whitehall with farce, the Stoll with musicals and Covent Garden with ballet and opera. At the Mermaid people will find a variety of theatre and that is why we have included a number of well-tried favourites in our opening programme. If we were to simply stick up a notice board saying "*Antigone* by Sophocles, *Galileo* by Brecht and *Les Justes* by Camus" we would just attract the audiences of the London art theatres, and that is not our aim.' Under the new concrete roof of the Mermaid rehearsals are under way for the opening production – a musical with a City background called *Lock Up Your Daughters*. Producing this adaptation by Bernard Miles of the Henry Fielding satire is Peter Coe, a young producer putting his ideals into practice in this dramatic experiment at Puddle Dock.

Keep Britain Black

Richard Buckle reviews The Hostage *and* The Complaisant Lover.

What greater contrast could be found than between Mr Graham Greene's clever, praised and successful *The Complaisant Lover*, now running at the Globe, and Mr Brendan Behan's clever, praised and successful *The Hostage*, currently at Wyndham's? The one, written by the Senior Classics master, directed by the Head Prefect and acted by the Sixth Form for the delight of rich and doting parents: the other, inspired by stolen hooch, improvised by the common scholarship boy with the help of the mad girl from over the wall, banged out just for the hell of it in the school lavatories on Saturday night! The Greene play is all intelligence, the Behan all blood and guts; and the latter is my choice every time.

The Complaisant Lover holds absolutely no surprises. I know it could be said that most of the newspaper-addicted public go to most plays knowing what they are all about and exactly what to expect – but, even so, this play holds less surprises than the majority. Within a few minutes of the curtain rising on the aftermath of this dentist's dinner party we know without the possibility of doubt that his wife will go off with the bookseller, that the dentist will find out and forgive, that the habit of marriage and her children will prove more important to her than a weekly night on the tiles. The final gimmick, if such it can be called, of the husband allowing his wife her extra-mural romance, is pretty well predictable too.

After the first scene I thought 'Is it really worth going through all this tedium just to see Richardson give a moving and masterly display of acting in the inevitable aria of forgiveness at the end?' After the second scene, in the Amsterdam hotel bedroom, I had to admit it was rather amusing to have introduced a touch of French farce, with the unexpected (God help us) appearance of

Graham Greene's *The Complaisant Lover* with Ralph Richardson, above, and, right, with Phyllis Calvert and Paul Scofield

husband, bewildered hotel valet and comic foreigner speaking no known language. Nevertheless, during the interval, when a quiet American strolled from the street into the stalls bar (rather bold, I thought) and, propelled by a sure instinct towards your critic, asked whether I could recommend the play, I told him I thought he'd find it heavy going. (Buckle strikes again.) After the third scene I thought 'They really do act well together – it's team spirit to the degree of a jig-saw puzzle.' And after the fourth and last scene I thought 'Was it really worth while going through all that just to see Richardson, Scofield and Phyllis Calvert give wonderful performances?'

It seems churlish not to be thankful for a perfect cast, perfectly directed, but I know that with me the answer is: I'll put up with a good deal provided I'm made to laugh or cry – and I wasn't. No doubt whatever that what the British theatre needs is to become less damned British. Anyway, thank God for Callas and Russia and Liberace. Thank God for Brendan Behan and Joan Littlewood, whom I suspect of being a Wop in disguise, probably an illegal immigrant – Giovanna Boschetto. Keep Britain black!

Sir Ralph Richardson's playing seemed all the more subtle and craftsmanlike for coming after his hammy though more spectacular disportment in that futile drama *Flowering Cherry*. A portrait in the round is what he painted – of this successful dentist with his fatuous good nature and addiction to practical jokes, his devotion to his job, his ordinary life hedged in by happy habit; then his incredulous eye-opening, his crumpling up, his ultra-British rising to the occasion, the final grandeur of his acceptance of the woman's need to live two lives, made possible for him by love. To present so true a mixture of intelligence and stupidity, of assurance and doubt, of commonness and nobility – in fact, to present a complete human being – is a feat only possible to an actor who knows his job and has a touch of genius besides.

Miss Calvert's performance in a difficult part was no less extraordinary. She suggested the struggle between the two loves –

the love of dull husband, home and kids, the love of romantic adventure and fresh desire; and although the drama of her choice, her longing to have her cake and eat it, was forcefully conveyed, it was conveyed in terms of absolute naturalness, with charm and style. Paul Scofield edged his way in and out of his caddish part with the plummy croak and faltering assurance which have for a decade proved irresistible to women of all ages. 'What I like about him, my dear, is that he's always the same.' *Semper eadem*! Oh England! Oh Aunt Edna! 'Oh chintzy, chintzy cheeriness half dead and half alive!' (Early Betjeman.)

> Oh the after-dinner coffee!
> Oh the neighbours dropping in!
> With *The Times* and children's bedtime
> Is there *time* for us to sin?
>   (Late Buckle.)

Before I get carried away I must say how pretty and distinguished Polly Adams was as the other girl – not a trace of RADA. All the cast were fine, though, and Gielgud's direction was as painless as perfect dentistry. The red-papered hotel bedroom of Carl Toms was a good set.

My burst of song above was no doubt a result of Brendan Behan's play, which is one third sing-song and which has changed my life. I keep sending out for more Guinness, breaking into rousing choruses and filling the house with whores. The other delightful thing about *The Hostage* – apart from its being one-third sing-song – is that the author takes the mickey out of English and Irish in equal proportions.

Of course with Miss Joan Littlewood's Theatre Workshop productions one never knows how much is author and how much inspired, swashbuckling director – but that is ideal so far as I am concerned. I'm all for everybody mucking in. *The Hostage* seems to be the triumph of mucking in. It doesn't read as well as it acts, but why should it?

Everything about *The Hostage* is fun – good dirty fun. You have to hand it to Behan – to take the last night in the life of an English soldier held as a hostage by the IRA and shot at dawn, then to turn it into a farcical musical comedy is some feat. There are marvellous crazy ideas in the show, not least that the action takes place in a lodging-house in Dublin run as a brothel (male and female) without the knowledge of its owner, a barmy idealist Englishman who has espoused the cause of the IRA, who plays the pipes and is called Monsewer, but still has pangs of nostalgia for cricket at Harrow on summer afternoons. He is the only character who can speak Gaelic. The others – thieves, whores, ponces and queers – don't know what he is going on about half the time, but respect his mania. Howard Goorney as the adaptable caretaker and Eileen Kennelly as his sharp-tongued partner are admirable and carry half the play. The Cockney hostage in his ill-fitting battledress is a darling, and his one-night romance with the orphan skivvy jerks a few welcome tears from a house exhausted with laughter. Alfred Lynch, who was good as the Welsh boy in Lindsay Anderson's amazing production of *The Long and the Short and the Tall*, has popped across the courtyard to take on with zest this smashing part and to voice the feelings of us all in his immortal reply to Miss Gilchrist, the social worker:

MISS GILCHRIST:
    Would you live on woman's earnings
    Would you give up work for good
    For a life of prostitution?
SOLDIER: Yes, too bloody true, I would.

When you like a show very much you sometimes get annoyed with yourself for carrying on about it at length, without really succeeding in suggesting its special flavour, and you want to fall back on quoting great chunks. In case I forgot to say so before, *The Hostage* is packed with humour, life, poetry and satire; and it's just my slice of salami. We Irish are just a lot of hopeless, useless, loud-mouthed Turks and layabouts, and we English are just plain bloody; but sure 'tis a fine thing after it's fighting each other we have been all these years that we can get together in a public place and enjoy a laugh and a cry over each other and the hate we bear to each other.

Could *The Hostage* be given in Dublin? I ask because I want to know. (Somebody leans over my shoulder and says 'They'd laugh their heads off at the jokes against themselves, but the sex part wouldn't get by the censor.')

OCTOBER
1959

Coventry Makes Theatre History

Bryan Bailey, The Belgrade Coventry's first artistic director, all too soon to die in a motor accident wrote the following account of Britain's first post-war municipally-built theatre which had opened on 28 March 1958.

Amongst theatregoers much is already known about the Belgrade Theatre. It has now been in operation for exactly 18 months and there is a natural temptation, in writing about it at this stage, to list the work that has been done and the achievements of which we are proud. In a short article, however, that would seem merely like an annual report. I prefer to select only three or four main aspects of the work here and to relate their significance to contemporary theatre and to likely developments in the future. Facts first. The Belgrade Theatre, so named in appreciation of the Yugoslavian gift of timber which has added elegance to the decor, was designed by the Architects Department of the Coventry Corporation. It was built by the City, thus becoming the first theatre to be built by a Municipality and also the first full-scale professional theatre to be erected in this country since before the war. Its cost was £300,000. It is not administered as a department of the City Authority, its management being the responsibility of an independent Theatre Trust.

The Theatre was opened by the Duchess of Kent in March, 1958; there is no doubt that at that time and subsequently it has pinpointed attention on the whole question of State and Municipal Aid for the Arts. The boldness of the venture, coming as it did when people were being made constantly aware of the closure and demolition of many theatres, made a vivid impact on the public imagination, encouraged those other authorities, such as Nottingham, which were considering similar undertakings, and provided occasions for many articles, broadcasts, talks and lectures, all of which have brought about a substantial development of public opinion towards a more generous acceptance of the principle of subsidies for the arts.

The Belgrade Theatre, by its success as a contemporary building with facilities and amenities beyond those of a mere playhouse, has grown into a social and community centre as well as a theatre centre. The ample provision of foyers, restaurant and bars, has enabled the theatre to provide catering services which contribute greatly in financial terms and in the creation of a friendly and intimate atmosphere. The public is encouraged to spend a whole evening at the theatre. By thus making a visit into an 'evening out' in the fullest sense, with opportunities for meeting friends, for leisurely conversation and discussion, it has been possible to overcome at least some of those barriers, often unconscious but none the less real, which have prevented theatres in the past from making a real and vital contact with many members of the community.

The social significance of the Belgrade is, therefore, of importance and it has been possible to link this with the development of a true theatre centre – a headquarters towards which all those interested in the arts will look and from which can come advice, help and encouragement for those concerned with the place of theatre arts in the community.

The additional activities and services provided by the Theatre have emerged naturally and gradually, stimulated by the requests and interests of theatre patrons and others. They have never been imposed or allowed to affect the basic purpose of the theatre, the presentation of plays. The series of exhibitions, the provision of Sunday concerts of music, lunchtime poetry readings, lectures and talks on theatre and drama, the conception of a theatre bookstall, the organisation and staffing of training courses, and co-operation with the amateur theatre movement are all aspects of the Belgrade's work which have emerged in a relatively short time.

The Theatre is a living building much of the day, bringing into its orbit increasing numbers of people. The part played by the new building itself in all this is, of course, paramount. It is also the foundation of the other most exciting development – the early and whole-hearted winning of a young theatre audience. A consistent policy for young people has been adopted and its success suggests there is much to be done in every theatre to attract and hold the younger sections of the community.

The policy is based, as in many other repertory theatres, upon close co-operation with the Local Education Authority and the purchase of certain matinée performances by the Authority. There is a Committee of Head Teachers working with the Theatre Director, to advise on this co-operation between theatre and schools. It has been encouraging to find so many teachers actively encouraging young people to link themselves with the Belgrade Theatre and the theatre staff, in its turn, visits and helps schools with their own productions. Secondly, everything possible is done to encourage young people to attend apart from the 'crocodiles' that march into the special matinées. By developing an Under-20 Club, with concessionary prices for all between 13 and 20, young

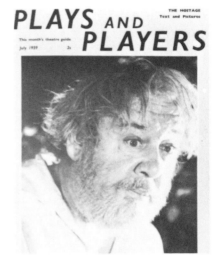

PLAYS AND PLAYERS
THE HOSTAGE
Text and Pictures
This month's theatre guide
July 1959 2s

people in their last years at school and immediately on leaving come to the theatre individually, in pairs or with small groups of friends. By joining with an adult audience they regard theatregoing as a natural and regular leisure time activity. At no time has the behaviour of these young people (the Under-20 Club numbers 3,500) occasioned comment or complaint. It is an integrated audience.

To remedy the lack of personal contact between the theatre's staff and the young people, and to create a selective and critical young audience, a series of 'Theatre Holiday' sessions has been held. These sessions (for convenience the attendance at each is limited to 200) give opportunities to demonstrate and discuss various aspects of a theatre's work. Their success at holiday times has led to a regular series of Saturday morning meetings. The young people attending gain a better insight into theatre methods and, whilst no attempt is made to turn these sessions into occasions for training young actors and actresses (indeed every effort is made to stress the problems of the profession) or needlessly to dispel the glamour and magic of the living theatre, what is being achieved is real practical training of an audience for the future. Training an audience may sound formidable, yet there is no doubt that theatres generally, and repertory theatres in particular, must remember how much needs to be done to encourage present-day theatre patrons to understand their responsibilities as audiences. With so much mechanised entertainment, with cinema and television requiring little or nothing in the way of positive audience response, we need to restate the importance of audience behaviour and reaction. A theatre audience must give a live, immediate, friendly yet selective response to the flesh and blood actors on the stage. Many of the Belgrade's audiences come from the 20–25 age range – a group not greatly found in theatres. Here again it is the contribution of the building itself, with its opportunities for the full 'evening out', that has been vital.

The Theatre Trust is working to an initial three-year plan, within the general framework of a fortnightly repertory company. However, the opportunities presented by this new building suggested rethinking many of the problems and basic assumptions of the present repertory system. People have for long accepted the principle that it is sensible to travel distances to the theatre if the attraction is sufficiently strong. Within this area of the Midlands there is already the magnet of Stratford and two repertory theatres in Birmingham. The Belgrade need not be 'just another repertory theatre', duplicating and imitating others' programmes. It can seize the chance of providing for the Midlands a third point of an exciting triangle of play-producing companies. Within the provision of a widely-based programme, it is the Trust's policy to establish a special emphasis which will make the Belgrade's contribution to theatre in this area, and to the repertory movement, definite and clear-cut. This emphasis is the encouragement of new plays by new writers.

Within the 18 months that the Theatre has been open, twelve new plays have been seen. Of these, two have been produced in London, one has been sold for television, one has been extensively produced by other repertory companies, one sold for a pre-London tour and then for publication.

The success of Arnold Wesker's *Roots* is proof of the value of the new play policy. Both this play and the author's first play – *Chicken Soup With Barley* (presented at the Belgrade in July, 1958) were rejected by London Managements and the critical acclaim so rightly given to Arnold Wesker underlines the importance of provincial theatres encouraging the new writer. Consistency in this policy is also vital as the new author needs help quite as surely towards his second and third play.

The Theatre Trust set aside the initial and generous grant from Associated Television Ltd, as a fund for the commissioning of new plays (in this respect an experiment was made by attaching for two months a writer to the staff and commissioning a play from him, which will be presented early in 1960); for the purchase of options and to meet the additional expenditure involved in the mounting of new plays. The Theatre works closely with the Arts Council in this respect and has benefited from the Council's schemes to aid new writers.

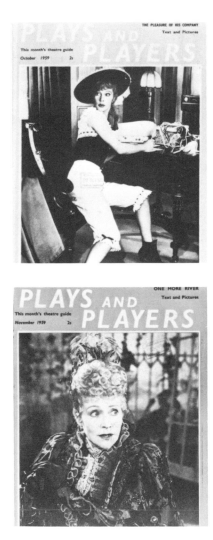

It would be gratifying if, in due course, a Midland group of playwrights emerged. Such may come about in the fullness of time; for the present every effort is made to meet, help and advise those playwrights who live in the Midland area.

In repertory work it is always dangerously easy to allow the ease of routine to become too dominant. By retaining a flexible programme, arranging for the company to undertake occasional, limited tours, by introducing specialist touring productions every effort is made to vary the programme offered to theatregoers and to provide the artists with varied opportunities and 'breaks' in the monotony of a strict repertory system. The programme of plays during the past year can be analysed as follows:

Six first performances and two English premières.

Three virtually unknown plays.

Four plays immediately following their release from London.

Four established repertory successes.

Seven modern and period 'classic' works by Shakespeare, Wycherley, Eliot, Ibsen, O'Neill, Shaw and Maugham.

Much more could be written about other aspects of the theatre's artistic policy, such as its reasons for working with guest designers, the advantages and problems of its guest producer policy and so on. There is space, however, only for stressing the Trust's anxiety to create conditions of work and an environment, in which its company of young artists can enjoy opportunities for stimulating and varied casting and for continued technical training and exercise in an atmosphere in which artistic integrity is respected and fostered.

Lines of Communication

Caryl Brahms reviews Serjeant Musgrave's Dance *at the Royal Court*

For an outstandingly important play, *Serjeant Musgrave's Dance* has had a very mixed press. There have been those critics of Mr John Arden's piece who have boasted that they could understand it but disliked it. Others have admitted that they could not understand it but disliked it. And so it has been left to an enlightened few – among whom I have honour to make my stand – to salute the quality of greatness in it. And why not? Since when has it been necessary to understand a work of art before being exhilarated, astonished, even transported by it? Nice, yes; necessary, nonsense! That symphony which cannot keep its secret; that picture which immediately tells its story; that poem with no thought in any line left to the future to bring, in its good time, home to the heart – these are all works concerned with surfaces. Perception can delve deeper.

There can be, however, too much of the prevalent passion of playwrights for not stating in plain terms the things they mean, for the sake of seeming to be clever, or out of pride, or carelessness, or the pressure of strong emotions too mixed up to be clarified; and of some or all of these Mr Arden cannot entirely be exonerated.

'Take no notice of anything your mother may say when she is out of sorts, my dear. It will have very little to do with what she thinks and nothing at all to do with what she feels.' I am reminded of this perceptive comment of my father's as I mull over what Sarn't Musgrave seemed to me to mean by what he did and said. Not until the last fifteen minutes of this mystifying but enthralling play did I begin to get the message – or what, for the purposes of this critique, I intend to settle for as being the message.

Let us confine ourselves, therefore, to the exciting surfaces of the play – for it was exciting even while to me, it was incomprehensible – exciting to the eye, ear and mind. A sergeant of Militia in charge of a company of three red-coats arrives in a small North Country mining community in the days when Grandma Moses was a slip of a girl with a grandma Moses of her own – say, 1870. There is unrest in the mines and the leaders think the redcoats have arrived to break the strike. But when Serjeant Musgrave stands all-comers drinks at the local as an inducement to them to take The Queen's Shilling they suppose he has come to them on a recruiting campaign.

Last scene of all – and that at which I got the message, he stands revealed as our old friend the fell Sergeant Death. For turning on the townsfolk what I like to think of as a cannon he hoists a skeleton to the flagpole. It is the skeleton of a local lad, recruited from the town and sent abroad to die in a colonial war. This lad, Sarn't Musgrave says – and to give him his due he has been saying this for quite some scenes now, to anyone with the ears to hear, this lad was killed to keep a colony for you. And to avenge his death four other men were killed. So now the fell Sarn't who turns out, definitively – I think – to be a deserter has brought the bones home to the Skeleton's own-and-native, and now prepares to mow down twenty-five members of the mining community.

And if the message isn't twenty-five eyes for an eye and twenty-five sets of teeth for a tooth then it must be contrarywise – e.g. that war is wicked and must cease. Not a new message, but can it be repeated in this world and at this time too often? And Sarn't

Musgrave brings home to us his creed in a crescendo of terror and theatrical excitement, but not without pity and laughter and the dim beauty that lies in some sorts of ugliness. Terror, laughter, excitement, an ecstasy of words, pity and beauty – do not these quantities amount to what we seek in the theatre? Can we not escape into them? Are they not 'entertainment'?

This piece, impeccably acted at almost every level, was playing when I saw it, in the second week of its run, to a house which was something more than three-quarters empty. Playgoers, I'm here to say that I'm ashamed of you – and I don't care what you say to me in correspondence columns. Surely you, the men and women who have time to live and feel and put your toes up and reflect – surely you should show more sense than a lot of word-obsessed and clock-ridden critics. You must not let us keep you from this or any play of passion and poetry in prodigious confusion.

Mr Lindsay Anderson, who directed *The Long and the Short and The Tall* without, I thought, sufficient definition, must not be blamed for the obscurities of this play. For he has allowed the piece to gather its own pace and given it time to roar its thunder; and he has let his actors find their strength and speak with it.

In this he has been greatly helped by certain incidental sounds and songs composed by Mr Dudley Moore (I hope to have the good fortune to work, some day, on a piece for radio – the most intent of all dramatic media – with this composer whose work I have not heard before) and by the stark, spare, coloured beauty of Miss Jocelyn Herbert's sets.

And now to the most impressive performance to be seen on the stage today. Mr Ian Bannen's Serjeant Musgrave owes nothing to what I beg leave to describe as Mr Ian Bannen's Ice-man – if 'e cometh. He is a ghastly grin, an illness in the mind, a puritan, a drum-beater – one who abrogates to himself the final function of the Lord which is to mete out death. He will die with his boots on.

He is admirably supported by James Bree, a stubby limping, jumpy little fellow of a man, like a chirpy undertaker on the way home, malicious as a ferret, gay as a cause so irretrievably lost as to leave nothing much for tears. I have never been commissioned to write my version of the Macbeth story – I've often wondered why – in which the Lady is a housewife, probably the mother of a ballerina, and the three witches her Bank Manager, her Hairdresser and her Psychiatrist. But if ever a management comes along I shall have Miss Freda Jackson in my contract.

As a raw-boned mainly silent woman behind a law-abiding bar she is, in her way, almost as terrifying as the fell sergeant. Set her brooding at a window and who could tear their eyes away to the procession. Miss Patsy Byrne, who I have seen and I hope praised, at the Belgrade Theatre, Coventry, playing a sex-fed slut, is one to watch; and in a part that calls for but cannot get Miss Joan Plowright, might well establish a line of Patsy Byrne parts. I went to see this play unwillingly and as an act of grace to an editor who has never been less than wonderfully considerate to me. I am grateful that I listened to the small still voice . . .

Credits and Discredits for 1959

Personality of the year: Sir Michael Redgrave for his dramatisation of *The Aspern Papers* and his performance in the leading role.

Success story of the year: Bernard Miles's Mermaid Theatre.

Mistakes of the year: *The Love Doctor, The World of Paul Slickey.*

Best performances of the year: Sir Laurence Olivier in *Coriolanus*; Flora Robson and Beatrix Lehmann in *The Aspern Papers*; Patrick McGoohan in *Brand*; Joan Plowright in *Roots*; Barbara Jefford in *The Cenci*; Sir John Gielgud in *The Ages of Man*; Sir Ralph Richardson in *The Complaisant Lover*; Paul Rogers in *One More River*; Kenneth Williams in *Pieces of Eight*.

Disappointments of the year: Paul Robeson's Othello; Fay Compton's Lady Bracknell; and *Candide*.

Better late than never department: the production of *Cock-a-Doodle Dandy*, which Sean O'Casey wrote more than ten years ago.

Most enterprising management: the 59 Company.

Pull up your socks department: the Arts Theatre.

Lesson of the year: the magnificent style of the Comédie Française.

Damp squibs of the year: *Moon on a Rainbow Shawl* and *A Raisin in the Sun.*

Bravest Try of the year: *Kookaburra.*

Plays we should like to have missed: *The Darling Buds of May, Beware of Angels* and *From the French.*

Disaster of the year: *A Man's Job.*

Was it worth it? department: William Douglas Home nursing his sick Aunt Edwina.

Black marks: to the public for failing to support *Roots, Serjeant Musgrave's Dance* and *One More River.*

Names we have missed: Eric Portman, Peter Ustinov and Emlyn Williams.

Welcome to The Establishment: John Osborne.

Talking points. Above: Kenneth Williams with Fenella Fielding in *Pieces of Eight*. Top: the Royal Court production of O'Casey's *Cock-a-Doodle Dandy*. Right: Ian Bannen as John Arden's Serjeant Musgrave (with Freda Jackson)

1960

The year of the Sharpville shooting and the attempted assassination of Verwoerd in South Africa saw Brezhnev become President of the USSR whilst Kennedy became the first Roman Catholic President of the USA. 1960 was also the year the Israelis captured former Gestapo Chief Eichmann.

In Britain it was the year Princess Margaret married Anthony Armstrong-Jones. The farthing stopped being legal tender and the last English tram ran in Sheffield. The 56-year-old Barbara Moore walked from John O'Groats to Land's End. The film Saturday Night, Sunday Morning *with Albert Finney brought prestige to the British film industry whilst Pinter's* The Caretaker, *Wesker's* I'm Talking About Jerusalem *and Bolt's* A Man for All Seasons *ensured that the new British Drama continued to be talked about.*

1960

Actress 1960

by Caryl Brahms

In honour of the early weeks of the new decade I have gone back to the files in search of the first issue of PLAYS AND PLAYERS'. It appeared in October 1953. In it I was writing about the young actresses of seven years ago.

'They are standing in the wings of the Theatre Royal of my imagination, the younger generation of actresses, the Misses Siddons. Their names are Eileen Herlie, Pamela Brown, Yvonne Mitchell, Claire Bloom, Dorothy Tutin, Joyce Redman, Margaret Leighton.' There is something bravely defiant, something almost Lost Legion about that list of names, now that we come upon it, seven years later. One muses on it with the same amused tenderness as the ladies who smile a little stickily at one from the pages of an out-of-date *Spotlight*.

It would of course be plain silly to feel sorry for some of them – for Miss Eileen Herlie, for instance, queening it in her Broadway Musical, *Take Me Along* (produced by our own lost – or so alas! it seems – Mr Peter Glenville). Or for Miss Yvonne Mitchell who has made a corner in the tempestuous ladies of the larger screen. For Miss Claire Bloom, who is said to have said that she prefers to live in America and recently married Rod Steiger and will no doubt continue to work where her domestic life is settled. Miss Dorothy Tutin, bless her, is with us still, and fortunately no farther off than Stratford-on-Avon, where she will play Portia and repeat her Viola and where one will look forward to seeing her. Miss Margaret Leighton is about to burst upon us in the first full-length Mortimer play. Miss Joyce Redman comes and goes.

Only Miss Pamela Brown remains for tears – is it bad health or bad luck that has caused those long absences from our stages? Recently she has been appearing in *Heartbreak House* in Sir John Gielgud's production on Broadway. But though she has shone out in *The Lady's Not For Burning* and coruscated in the fabulous Gielgud season at the Lyric Hammersmith, she is more of a legend than an ascertainable fact.

Where should we look to find our next Dame Edith Evans if not in the direction of Miss Brown? But if we never see her how are we to recognise this, or she to continue to develop? Not in these wordless parts in which with subtle smile and well-timed eyelid – and her native wits she steals the film from some orating Miss. But this was not meant to be a lament to a lady who could scintillate like golden rain down the night sky on the 5th of November, but a space in which to consider the young actress 1960. And first of all who is she?

One name comes immediately to mind. She is Miss Joan Plowright. Or if she is not quite Miss Plowright yet, Miss Actress 1960 is doing her nut to emulate the movement of the tiger. She is the new, Chelsea Fringe Untidy Anonymous, the All-Purposes Actress, called for by the 1960 dramatist for his latest kitchen-to-living-room, Sloane Square play. The girl next door to end all girls next door. In short she is The Bleatnik. Unless, however, she is Miss Mary Ure, an actress of a honey-coloured, smooth, well-modulated beauty, who derives from the Herlie, Mitchell, Leighton, personality or star group, rather than that of the dialectic drearies. Miss Ure works with courage and conviction, attack and confidence and, where she needs it, pathos. However, she has not the style and vocal resource for Shakespeare. She cannot quite shake – would it be the Midlands? – from her accent, nor the Film-Fan Gossip from our minds.

There are no black woollen stockings in the lively art of Miss Maggie Smith, stylist and wit. Of all our younger actresses Mark 60, she is the only one who could appear at The House of Molière without our suffering an agony of shame – or any shame at all for her – 'if it wasn't for the langwidge in between.' She is by definition a satirist – but one who has been much in the sun so that her wit springs from her sense of fun and not from any bitterness of spirit. She works, as it were, in enamel, covering the surface of her characters with the lacquer of her voice (and this has an edge to it) and the smooth gaze of her wide blue eyes. And she has a considerable technique for that virtuosity which Hamlet asks in his players – she pronounces the words trippingly on her tongue.

Miss Joan Plowright is the girl who changed the pace of acting in the fifties. And this she did involuntarily and by the most simple and direct means: in fact, by getting down to it and acting. She is a provincial dumpling of a young woman, the epitome of the all-purposes player – all purposes save glamour. She is a ravenous actress – not ravening in the sense that Miss Flora Robson falls upon and devours a part, and having consumed a character ravens for yet more to act; but pouncing on whatever is on her plate. She knows well how the humble girl thinks and feels and what is important to her – what she says and why, as well as how, she says it. She can be funny or sad, *and* funny and sad. She seems to look at life and ask a question – but she knows that the answer can come to her only from deep inside the person she is acting. She has no overwhelming personality of her own and is content to be a day-to-day, and not a High Day Actress – that is to say, I hope she is content; for she is no gala-girl. But she brings to the right kind of everyday part so steady an understanding that her name is Legion. And her miraculous performance as the old lady in Ionesco's play *The Chairs* has passed into a contemporary Theatre History.

'That girl is going to be the next Joan Plowright.'

'Oh – I thought she *was* Joan Plowright.' But it was Miss Frances Cuka on the first night of the transfer of *A Taste of Honey* from Theatre Workshop to Wyndham's. Previously I had seen her in a Samuel Beckett Dust Bin at the Royal Court Theatre. I, too, thought she was Joan Plowright then, till I checked with the programme. Soon Miss Cuka, square, homely, raw and happily-gifted, will be seen at Stratford-upon-Avon and after this we should be able to tell what in her splendid performance of a Salford brat was old Svengali-Littlewood at work, and what was her own original, offbeat, talent. But I do not expect ever to find her performance anything less than admirable, for even in these, her plain and puppy-fat days, she is *en rapport* with her audience and can make them laugh and cry.

Miss Heather Sears was just beginning to show a strong and dedicated talent when along came husband, film-contract and baby, and so we do not see her unaffected, candid performances on our stages any more.

Miss Wendy Craig is making a girl-next-door name for herself with her sympathetically handled young girls in all the usual mental and emotional dilemmas. And of course we have high

hopes of Miss Ann Beach, the Theatre Workshop girl with a load of Weirdies. Miss Beach is one of Nature's Actresses. She has great potential power but little discipline. She is a genuine 'Weirdie' and has her own short cuts to magic. I would rather watch her, not without dismay, doing so many things all wrong, than a number or more tame and docile girls getting them right. For she has the true excitement of the boards and limelight and brings gusto with her even if she is at times a little wild.

Miss Geraldine McEwan is no girl next door; though many a would-be neighbour will be found to wish she were. She is an actress with a pert face and a cut-through voice who is unusually gifted in crack-and-come-back dialogue. Her Stratford Hero was accomplished and much admired. But her loose limbed and gangling adolescent Member of the Wedding still haunts me with the uncertainties and anguishes of trying to grow up.

And so we come to Miss Dorothy Tutin – the only name from my earlier list to appear, too, on this. For she is that strange thing an ageless one – ageless as Dame Edith, in her very different way, is ageless – ageless as Madame Edwige Feuillère. Miss Tutin is a small-scale hurricane. And once she is unleashed upon a part there is bound to be, one feels, a short, sharp tussle. But Miss Tutin comes out on top, and having subdued it to her temperamental and technical measure, parades in it, all smiles and sequined tears. She can be gay, pathetic, lively, stunned – part minx, part poet, and part sex-kitten. A comedienne of skill and a pint-sized tragedienne. I hope some day she will be given the chance to tackle Lady Macbeth. Meantime her Juliet holds all of Spring and quite a deal of Summer.

Oxford Triumphs

In the wake of several West End transfers from the Oxford Playhouse Plays and Players *ran this interview with Frank Hauser, director of Oxford Meadow Players*

'When is a repertory theatre *not* a repertory theatre? When it is a success.' That is supposed to have been one of Beerbohm Tree's favourite little jokes about the Repertory Movement when it was still in its infancy. Today, it does not strike one as being very funny, though nobody can pretend that Tree's suggestion that repertory rarely pays is no longer accurate. At a time when every repertory company in the country is having to put up a struggle for existence it would be foolish to pretend otherwise. There are far too many gallant failures.

Back in 1956 Tree's little joke could well have been cracked in Oxford. For the management of the Playhouse Theatre there had run into financial difficulties and in April that year had been forced to shut up the theatre. This was all the more regrettable as the building was no monster white elephant. A neat little theatre seating 592 (about half a capacity audience at the Old Vic), it had been built as recently as 1938. Set in a university city like Oxford, one would have supposed it to have been a gem, a regular little gold-mine. But for five months the Playhouse doors remained closed. Then a non-profit-making-distributing company, known as the Meadow Players, was formed under the chairmanship of Alan Bullock. Thanks to a gift of £2,000 from Richard Burton, once a wartime student at Oxford, £1,500 from the Arts Council, and

£600 from a University fund, this company was able to reopen the Playhouse on 1 October 1956 with *Electra* by Giraudoux, translated by Juliet Mansel.

When Frank Hauser was appointed the new Director of Productions there was, of course, one question uppermost in the minds of all Playhouse habitués. What was his policy going to be? After the failure of the previous management the best that could be expected was a play-safe policy. Plenty of West End successes with the odd revival of a popular comedy from the thirties was undoubtedly what was expected. As the hoardings announced not only a series of new and unknown plays, but also a liberal supply of translations from contemporary European dramatists and from the classics, Oxford must have first been surprised and then staggered at the survival of its new Playhouse management. One elderly devotee of drawing-room comedy looked down the list, which consisted of Giraudoux's *Electra*, Canetti's *The Numbered*, Nicholas Moore's *Lock and Key*, Anouilh's *Medea*, Obey's *Frost at Midnight*, Aristophanes' *Lysistrata*, and Robert Bolt's *The Critic and the Heart*. 'At this rate, they'll close the theatre for good and ever,' she remarked. Time, however, has proved that Mr Hauser's policy was the right one. He was quick to realise that many of the Playhouse's regular patrons were in the habit of going up to London where they would have already seen the big West End successes. He wanted, anyway, to break his theatre's reliance on what went down well in Shaftesbury Avenue. He wanted to put a stop to the process whereby repertory theatres just produced carbon copies of London successes, so that what was in London this month invariably turned up at Oxford next month. And, indeed, as time went on, he succeeded so well that he even managed to reverse the process. Now, there is a good chance of seeing in London today what Oxford saw yesterday. *Dinner with the Family, Lysistrata, The Hamlet of Stepney Green* and *Rollo* were all applauded at the Playhouse before coming up to London.

Mr Hauser realised, of course, that the public don't like to see what they have never heard of. But, by the very audacity of his policy, he was able to interest the national press in what was being presented in Oxford. Playhouse audiences soon got into the habit of reading about their local theatre's new play in their daily papers. There would invariably be mention, too, of a familiar star name, for Mr Hauser was able to tempt the big names to Oxford with a succession of exciting new roles. He was not able to pay star salaries, but he was able to offer big new parts in new plays, with the added attraction of a possible transfer later to the lights of London. Joan Greenwood, Catherine Lacey, Mary Morris, Yvonne Mitchell, Jill Bennett, John Justin, Leo McKern, Dirk Bogarde, Constance Cummings – these are only some of the actors and actresses who helped to make Mr Hauser's adventurous policy a successful one. And since he first began at Oxford, this policy has remained unchanged.

'The only thing I've learned,' he says, 'is that to try to leaven a "heavy" programme with revivals of light comedies is disaster. You lose just as much on an old play as on a new one, without half the fun.' The secret of the success of this policy is not, of course, the devil-may-care attitude of the director who says 'I'm going to give them what they ought to like'. It is a success that is

based on sound economy. To break even a small theatre like the Playhouse needs 80 per cent attendances throughout the year. This is a virtual impossibility when the director of productions tries to experiment with a new play every fortnight. The first step, then, for Mr Hauser, was to try to stop the constant drain on capital by extending the run of each play. Accordingly, the Playhouse Company got into the habit of playing every third week outside Oxford (usually at Cambridge) when their theatre was let to an outside organisation. In this way, they were able to step up from fortnightly to three-weekly runs. Important though this proved to be, it was a relatively small saving. What helped much more to keep the Playhouse coffers full were transfers to the West End, like *Lysistrata* and *Rollo*.

By December 1957 this twofold economy based on three-weekly runs and West End transfers has paid handsome dividends. In that month the Playhouse had three companies performing simultaneously, *Dinner with the Family*, *Crime on Goat Island* and *Under Milk Wood*. Such a state of affairs would have seemed impossible when the abandoned Playhouse was reopened in 1956, and Mr Hauser admits it still did seem incredible when it happened. Twelve months later, however, the Playhouse was able to afford the greater luxury of European tours. Holland, Italy, Switzerland, Portugal and Denmark welcomed Playhouse productions of Shakespeare in 1958 and again in 1959. India, Pakistan and Ceylon have quite recently also welcomed its productions of Shakespeare, Shaw and Eliot. In fact these tours, together with the World Premières and the transfers to the West End, have given a fine flourish to the activities of the Oxford company. But the future is still far from certain. Everything depends on money. What Mr Hauser would like to do depends on his being able to pay his actors more than in the past.

His own interests are greatly with Shakespeare, Ibsen and Greek drama, but they are all three very heavy on casts and costumes. He would like to produce them with a fairly large permanent company – not, as in the past, with a specially assembled cast. But there can be no permanent company without more money, though Mr Hauser admits that he has an interesting repertoire to offer an actor. 'To be able to offer a new actor to Oxford Iago, Lopakhin, Agamemnon and a big part in a new play would tempt all but the rabidly TV-minded.' Last year's Arts Council grant to the Playhouse was £3,000. With the evidence of what Mr Hauser has achieved on his shoe-string budget, all who take the smallest interest in repertory in Great Britain will wish him every Arts Council blessing. These are hard times for Repertory in this country, but he has proved that a Repertory Theatre is still a Repertory Theatre, even when it is a success.

The reasons why every passionate playgoer should somehow get to see *A Man For All Seasons*, Robert Bolt's play about the trials which led to the Trial of Thomas More (who opposed Henry VIII's divorce, and by opposing, ended), are many and to my mind overwhelming.

It must be seen because as Thomas More Paul Scofield gives the finest of a career of fine performances. More is in safe hands, true hands, being in Mr Scofield's hands. For Scofield knows him with his mind and with his heart which means that he completely convinces us that he *is* that grey, dry, loyal, wise and witty man; and that if in life More was something less grey, dry, loyal, wise and witty, it is life and not the actor who has failed to show us the whole truth.

'I am not the stuff that martyrs are made of!' says More – yet history reports and Scofield shows that conscience – the stuff of martyrdoms – made a martyr of this man; and that it could not have been otherwise with him. For he was steadfast.

It must be seen for Mr Noel Willman's fine production. For in it Mr Willman proves himself to be not only a sensitive, intelligent and highly theatrical man of the theatre (these things we have long known him to be) but to have taken the fashionable art of alienation and, by integrating it into the play with unfaltering tempo and many a *coup-de-théatre*, has proved himself not its slave but its master. In the exact proportion that *The Caretaker* owes its tensions and its shape to McWhinnie, its producer, *A Man For All Seasons* owes its flow and its shape to Mr Willman and under his direction the well-known mannerisms of certain members of the cast gave ground to acting – real, even at times antagonising acting.

It must be seen because someone – was it the author or producer or designer (Motley)? – has conceived Henry VIII not as the paunchy monarch of the Holbein, but as one of those quite literally golden lads who must, as chimney sweepers, come to dust – but in the case of the young king, as Mr Richard Leech sees him, thoroughly spoilt, and with a darting mind, it somehow seems the more incongruous.

It must be seen for Mr Leo McKern's clowning and relish in his own cupidity and for the quietly assembled truth of Miss Pat Keen's daughter Margaret; and also for the elegance of speech of Mr Willoughby Goddard as the fleshliest Cardinal in the business – where was Mr Goddard when the casting for the Oscar Wilde of the films was in progress? He might, I think, while not bettering the Wilde of Mr Robert Morley, have bettered that of Mr Peter Finch.

It must be seen for Mr Geoffrey Dunn's silken Spanish Ambassador. And, too, it must be seen because, almost in spite of himself, Mr Robert Bolt has written an exciting and moving piece. Be seen, in spite of the somewhat self-consciously measured iambs of the prose of the early scenes. Be seen, because it is better observed and truer than *Flowering Cherry*. Be seen because I would place it third to *The Caretaker* and *Ross*, in a list of performances of great distinction, tying with *Roots*; with the Lunts in *The Visit*, and the Kilties in *Dear Liar* following hard on, at least so far as the London playgoer is concerned.

A Man For All Seasons at the Globe

Reviewed by Caryl Brahms

The Theatre in Shipbuilder Street

Gerald Frow, then personal assistant to Bernard Miles at the Mermaid as well as the theatre's lively press and publicity officer, wrote this account of a visit to the Berliner Ensemble in East Berlin made in connection with the Mermaid's production of The Life of Galileo.

The first thing that struck us about the home of Bertolt Brecht's Berliner Ensemble was the similarity of its situation to that our our own Mermaid Theatre. The theatre is called the Theater am Schiffbauerdamm – the Theatre on Shipbuilder Street. It stands just inside the Eastern Sector of Berlin in a workaday bomb-scarred area not at all unlike our own corner of the City of London. A few hundred yards up the road, trains thunder out of a station perched on a river bridge, as Blackfriars is, and in front of the theatre the River Spree carries the long barges past the door as the Thames carries the 'flat irons' past our restaurant at Puddle Dock. Brecht had used this theatre long before the formation of his Berliner Ensemble – as far back as the '20s in fact, when his *Threepenny Opera* was staged there. It was by an odd stroke of coincidence that he secured the same building for his permanent company when he returned to Germany in 1949 after 15 years in exile. The theatre itself is an unpretentious building, dressed in grey and carrying only the most unobtrusive poster displays. The actors are given no individual billing outside. At night, the words 'Berliner Ensemble' set in neon letters revolve in a hoop of white light high on the roof. (A German cartoon showing Brecht himself sitting in the bowels of the theatre turning this sign through a nightmare system of pulleys, ratchets and wheels, was among his treasured possessions!)

Our appointment with Brecht's widow, Frau Helene Weigel, was at 11 a.m. on our first morning in Berlin. A taxi from our hotel in the West, swept us through the Brandenburg Gate, past the faintly foreboding notices which warn, 'You are Now Leaving the British Sector' and into east Berlin, our pockets bulging with packets of English tea, which is a special weakness of Frau Weigel's. We met her in her office looking out over the courtyard at the back of the theatre. As we entered, grandchildren were swept from the room, and in a matter of minutes the kettle was on for English tea. Then it was down to work. We showed her the designs that Michael Stringer had done for our production of *The Life of Galileo*; we showed her pictures of members of our company; we showed her a model of our stage and told her how the play was to be worked. Then came the questions – acute, probing, aimed at helping us to achieve some effect essential to the play. How were we to get the pacing stone effect on our stage? A stage cloth? No, there is a better way. And a shout from the window brought a stage hand in with a sample of the tiling they used. 'Take it, it may help you.'

Frau Weigel is a small woman, lean and wiry, with a face of quite outstanding strength and beauty. Her English is impeccable. From her room above the courtyard she now controls the vast theatrical workshop that is the Berliner Ensemble – a theatre employing 270 people, with a nation-wide audience, working a different play each night. She and Brecht left Berlin on the night after the Reichstag Fire in 1934. (Brecht was at one time fifth on the Nazi extermination list). For the next 15 years they wandered the world as refugees – Switzerland, Denmark, Sweden, Finland and America. It was during these years that Brecht wrote the plays which have since made his name – *Mother Courage, The Good Woman of Setzuan, The Caucasian Chalk Circle*, and *The Life of Galileo*. During all this time the enormous talent of Helene

Weigel went unused. Eventually, at the beginning of the '50s, they returned to Berlin, where Brecht was at last able to get together the Ensemble he had dreamed of; able to put into practice his ideas of an imaginative epic theatre; able to stage the plays that he had carried with him for so long. And Helene Weigel was able to act – able to stun the world with her performances in *Mother Courage* and *The Mother*. Unfortunately, Brecht had very few years left. He died of coronary thrombosis in 1956 – a few weeks before his company visited London for the first time. The house in which he lived is now the Brecht archive, where a staff of half-a-dozen girls work all day and every day photostatting the plays, arranging the letters, filing, documenting, ordering. The room in which Brecht worked and died remains as it did in his lifetime – on the wall hangs the Chinese scroll painting of Confucius which Brecht carried throughout his exile; beside the bed lie the German and foreign papers which he was reading on that last morning. Simply, almost sparsely, furnished, the room looks out over the old Hansa cemetery in which the playwright is buried.

The interior of the Theater am Schiffbauerdamm contrasts oddly with the simplicity of Brecht's stage designs. Built in the late nineteenth century, it is a decorative Prussian theatre – all red plush and fleshly heavy statuettes. It seats about 700. Brecht's first job when he moved in was to knock out the back wall of the stage and move it as far back as he could. The present stage is almost exactly opposite of the Mermaid's in size – it is about as deep (50 ft) as ours is wide, and about as wide (20 ft) as ours is deep. Unusual features of the theatre are its raked revolve installed by Brecht after he had overcome some frantic technical difficulties, and its battery of lights which flood from every direction to bathe the stage in bright white light throwing virtually no shadows. Around the theatre cluster the workshops and scene dock, and there is also a canteen in which members of the company and staff can get a square meal very cheaply. The beer here is excellent!

The actors in the Ensemble are employed on a yearly contract at a fixed salary, and as the plays are changed every night, they seldom work two nights running. Their time is filled with rehearsals. They are also free to do television appearances. One of the jobs on hand when we were there was the filming of *Mother Courage* – both for record purposes and also as a feature film for the East German cinemas. Directors from the Ensemble are also sent to other towns in Berlin to produce Brecht's plays. At the moment, all the plays in the repertoire are Brecht's, but a new play by a young German writer is scheduled for production later this year. One of the most talked-of features of the theatre's work is the amount of time devoted to rehearsals. It is true that many of the plays are rehearsed for what, by our standards, is an abnormally long time – six months is the minimum. But then the whole business of production is a much more leisurely and Germanic business, and we were told by a member of the company who knew the English theatre that no German actor would tolerate the sort of concentrated hard work expected by a British director.

In our three days in Berlin we saw three of the Ensemble productions – *The Threepenny Opera*, *Mother Courage*, and *The*

Resistible Rise of Arturo Ui, Brecht's satire on Hitler expressed in terms of Chicago gangsters. They were, of course, superbly exciting. And the audiences? From the East, school parties, trade union parties, large parties from the services. From the West, a flood of tourists from all over the world. The theatre does undoubtedly attract a large local audience, and this does not mean that it is full of blue-dungareed navvies smoking clay pipes. Sitting there in the Theatre am Schiffbauerdamm in East Berlin was no different from sitting in any theatre in Shaftesbury Avenue – except, of course, for the play!

Final impressions? Well, very strongly, Helene Weigel's hope, expressed in parting, that Brecht should remain alive and not be buried by either his own archive or the theorising of Western critics.

'Brecht', she told us, 'was not a solemn man. He had an enormous sense of fun. He loved a joke. At his rehearsals there was laughter.' She is afraid of the pall of solemnity which hangs over him – 'I am afraid he will become a plaster saint'. Outside in the sunlit cemetery near his home, we stood in front of the rough-hewn stone that bears only two words: 'Bertolt Brecht'. Beside us in the house, the girls worked at the archive. But in his theatre on Shipbuilder Street they were preparing for another play. Brecht's immortality was being hammered out there in the bright white lights of his theatre.

1960

Roots at the Royal Court

Reviewed by Peter Roberts

When *Roots* first appeared at the Royal Court Theatre a year ago, later transferring unsuccessfully to the Duke of York's Theatre, we saw it as an exciting but isolated play. Now it has returned to Sloane Square in its proper setting as the second part of the Wesker Trilogy, so it can be measured against *Chicken Soup with Barley*, which appeared there last month, and *I'm Talking About Jerusalem*, which will be seen a few weeks hence.

'*If you don't care, you'll die,*' were the closing words of *Chicken Soup With Barley*, spoken by Sarah Kahn to her poet son, Ronnie. Wesker takes this theme up again in *Roots* when Beatie Bryant goes home from London after a three year affair with Ronnie to her family of farm labourers in Norfolk. None of her Norfolk relatives are people who *care*. None of them is *engagé* like Beatie's boy friend, who was such an important figure in the first play of the trilogy. Beatie tries to get her family to be interested in art, politics and current affairs by repeating, without fully understanding, what Ronnie has taught her. Only when the boy ditches her by post just when she has assembled the family to meet him is she able to stand on her own feet and think with passion and conviction for herself.

Although these first two plays of the trilogy have the same underlying theme they are very different in form. The first marks the growth of apathy in a number of people whilst the second marks the death of apathy in one. The first spans 20 years, the second as many days. In the first Wesker's touch is not always sure, in the second it is always so. Where the Kahns sometimes

Right: Joan Plowright as Beatie Bryant
with, above, Gwen Nelson in *Roots*

spoke with a hollow ring that betrayed the imperfect integration of Wesker's idea and his sense of character, the Bryants never utter a word that is out of place.

Though the setting is Norfolk, theatrically speaking the play comes very close to the old Lancashire family comedy. It is in fact just this kind of play, but with a theme and with real people. That is why I should not care to see *Roots* in an inferior production with an inferior cast who might well turn the Bryants into music-hall caricatures. One could easily see it happen with Mum and Dad who squabble and relatives who are not on speaking terms – not to mention neighbours with weak bowels. John Dexter's sensitive production never lets the comedy run away with life, and Gwen Nelson and Joan Plowright repeat their wonderful work as mother and daughter. Their scenes together are the best in the play and I shall not easily forget the figure of Miss Plowright dancing to the handclap of her mother at the close of the second act.

119

The Best Plays and Players of 1960

by Alan Dent

Hearken to this:

'You remind me of my uncle's brother. He was always on the move, that man. Never without his passport. Had an eye for the girls. Very much your build. Bit of an athlete. A long jump specialist. He had a habit of demonstrating different run-ups in the drawing room round about Christmas time. Had a penchant for nuts. That's what it was. Nothing else but a penchant. Couldn't eat enough of them. Peanuts, walnuts, brazil nuts, monkey nuts, wouldn't touch a piece of fruit cake. Had a marvellous stop watch. Picked it up in Hong Kong. The day after they chucked him out of the Salvation Army. Used to go in number four for Beckenham reserves. That was before he got his gold medal. Had a funny habit of carrying his fiddle on his back like a papoose. I think there was a bit of the Red Indian in him. To be honest, I've never made out how he came to be my uncle's brother. I've often thought that maybe it was the other way round. I mean that my uncle was his brother and he was my uncle. But I never called him uncle. As a matter of fact I called him Sid. My mother called him Sid too. It was a funny business. Your spitting image he was. Married a Chinaman and went to Jamaica . . . I hope you slept well last night.'

This is an absolutely typical snatch of the dialogue in the year's most successful play, *The Caretaker* by Harold Pinter. And by 'successful' one means triumphant with the critics as well as with the public.

Is it literature? Obviously not. Is it dramatic – in the old sense whereby each sentence carries on the action? No. But is it dramatic – in the new sense whereby each sentence or half-sentence reveals the character of the speaker? Yes, it *is* rather. But the person to whom this tramp called Davies is speaking at such length now, interrupts with: 'Listen! I don't know who you are!' Some of the audience read deep and subtle meanings into *The Caretaker*. It is a play about three men in a shapeless and charmless room who cannot communicate with each other at all. Alternatively it is a play about three men who would not communicate with each other, even if they had the desire. It is all about nothing, and all about everything. Or is it a play about a man who is dead already – the tramp – and two other men who don't want to have anything to do with him because they are still alive? Mr Pinter then confounded us all on the radio by saying that it was not this, or that, or any other thing – but just a *play*. He just sat down to it and it wrote itself. It is just as much without symbolism as it is without life or action. It is all just talk and pauses – especially pauses. It is most certainly a strange, fascinating, bizarre business – and the direction by Donald McWhinnie and the acting by Donald Pleasence, Alan Bates, Peter Woodthorpe make it something *unmissable* – full of grisly wit and still more full of pregnant pauses.

The other truly successful playwright of the year has been Robert Bolt, who has the rare honour of having two successful plays running side by side in Shaftesbury Avenue – *A Man for All Seasons* and *The Tiger and the Horse*. The first – a singularly satisfying production – gave us Paul Scofield as Sir Thomas More, a serene philosopher in troubled times. The other – less completely satisfying – gave us Sir Michael Redgrave as an Oxbridge professor brought up against the realities of modern existence because (*a*) his wife had lost her reason in trying to reason with it, and because (*b*) his daughter had let herself be seduced by a young University man who may be said to loll in an armchair in protest against all the Professor stands for. There was a deeply moving performance of the daughter by Vanessa Redgrave.

The Royal Court Theatre boys did not do so well. John Mortimer had only a near-success with *The Wrong Side of the Park*. We believed in Margaret Leighton's unhappy neurotic wife sighing for a dead husband who was no good. We believed in Richard Johnson as the second husband, a worthy chap whose wife ran away for twelve hours just because he had forgotten an anniversary. We believed in his parents – in Charles Heslop as the father who addled his brains with reading, and Joyce Carey as the unimaginative mother whose kitchen was the whole of the world. But the action of the play was at fault. It sagged, staggered, stopped dead, and then started again with a jolt. This kind of thing can only be allowed in a room without windows – in a play of the Pinter school. Mr Mortimer had windows looking out on the unfashionable side of a recognisable park.

More successful – in its own mad way – was N. F. Simpson's *One Way Pendulum*, a rare sort of surrealistic farce. Solemn and responsible people thought this excruciatingly funny; gay and irresponsible ones thought it a macabre and unfunny joke. People who were bored by this fantasy declared it to have deep, subtle, and sinister meanings. People who revelled in it said that the chief of its many virtues was that it had no meaning whatsoever. But everybody agreed that Alison Leggatt was deliciously sane as a housewife who saw nothing at all extraordinary in a husband who built a replica of the Old Bailey in his living room or in a son who taught weighing-machines to sing Handel choruses.

Only a trifle less insane was a long-winded parable by Eugene Ionesco called *Rhinoceros* in which everybody – with the diffident exception of Sir Laurence Olivier – turned into whatever is the plural of 'rhinoceros' one sultry summer morning in a little French town. Sir Laurence began this play as a most amusing alcoholic whose very moustache was tipsy, and concluded it as a rather terrifying and isolated man struggling to remain human among the inhabitants of a world turned into thick-skinned beasts. This was another Royal Court Theatre offering. So was *Platanov*, a first play written by Chekhov when he was a young medical student – a tentative farce about a small-town Don Juan plagued to death by all the women he had satisfied and abandoned, or dissatisfied and abandoned. This turned from farce into tragedy, and then back into farce, in a way which was too much for everybody but Rex Harrison, who managed somehow to make a personal success out of a play which might as well not have been exhumed. It was interesting to the drama-student – as *Two Gentlemen of Verona* is interesting to the student of Shakespeare. It showed the shapes of better things to come.

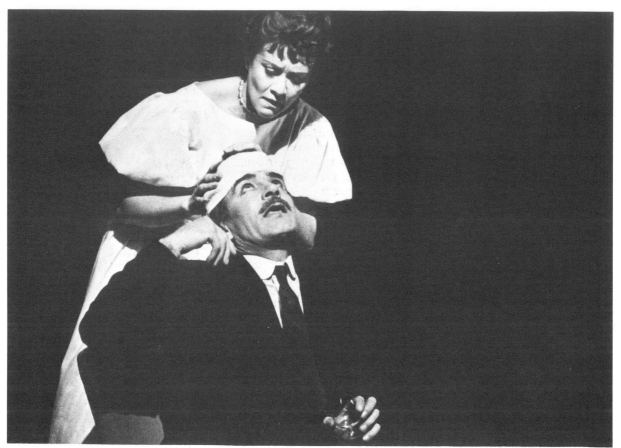

Joan Plowright and Laurence Olivier in Ionesco's _Rhinoceros_

The world of the theatre is so clamantly young these days – like the big world itself – that to be forty is to be aged, and to be sixty is to be decrepit and doddering. The aged Mr Rattigan gave us in _Ross_ an arresting play that showed us Lawrence of Arabia (disguised as Sir Alec Guinness) discovering his real self only after the unspeakable Turks, who took him prisoner, had finished with him. The doddering Mr Coward – still the blithest spirit in the theatre whatever the fledglings may say – gave us in _Waiting in the Wings_ a heart-aching and subsequently heart-breaking sentimental tragicomedy about aged and more or less venerable actresses spending their last days in a comfortable shelter and putting up a more or less gallant fight against the humiliation of not having died on the stage. This one was particularly savaged by those two intensely bright young daily-paper critics whom _The Guardian_ has happily termed 'our two tiny Hazlitts'. Yet it ran and ran – because people still like to be moved directly as well as indirectly, and because it contained – besides the gorgeous Sybil Thorndike and the superb Marie Löhr – such lovely old actresses as Nora Nicholson, Maureen Delaney, Una Venning and others.

E.M. Forster – who being over eighty must be considered by the young to be a positive Methuselah – also had a tremendous success with his _A Passage to India_. This was, admittedly, only a dramatisation – carried out very ably by Miss Rama Rau, an Indian writer of skill and sensibility. But Mr Forster was seen beaming in the audience at the first night and looking energetic enough to write a play on his own. And why not? We have far too few imaginative writers of any sort.

Two other veterans – Alfred Lunt and Lynn Fontanne – brought to us from America their very successful German play about revenge, Friederich Dürrenmatt's *The Visit* – a laccrating, almost Volponesque exposé of human vindictiveness and human greed. This very powerful piece – memorably well directed by Peter Brook and, as goes without saying, searingly well acted by the Lunts – scandalised and froze in their seats the unthinking public – especially matinée goers – who came to the brand-new Royalty Theatre expecting to see these two old favourites in their usual sort of vivacious comedy. Another new theatre, the Mermaid, was burningly occupied for several months by Brecht's *Galileo* with Bernard Miles, the theatre's jovial builder and owner, as the dedicated astronomer-philosopher-scientist.

That was about all that mattered. Some staggeringly dull American musical plays throve on advance-booking types of

Sybil Thorndike and Marie Löhr in Coward's *Waiting in the Wings*

audiences, and thrive still. The indigenous Lionel Bart had a tremendous and much-better-deserved success with a musical version of Dickens's *Oliver Twist* called *Oliver*! This brought not only Mr Bart's talent to the fore, but also the acting talent of Georgia Brown, who played Nancy, and the scene designing talent of Sean Kenny.

A rising favourite, Albert Finney, made a great hit in a rather feeble farce called *Billy Liar*. An accepted favourite, Ian Carmichael, had a lasting triumph in a murder-farce called *The Gazebo* (for which few critics had a word of praise). And an all but venerable favourite, Robert Morley, partnered the seasoned and satisfying Molly Picon as a modern Pooh-Bah offering hospitality in Tokyo to a shy little lady called Mrs Jacoby (on a visit from the USA). These were almost all the good things. But there was also an almost unprecedented number of bad things – sometimes almost as bad as 'our two tiny Hazlitts' said they were. The sudden demise of the *News Chronicle* in mid-October summarily stopped this present critic – now fifty-five and therefore practically senile – from saying *anything*, from trying to find fault with all those good things, or from trying to make excuses for all those bad ones.

Credits and Discredits for 1960

Personality of the Year: Arnold Wesker, whose Trilogy at the Royal Court Theatre was the most memorable theatrical experience of the season.

Musical of the year: Lionel Bart's *Oliver!* at the New Theatre.

Best team-work of the year: Donald Pleasence, Peter Woodthorpe and Alan Bates in Harold Pinter's *The Caretaker* at the Duchess Theatre.

Best performances of the year: Paul Scofield in *A Man for All Seasons*; Sir Alec Guinness in *Ross*; Peter O'Toole in *The Merchant of Venice*, at Stratford-on-Avon; Albert Finney in *Billy Liar*; Margaret Leighton in *The Wrong Side of the Park;* Siobhan McKenna in *The Playboy of the Western World*; Celia Johnson and Anthony Quayle in *Chin-Chin*; Sir Laurence Olivier in *Rhinoceros*; Barbara Jefford in *Saint Joan*.

Impersonation of the Year: Micheal MacLiammoir as Oscar Wilde.

Bores of the year: those dreary princesses in American musicals.

Miscasting of the Year: Lynn Fontanne in *The Visit*.

John Mortimer's *The Wrong Side of the Park* starring Margaret Leighton (seated)

Waste of talent: Sir John Gielgud and Sir Ralph Richardson in *The Last Joke*.

Disappointments of the year: *Toys in the Attic* and *Over the Bridge*.

Disasters of the year: *Joie de Vivre, Horses in Midstream, Out of This World, Bachelor Flat, The Golden Touch, It's in the Bag, Call It Love* and all those impossible plays at the Westminster Theatre.

Mistake of the year: the decor of the new Royalty Theatre.

Mysteries of the year: the long runs of *Flower Drum Song* and *The World of Suzie Wong*.

Above and left: Terence Rattigan's *Ross* with Michael Bryant who took over from Alec Guinness as Lawrence of Arabia.
Right: *Flower Drum Song*

Rumour of the year: that Elvis Presley will be the Old Vic's new Hamlet.

Names we have missed: John Osborne, Dame Edith Evans, Peter Ustinov and Emlyn Williams.

1961

The year that the Russian Yuri Gagarin became the first man in space was the year that East Germany erected the Berlin Wall. It was also the year that South Africa left the Commonwealth and the year the USA made an unsuccessful attempt to invade Cuba. The old Orient Express made its last journey from Paris to Budapest.

The publication of Graham Greene's A Burnt-Out Case *and Muriel Spark's* The Prime of Miss Jean Brodie *helped focus attention on the British novel. The newly formed Royal Shakespeare Company presented John Whiting's* The Devils *in its new London home at the Aldwych. But Sloane Square remained a mecca as the Royal Court premièred Osborne's* Luther *with Albert Finney in the title-role. The forthcoming 1960s satire boom was launched when* Beyond the Fringe *opened in London.*

George Devine, by virtue of his work as Artistic Director of the English Stage Company, can now undoubtedly be hailed as the High Priest of Contemporary Drama. Since he took over the direction of the Royal Court Theatre in April 1956, the English Stage Company have launched, among many other dramatists, John Osborne, N. F. Simpson, Arnold Wesker, John Arden, Willis Hall and Harold Pinter. In consequence, Devine's Company can claim with justice that they have truly inaugurated an era in which the young and unknown contemporary-minded dramatist has never had it so good.

Strangely enough, Devine's own formation in the theatre has been anything but contemporary. In the early thirties after coming down from Oxford, where he had been President of the OUDS, Devine began his career as an actor, and as a result of his work with John Gielgud, Komisarjevsky and Michel Saint-Denis he worked almost entirely in a classical field very far removed from the rough and tumble urgency of the Angry Young Man. It was not until just before the war that Devine began to produce plays, but his work in this direction was then immediately interrupted by the war, which resulted in his serving in the artillery and going off to Burma. During this period he severed all connections with the stage. 'I didn't want to do any of that ENSA stuff – it bored me. I did not want to *play* at the theatre – I liked it too much and didn't want to do just concerts.'

After the war he joined Michel Saint-Denis and Glen Byam Shaw in forming the Old Vic Theatre Centre with the Old Vic School and the Young Vic Company – a project which came to a much regretted end in 1950. Thereafter Devine was at liberty to strike out as a free-lance artist, and he directed Shakespeare at Stratford-on-Avon and at the Old Vic and opera at Sadler's Wells and Covent Garden. For a time he returned as an actor, appearing notably as Tesman in *Hedda Gabler* with Peggy Ashcroft. At this time the idea of doing contemporary theatre occurred to him. 'I was feeling', he says, 'that the classical theatre really occupied nearly all our biggest talents and was so successful that people were just using it as a way to get away from life – in the bad sense.' He felt there were so many terrible things happening, the times were so urgent, that the theatre simply had to be more in touch with life. He remembered all too well that during the period between the two wars people had just got on with their work and had not cared what was going on around them.

A television engagement brought him in contact with Tony Richardson, who felt the need for a contemporary theatre just as keenly and who invited Devine to take charge of the Royal Court Theatre which, he confided, he had an opportunity of taking over. Unfortunately the success of *Airs On A Shoestring* at Sloane Square at this time pushed the price of the theatre up to such an extent that the project had to be abandoned. For the next 18 months Devine and Richardson continued to try to interest people in their plan, even approaching the Stratford Memorial Company to see if they would like to have a theatre in London. They did not get anywhere, however, until, out of the blue, they were approached by a body called the English Stage Company which had been set up as an equivalent of the English Opera Group. An influential business man, Mr Neville Blond, had agreed to interest

Contemporary Godfather

Four years before the struggle to establish and maintain the English Stage Company led to his early death in 1965 at the age of 55 George Devine gave this interview to Peter Roberts on the background to the formation of the company.

Opposite: George Devine

himself in the Company if they found themselves a theatre and an Artistic Director. By this time things were not going so well at the Royal Court Theatre and it was consequently obtained on more reasonable terms. Devine then agreed to become Artistic Director of the new company as its aims coincided with what he himself was feeling about the theatre at that time.

When the venture opened in April 1956 and got off to a flying start with John Osborne's *Look Back In Anger*, Devine says he was determined to keep the theatre open at all costs and bash his way through with quantity as well as quality to show that it *could* be done. Accordingly productions were limited to short runs of sometimes four, sometimes six and very rarely eight weeks. In the second year, Sunday 'performances without decor' were introduced, and although all these productions were not always on the same level, they exerted a tremendous influence.

'We simply made an onslaught,' Devine says, 'and this has resulted in the writer in the English theatre being in a better position today than he has ever been within my memory.' The position of the English Stage Company is now an odd one, for they are finding themselves in competition with many commercial managements who, before *Look Back In Anger*, would not look at the kind of play to be seen in Sloane Square.

The English Stage Company have had an Arts Council grant which has varied from £2,000 to £8,000 a year, but which, according to Devine, 'is really nothing when you are doing experimental work'. In order to subsidise themselves and pay their way, the Company have invented what they call the 'Pylon System'. In other words, every now and then they have cast-iron star pieces which pack the theatre for six weeks, and between these successes they string experimental work. The function of the pylon is not only to have the theatre full for six weeks, but also to have a possible transfer which could then earn extra money to subsidise more experimental work. Devine's personal feeling now is that the English Stage Company have reached a stage and status when they ought to be more heavily subsidised. Their present position creates a 'constantly anxious situation' and makes it difficult to go on doing experimental work. A dramatist like John Arden, whom the English Stage Company absolutely believe in, has cost them a lot of money. But they continue to invest in a man they believe in without any particular return, except the knowledge that they are doing what they think they ought to do.

In the course of a year approximately 1,000 plays are submitted to the English Stage Company. Every week at least 20 arrive in the office of the assistant director in charge of the script department. The director gives each play a brief examination to decide on the kind of work it is and then sends it out to the appropriate reader. The readers concerned are either young directors or dramatists, or people of that sort. The reader's comments are always double-checked by the assistant director of the script department, and if there is any doubt a second reader is suggested. After this preliminary sifting, the play goes to Devine himself, who takes a script home with him each night to read before going to bed. He decides whether the play submitted is to be rejected or taken further.

The result of the report by the English Stage Company readers are various. All that might be done is to send an encouraging letter to the author. Alternatively, it may be suggested that someone should see the author, talk to him and find out more about his work. On the other hand, the play might go through to one of the Sunday night performances or it might go through to the top, in which case it will have to be read by one or two people on the artistic committee before it is given a full-scale production. A writers' group has been formed so that would-be writers can learn about acting and other aspects of stagecraft by meeting once a fortnight with the young directors of the English Stage Company. If a script is particularly promising, Devine may decide to give the author a writer's pass – a little card entitling the owner to have two free seats at any performance at the Royal Court as many times as he or she likes, plus attendance at rehearsals.

In this way would-be dramatists, many of whom have never set foot inside a theatre before, are provided with a contact with the live theatre and are able to see a play both in rehearsal and performance and are made to realise how it varies from night to night. They are given, too, the feeling that they have some sort of cultural home. As far as Mr Devine is concerned all this is quite inadequate. At the moment there are only 40 names on the writers' pass list, many of whom have difficulty in coming to the Royal Court because they have to work during the day. The trouble, Devine says, 'is that none of us have enough money to organise things properly.'

Not with a quite easy mind does one come to Stratford-upon-Avon for the high days of the local cult. These words, which mirror my own feelings, are in fact by C. E. Montagu, writing of an earlier Stratford season. Not with a quite easy mind did I approach the first night of Zeffirelli's *Othello* with Sir John Gielgud as the Moor. I have often detected an over-elaboration in this director's work, notably in his *Falstaff* at Covent Garden; again at Glyndebourne with *L'Elisir d'Amore*; and at times in the widely proclaimed *Romeo and Juliet* at the Old Vic. And then Gielgud as a Moorish man of arms and action, forerunner, as James Agate pointed out, of the Sheik (Oh shade of Araby, pale and flickering and flashing with the frenzy that was Valentino!) How would the foremost Hamlet of his times acquit himself in the heat and breadth and writhing guts of foaming Othello?

I fortified myself with Coleridge's wise reminder that rules are but means to an end. Let Gielgud break the lot, I vowed; so he is Othello what does it matter if his Moor does lack the robustness of Valk, the violent immediacy of Wolfit. It will be lofty. For to see Gielgud stalk the stage and shine is one of this age's glories. And did not Hazlitt write of little heroic Kean: 'Othello was tall, but that is nothing. He was not black, but that is nothing.' Compensation, Lewes tells us, was to be found in the actor's lion-like power and lion-like grace. Well, Gielgud would have power and grace and be a lion. I told myself the way to approach Sir John's Othello was to value it for its gifts rather than to diminish

Oh, The Pity of It, Zeffirelli!

Caryl Brahms reviews Gielgud's Othello *at Stratford-on-Avon*

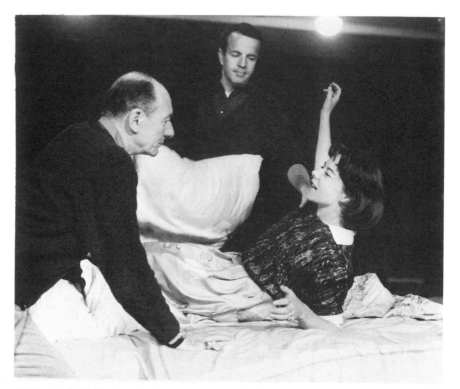

Othello with Zeffirelli rehearsing Dorothy Tutin and John Gielgud and, below, in production with Peggy Ashcroft and Dorothy Tutin

it by what would never be his to give. I greatly longed to cherish the plant and not allow any frost of mine to touch the flower.

And yet the evening was the most uniquely miserable that I remember to have spent in a theatre. Did my perception fail me, then? Was I too close to that weariness that is the aftermath of an operation, in which one feels emptied of all save the need to rest, too tired still to make the effort to open mind and heart to take in a new glory? I, who had seen Tearle and Wolfit? Wolfit, of whom C. E. Montagu might have been thinking when he wrote: 'Coquelin's acting was nothing but acting . . . a passion of joy in the thought of the character acted.'

There were some qualities that were foreseeable in Gielgud, and most of them in the event were there. One knew, for instance, that Sir John's Othello would conceive, as Agate has laid down, the death of Desdemona, not as a murder but as a sacrifice and that he would kill her, not out of passion but because her conduct has shaken the world from its propriety and, as Agate noted in Baliol Holloway's acting of the part, this Othello would be wounded not only in his love but in his *armour propre* – and most of all in his sense of property. Othello was, and we must not forget this, a very Eastern husband. Gielgud one foresaw would not fail to see Coleridge's argument that jealousy was not the point in Othello's passion; but rather an agony that the creature whom he had believed angelic should be proved impure and worthless. What one did not foresee was that in the throes of epilepsy Sir John would go into reverse and shunt a circle backwards before falling on his face and seemingly slumbering.

That Gielgud would have authority was never in doubt. One would have no anxious moments lest first-night nerves and the steep impetus of the Anthropophagi speech send him helter skelter down slopes better saved for later in this magnificent mountainside of a tragedy. Othello, dark-skinned commander of a battle force, must start quietly, with strong self-discipline, so that his disintegration, later, be the more spectacularly catastrophic. Moreover one knew beforehand that the fine orchestration of Sir John's delivery would make a nonsense of bluff Othello's 'rude am I in my speech'.

And so it was.

But Gielgud, as so often on a first night, stood aloof from himself, parted from us by his nerves and ours, watching himself, from his self-made limbo, going emptily through the motions. But that when we longed most to be with Othello, committed to playing our part of being with him in the scenes, we were most alienated, Gielgud was not to blame so much as Zeffirelli.

Where is the Othello who could bind us to him while hollow pillars rock and iron gates topple? Without blackouts taking their time in the light of eternity separate racing scene from racing scene? And where, for that matter, is the company that could renew the tension by winning us back instantly from the first and more lethally placed interval?

'I think of *Othello*' writes Mr Kenneth Tynan, 'as a theatrical bullfight, in which the hero is a noble bull, repeatedly charging the handkerchief in the wristy grip of Iago, the dominating matador.' I think of Sir John Gielgud's Othello as a handkerchief in the wristy grip of Signor Zeffirelli flickering in an empty arena in the dark of the night.

The lighting, like Iago's words on the first night, failed Sir John. Whenever there was a darkness over the stage – and not since *Anna Christie* have I seen a more pronounced or prolonged lack of light, there Sir John would seek out blackness and cleave to it so that his head, face, cloak became one prune. By the brief candles that the stage lighting afforded us one could discern his likeness to Kean in the role.

But as to stature, how is one to measure Gielgud, seeing him only on one disastrous first night, against the rock of ages that was lion-hearted Valk (which was why his disintegration was the more fearful to watch) or the full diapason of Wolfit? No wonder that among so much amok half of his beard became, as it were, unmoored. Some lines he spoke for ever. And these I hope to hear again and much much more when the production comes to town.

And the Iago. Did my ears fail me or did I hear Mr Ian Bannen say something like 'Cassio is dead – I mean he isn't yet'? Later when this good actor has come to terms with his lines we may find an arresting and unusual Iago whipping on the play with a mixture of spleen and relish. But what we saw on the first night was a desperate player giving by and large and rather quick the meaning of lines whose words were strangers to him.

Only Mr Brian Murray, Stratford's last minute Romeo, was a Gibraltar in a black sea seething with flotsam and jetsam after Veronese. The young actor seems immune to first night nerves. His Cassio was convincing.

Miss Dorothy Tutin played Desdemona like the girl next door off to bed with the boy next door. And very nice, too. For the boy next door. But there is more than boys next door to Desdemona as Miss Rosalind Iden showed us many a time. There is a grace of spirit. Miss Iden had a candle lit within her, and its wax was docility and its light was truth.

Dame Peggy Ashcroft is a skittish Emilia, looking younger than her mistress and rather better bred. But was Emilia well-bred? I doubt it. Time and again Agate calls this the best part for a woman in all Shakespeare and this may well be so, in some hands; though I would stake Dame Edith's Nurse in *Romeo* against all comers in Emilia. Patsy Byrne, increasingly my heart's delight, made an impression with her Bianca; a Rubens lady, clothed and come to life.

And finally a thought on policy. Could not great Stratford, Royal now, and soon to be part of our National Theatre have taken thought before allotting a rehearsal period to this, the last production of a pretty chancy season and provided an extra week in which three periods could be given to cueing-in scene changes?

The backstage staff at Stratford is by no means the staff of the Royal Opera House. The rest of the time could well have been spent to advantage in going over Othello's scenes with Iago. One sometimes felt theirs was but a nodding acquaintanceship.

Zeffirelli's *Othello* with, left, Ian Bannen and John Gielgud and, below, one of the sumptuous sets designed by the director

Time for Action

The always controversial designer Sean Kenny (1932– 1973) best known for his Oliver! set who had had a busy year in London designing The Devils, The Miracle Worker, Why The Chicken, Altona *and* Stop The World I Want to Get Off *gave this interview to* Plays and Players *before setting off for a spell in Cuba in 1961*

When you leave London for Cuba this month you will presumably be turning your back on drama designs. What made you decide on this step?

Yes, for the time being at any rate I am turning my back on drama though I shall be coming back to London next year to do designs for opera, ballet and a musical. One is for Sam Wanamaker's production of Michael Tippett's opera *King Priam* at Covent Garden. I am going to design a ballet for Jerome Robbins, and I shall work on another Lionel Bart musical. But no more.

For some time now I have been saying 'Let's have better stages . . . Let's have freer stages . . . Let's have better auditoriums.' Either I must do something about it or I must shut up. And by going to Cuba I'm going to try and do something about it. Over there they plan to build small community centres with drama houses, and the idea would be to have several large companies in Havana which would tour to small villages and industrial areas. These centres would also, I hope, provide outlets for sculpture, painting and music too. And the scheme is to decentralise the arts so that they are available to everybody – not just a select minority in the capital.

All this must make a refreshing change from this country where a civic authority has recently made arrangements to give away £75,000 rather than have a municipal theatre on which work had already begun.

Yes this country could badly do with a decentralised theatre. One of the reasons why I would consider giving up the theatre altogether is the fact that one realises, and becomes more aware every day, that one's work is pointed to, is being paid for and is only being appreciated by a small precious minority – the two and a half per cent of our 54 million population who go to the theatre. One wants to work for the rest, but one's work is bought up before one can show it to anyone else. One is adopted by this small, heavily worked, heavily-mined little strata which so quickly becomes satiated. And that's that.

How does one make this minority into a majority?

The answer definitely is not now in the West End of London. It is in the provinces, where we can begin to build small civic theatres where the ritualistic side of theatregoing is cut out. One must have permission to build from the small bureaucratic parties that run small English towns and villages, and then theatre architects must be given the money to build as they like.

Civic authorities hold the purse strings for a very conservative-minded majority. How does one *persuade them to accept revolutionary designs?*

The only way will be to point to a pioneer venture that works. One must be able to show them that an exciting place can stand up and give people a great amount of pleasure. We are trying at the moment here with Centre 42, which is a group mostly of writers and artists to find a building where we can exhibit sculpture and painting, play jazz and classical music and have plays on at the same time. It would be a place where people can entertain themselves as well as be entertained. But even if we got the building right away and made it work very well, it would be at least 50 years before this kind of thing would be widely adopted or became any kind of success.

Do you think there is no other way of obtaining results more directly and more quickly?

The answer is in schools. It is no good fighting the older generation who are set in their ways and who only go to a theatre for Bingo. One must get at the younger people through the country's educational system. The only influence theatre has over education is through Shakespeare, and this is badly done because children are told Shakespeare instead of being allowed to discover him for themselves. And, what is more important, English courses should include playwrights like O'Neill and Miller so that children could discover writers who are commenting on social conditions of their own times. And they should be allowed to discover these playwrights in their own properly equipped theatres. At the moment modern schools are set up with marvellously modern laboratories, but the drama activities are mostly restricted to this thing called a gymnasium. It's neither a gymnasium nor a large public lavatory. It's nothing. It's just a building with a roof over it where children are supposed to run and jump or something.

I do not understand why organisers of the theatre are not aware of these things. One would think that from a purely selfish and commercial point of view it would in the long run be in their interests to foster the audiences of the future. There are isolated cases like Caryl Jenner with her Theatre for Children and Michael Croft with his Youth Theatre, where good work is done. But on the whole little or nothing is done to influence the people now who in 20 or 30 years would go to Bingo, to ensure that they would appreciate and enjoy theatre, painting and music as well. In the theatre we don't seem to be able to think of what is going to happen 20 years from now. We just go on working in the past.

Do you think the Association of British Theatre Technicians' conference in London in June on Planning Adaptable Theatre *was successful?*

It was a good idea, and very interesting it turned out to be. But in the end it wasn't much good. A lot of technicians talked to each other about the best kind of stage – whether it should be a revolve, machinery, lighting or what. But there were no outsiders there. There were no young people and very few of the right people – the people who could have profited by it, like writers and actors.

New theatre buildings are, of course, of major importance. In my work during the last two or three years a lot of the time was taken up trying to outwit the limitations of the existing houses. And a lot of the rest of the time was spent trying to compromise – or trying not to compromise with West End managers. Eventually, when what you set out to do reaches the stage, you find only fifty per cent of it is there. There is so much watering down in the process of production that you end up with very little of what you wanted.

Does your work in Cuba bring about any side consequences?

Yes. I am not now allowed to work in America. The American Scenic Artists organisation have said that I cannot work there at all. I did their test in New York, but they said I did not come up to their standard. That means that shows like *Oliver!* must not have my name on them. At least in this one is in good company. They would not, for example, allow Marc Chagall, Steinberg or Benshahs to go into their Union.

135

Actually the story of Chagall and the Union is quite strange. Jerome Robbins wanted him to design a ballet, but before he was allowed to do it he had to go up and join the union. So he went up and had to queue – there were a lot of young people joining. They asked if they could see samples of his work. He said he was sorry that he had not any with him but he would go and get some. So he went to the Museum of Modern Art and borrowed three of his pictures. He brought them back up and showed them. But when it came to the practical test, they failed him.

Do you agree that the Union movement is killing the American theatre? One hears that smash hits do not even pay for themselves in New York.

Yes, absolutely. Even with a set for a show like *Oliver!*, which needs only three people backstage to work it because it is electronically controlled, the Union step in and say that this is a musical and that you need 14 stagehands. And you have to take them and pay them. They sit back-stage every night and they do nothing. The Union gives you the quota you must take. And take it you must. Over here, of course, conditions are different, and the really important considerations for those who are concerned about the survival of our theatre is not with the artists' and technicians' unions, but with the audiences of tomorrow who are going to school today. It is with them and their schools that a move must be made – now.

DECEMBER
1961

Albee Interviewed

As London had its first experience of Edward Albee with the Royal Court giving his The Death of Bessie Smith *and* The American Dream *in a double bill* Plays and Players *ran this interview by Mario Amaya.*

Gelber, Kopit and yourself are considered the most interesting young playwrights in New York today, and yet all of you have been received badly here by the critics. Why do you suppose The Zoo Story *got such a poor reception?*

I think it was unsuccessful in London because it shocked a number of people in Britain who are chauvinistic. I was a little startled when one critic went so far as to say, 'We don't need this particular kind of American decadence because we already have Harold Pinter.'

Some said you were induly influenced by Pinter.

While I admire him very much, unhappily, I had not read him by the time I wrote *The Zoo Story* in 1958.

You find critics unfair?

All critics are label-happy, because they have to write so quickly and find a convenient tag for something to comfort an uninterested reading audience who want to know what things are like without coming to conclusions themselves.

Do you care what the critics think?

Anybody likes to be taken seriously. It's only one's due. A good or bad playwright deserves to be taken seriously for his intention. I like a critic if he likes my work for the *right* reason or if he dislikes it and he's an intelligent man, and his reasons hold water. I respect the critic for his own intelligence and not the way he feels about me. I was rather spoiled by critics at first, I imagine, because both in Berlin, where *The Zoo Story* was done first, and in New York, there were good reviews. The London reviews were my first unfortunate ones, so I probably over-reacted.

There is a difference here, since the success of a play is not necessarily dependent on what critics say. Here, plays can run for years with bad notices.

I've seen some plays, and I can understand that they might have had bad notices.

You say you think the Lord Chamberlain is being unduly harsh with your new plays. Is this something that could not happen in America?

I'm not even sure the Lord Chamberlain exists, but the Lord Chamberlain's Office seemed to me to be wickedly arbitrary in what it chose to delete from *The Death of Bessie Smith* and *The American Dream*. In the US theatre we have censorship based on good taste. It works, though I don't know why it should. On US television there is the unfortunate censorship based on advertisers' desires not to offend *anybody*. In the movies we have a whole host of critics and censors: the Catholic church and the Legion of Decency. In the New York theatre, it is assumed that grown-ups are going and things will take care of themselves.

Do you feel, then, that censorship in the London theatre is childish?

As I understand it, in this country there are so many watch and ward societies, all over Britain, that quite often it is to its advantage for a play to have the Lord Chamberlain's seal so that it can be performed outside London.

Wasn't there one particular line, taken out by the Lord Chamberlain, which disturbed you very much?

Yes, it was the line that went, 'There he is, my lance-high, love-smit knight.' In America there were no objections to it and I cannot see how there could have been anywhere else.

But you did mean a double entendre.

I wouldn't think of it that way. I meant a rather single *entendre*, phrased, I hoped, poetically.

What is particularly wrong with the commercial Broadway theatre today?

It panders and caters too much to lazy public taste and presents to people what they want, rather than what is true and difficult – what is escapist, rather than what is involving. It is the same problem that has always existed in all art forms.

You have strong feelings about the Broadway theatre as opposed to the Off-Broadway theatre?

The Broadway theatre is big business. Costs are terribly high; audiences are hard to come by and they are basically lazy audiences who want escapist entertainment; expense account people, theatre parties and groups. They demand big stars. The Off-Broadway theatre, on the other hand, existing in small theatres for intellectually curious audiences, produces at low budgets, without the advantage or disadvantage of big name stars, the better plays. The Broadway theatre is irresponsible because it should be producing the plays that off-Broadway is producing, since it has better facilities and reaches wider audiences. Broadway has been mostly mediocre since the 'forties, when *Death of a Salesman* and *Streetcar* were put on within two seasons of each other.

What are the biggest differences, do you think, between the American and British avant garde *playwrights?*

First of all, you have more of them. Then, of course, the new British playwright inhabits the central stream of the commercial theatre here, whereas in New York, the experimental playwright is peripheral, living as he does in the suburbs of off-Broadway.

Surely there must be more differences than that.

Well, I think the new American playwrights are concerned with 'values' that are pertinent to the times we live in, while for the most part, the new British playwright is discovering areas examined in the American theatre 25 years ago. I don't mean by that to suggest that anybody is better than anybody else, of course. It's just that the British theatre has finally discovered social realism and the working class, which is just fine, and about time. Now, with any luck, it will discover other things as well.

Even if this is true, as you say, does that necessarily mean British plays of social protest are any less good than those written in America a quarter of a century ago?

No. In fact I think the ones written today in England are a little better than those written by Clifford Odets and Elmer Rice. Those plays were not particularly good, since they were propaganda rather than art. However, playwrights in England are still a little primitive. For instance, a vastly talented man like Arnold Wesker is still something of a primitive playwright. In the next 25 years, I imagine, these plays will amuse one more than they are taken seriously now. I still think the level is higher, but then there has been so much more in 25 years to take from.

You feel, then, that John Osborne was influenced by the plays of American social realism produced in the 'thirties?

Osborne's emergence as a playwright was, I imagine, the emergence of a playwright for its own sake and based upon its own needs. I do not think that he was trying to be fashionable to the United States of 25 years ago.

Well then. Do you think that England is going to be 25 years late again in writing plays of psychological problems like those of Tennessee Williams?

Time moves more slowly in England, but I imagine that things will catch up very quickly, now.

That may be. But how much farther can deep psychological and soul-searching inquiry go in the theatre?

It can go right on so long as society presents that face. Unless you're the sort of person who does not want the playwright to whitewash situations, unless you feel that a playwright has a responsibility to his time, to reflect it, to comment on it, unless you believe that, then you should only have escapist entertainment.

You feel strongly that the playwright has a responsibility to reflect his times. But shouldn't he first consider entertaining his audience?

It all depends on your definition of entertainment. Ideally, entertainment is instructive, disturbing, and very good theatre.

A playwright must *have a sense of purpose?*

He ought to try to leave the theatre in some way altered from the condition in which he found it. There is no point in doing anything if you leave it where you find it. Old tunes, in whatever orchestration, can be comforting: but art develops only through innovation. As long as the playwright leaves the theatre altered in some capacity, that is the difference between creative art and creative imitation.

Do you think the theatre must be didactic?

It has certainly proved to be with, for instance, Brecht, Ibsen and Shaw.

But surely Shaw's success today is not so much on account of his comments on social conditions as his ability to amuse?

Shaw, in order to get his points across had to be what he called himself – 'a clown'. But the majority of his plays just don't survive at all. They are very well written, most of them, but some of them now have become exquisitely boring.

Well, I don't agree. But assuming you are right, do you suppose that is because he concentrated on social rather than psychological problems?

I don't know how you can separate a man's psychological reaction from his environment. Nobody should set out to write either a psychological or a sociological play. I don't believe in these playwright schools where they all get together and decide to write a social drama. It's artificial. I write a play and it comes out the way it does. These writers are so concerned with social message that they do not develop realistic, believable characters. They produce imperfect plays for that very concentration. If the psychological impact of a society on an individual is minimal, it makes for lesser plays.

Then, as an artist, you don't have any particular liet-motiv?

I think it is ridiculous for a playwright to concern himself with these matters. It produces a kind of unfortunate, inhibiting self-consciousness, and besides, I haven't written enough plays to know why I'm writing them. When I've written 10 or 15 plays, I will try very hard to resist the temptation.

It has occurred to me that your play The Zoo Story *does not have much physical action in it.*

It depends on what your definition of action is. *The Zoo Story* does have a great deal of action . . . *interior* action. And I see no reason why intelligent people in an audience cannot watch and listen to intelligent people on the stage. After all, the validity of a stage piece does not have to depend on how much running around on stage there is. That is a post-Ibsenite convention, which has been run into the ground.

Up to date your plays seem to be all in one act.

Yes, in the sense that it begins when the curtain goes up and ends when the curtain goes down. They are all in one action. However, the 'one-acter' has got a rather unfortunate connotation over the years. It seems to be a play concerned with lesser matters than a long, three-act play. Most plays should, in fact, be shorter, and it is not necessary to have the amount of intermissions that are demanded by the commercial theatre.

Is this part of your protest against the 'well-made play'?

Not aggressively so. The well-made play is grinding itself into the ground without assistance from anybody.

Well, perhaps the future of the theatre is in the one-act play?

I've noticed that Genet, Beckett and Ionesco, just to mention three, have worked effectively in this form. However, I think that any attempt to push the one act play form would be just as

PLAYS AND PLAYERS

This month's theatre guide
November 1961 2s 6d

AUGUST FOR THE PEOPLE
Text and Pictures

ridiculous as pushing the five-act play in the 19th century.

Or the five-hour play of O'Neill?

Every play has its own proper duration. The audience can receive its emotional and intellectual gratification in 10 minutes or 10 hours, provided it is written well enough. There is no ideal shape, no ideal form, no ideal duration for a play.

Do you think the subject matter of your plays is essentially American and may be misunderstood by the English?

Well, for instance, *The American Dream* is concerned with the substitution of artificial values for real values in society, concerned with cruelty, emasculation, vacuity. I don't imagine, even though I am a guest in this country, that England is free of these matters. Any audience that pretends not to understand them is living in an ideal society, which I doubt England is, or is completely self-deceived – and I don't think England is that either.

What about your new play, Who's Afraid of Virginia Woolf?

I haven't quite finished it yet and I don't like to talk about it. And I don't like to talk about my plays at all. The play is not about Virginia Woolf, so the title will have to sum up all I have to say about Virginia Woolf.

As a new, experimental playwright, where do you feel the future of the theatre, both in England and America, lies?

Granted that we're not all blown up, the future of the theatre is in the hands of the people who care desperately about the theatre – as opposed to a sedentary audience.

But it does rest ultimately on an audience.

Naturally. A play should have and must have an audience. But a play should be done as written, without compromise as well. There is always an intelligent and responsible audience, which is proved by the fact that the Off-Broadway Movement has gained such strength in the past several years.

What do you think makes up the ideal audience?

There must be malleability, a willingness to be involved in things outside of themselves; the desire to suffer an experience that need not be a pleasant one. To learn, to be put beyond oneself. An audience that is not concerned only with having its own values reaffirmed in the theatre. I like the objective involvement on the part of the audience, when they keep their intelligence awake as well as their emotional tract.

Certainly, that kind of ideal audience can solve a lot of the playwright's problems.

The only problem with the playwright is to keep his vision foremost and if he is a good enough playwright, he will find his audience during his time. The playwrights who get into trouble are the ones who pander to the lazy audience or the playwrights who sin in exactly the opposite direction: some of the terribly extreme *avant garde* types, who think that acceptance is a form of failure.

And, which do you think are the most interesting of our young English playwrights?

Osborne has been around for a while now, but is, even at his not so great age, the patriarch of the revolution in the English theatre. I think he has very great potential – but so have Wesker and Delaney. I think, though, that Harold Pinter impresses me most at the moment. He is certainly the most accomplished craftsman of the whole bunch. The fact that he has discovered and studied Samuel Beckett so carefully is a very good sign.

You're a great admirer of Beckett, are you?

Yes, I am – because he is an extraordinarily good playwright. I like him because I like the way he writes and what he writes about.

And what about America. Who do you feel is most promising there?

Jack Gelber, who wrote *The Connection*, has a new play coming up this winter in New York. Aside from a few Pirandello-esque quirks to it, *The Connection* indicates a rather exciting talent. Jack Richardson is another interesting American playwright who has not been seen in London yet. At the moment he seems to be dealing a little self-consciously with the French theatre of the 'thirties: a little like Anouilh and Giraudoux. But he's a big talent, I suspect.

And what of Kopit?

He had a play here last summer, the title of which ran longer than the play did. It was a sort of grab bag of European attitudinizings.

It was very poorly received in London.

I can't think of a half-way decent American play that *has* been received cordially in Great Britain in the last five years. Kopit's very young, but there's some life there, at any rate.

Younger than you?

Almost everybody is.

How old are you?

Thirty-three.

And the others?

Kopit's about 26, though American playwrights lie about their age so I don't know. Gelber is 29 or 30, and Richardson *says* he's 24.

PLAYS AND PLAYERS

AUGUST FOR THE PEOPL

This month's theatre guide

December, 1961   2s 6d

Text and Pictures

Credits and Discredits for 1961

Play of the year: John Whiting's *The Devils.*

Best performances of the year: Dame Edith Evans in *Romeo and Juliet*; Eric Porter and Christopher Plummer in *Becket;* Albert Finney in *Luther*; Michael Bryant in *Ross*; Sonia Dresdel in *Mourning Becomes Electra*; and Paul Daneman in *Doctor Faustus.*

Disappointment of the year: John Osborne's *Luther.*

Plays we have enjoyed: *The Kitchen, Progress to the Park, The Death of Bessie Smith, Altona* and the revivals of *The Oresteia, The Changeling* and *Heartbreak House.*

Plays we should like to have missed: *Bonne Soupe, The Geese Are Getting Fat, J.B.* and *The Long Sunset.*

Disasters of the year: *Dazzling Prospect, A Wreath for Udomo, The Fantasticks* and all those dreadful plays at the Arts.

Success of the year: *Beyond the Fringe.*

Noisiest musical of the year: *The Music Man.*

Play of the year: John Whiting's *The Devils*

Corniest musical of the year: *The Sound of Music.*

Mistake of the year: Bernard Miles playing John Gabriel Borkman.

Tragedy of the year: Zeffirelli's *Othello.*

Bores of the year: Noël Coward attacking modern drama; Lady Chatterley; and all those people who go on about Edwige Feuillère.

Names we have missed: Sir Laurence Olivier, Sir Ralph Richardson, Sir Donald Wolfit and Peter Ustinov (second year).

Mystery of the year: Why are the Royal Shakespeare Theatre Company so good at the Aldwych and so disappointing at Stratford?

Hopes for 1962: that new American musicals will be left in America, and that Tennents will find a play.

Problem for 1962: finding a new lost cause now that we have lost the National Theatre as a lost cause.

RIP: The Royalty Theatre.

Revue of the year: *Beyond the Fringe* with, left, Peter Cook, Dudley Moore, Alan Bennett and Jonathan Miller and, right, Bennett and Miller

1962

The year of the Cuban crisis with the USA and Russia in confrontation over the Russian missile base in Cuba was resolved when the Soviets climbed down and dismantled it. In the same year the USA established a military command in South Vietnam. An earthquake in Iran killed 12,000.

London's changing skyline had an addition with the opening of the London Hilton in Park Lane and in Sussex the Chichester Festival Theatre opened as Britain's first public arena stage. The year that Albee's Who's Afraid of Virginia Woolf? *was premièred was also the year of the unveiling of Pinter's* The Collection *and Wesker's* Chips with Everything.

1962

It's The Magic That Counts

Michael Annals, then a young designer on the brink of becoming a well-known one thanks to his designs for Macbeth *at the Old Vic and* Doctor Faustus *at the Edinburgh Assembly Hall, gave this interview to Peter Roberts.*

Much criticism has been made of the limited opportunities theatre designers have for training in this country. As a young designer whose training has been going on over the last ten years, do you agree with these criticisms?

Yes, I do, and this is something that I feel very strongly about. In the first place I do not believe one can study theatre design at all unless one actually works in a theatre with directors, actors and technicians. Theatre design is something that just cannot be taught at an art school – one has only to see the nonsense that comes out of the various schools to realise this. When I studied at the Hornsey College of Art I paid particular attention to painting and drawing but I didn't attempt really to study theatre design there as I felt it could not be so valuable away from the theatre. As soon as I had the chance I went to work in various repertory companies up and down the country such as York, Bedford, Tynemouth and Hornchurch. Then I went on to work with various West End designers such as Leslie Hurry, Reece Pemberton and Disley Jones before being invited by Michael Benthall to design his production of *Macbeth* which the Old Vic toured in this country and which they took to Russia at the beginning of 1960.

But the point about training and the young designer is that unless he is able to get out by himself into repertory companies

and then work with experienced designers such as Leslie Hurry and Disley Jones he has absolutely no opportunity to do any worthwhile training at all. One cannot help feeling that it is a great pity that companies like the Old Vic and the Royal Shakespeare, who are continually drawing on designers, are not able to organise some system of apprenticeship under which young people could work and gain really worthwhile practical experience.

In what way was your experience in provincial repertory worthwhile and practical?

Well, first of all there is the economic factor: you have to make a very little money go a very long way. And then one spends so much of one's time trying to make boring plays *look* interesting. This is all very valuable experience. No matter how dull the play is, I feel very strongly that people who have come out for an evening in the theatre must have something enjoyable to look at. For instance, when I was designing at Hornchurch we had a very dreary play, *Saturday Night at the Crown,* to put on. As it happened to be an anniversary of the theatre we were allowed to spend a little more on this production, so I transformed the whole thing, both stage and auditorium, into a monster, glorious and vulgar Edwardian pub cum music-hall, plastered with potted plants and cut glass vases. Everybody joined in for three days and three nights before the production opened to get it ready, and we all became very excited by it. And the audience saw something a bit different, which they always enjoy doing.

Do you think it would be to the advantage of both repertory companies and designers, if the various companies were to co-ordinate more and draw up a panel of designers for use at their different theatres? A designer might then be freed from the worst strains of weekly and fortnightly repertory.

I think that is a very nice theory but one that would never work in practice. The economics of repertory being what it is in this country, one has to use the same pieces of scenery again and again. One uses a door from one set and a window from another – bits and pieces that one gets to know and repaints in different ways. Only by working in one theatre over a long period can one make a little go a long way in this manner. Practical considerations rule your theory out, I think.

Your designs for Macbeth *have now been used for three productions, the one the Old Vic took to Russia in 1960, the current production by Oliver Neville in the Waterloo Road and the production that Michael Benthall is taking to America with John Clements in the title-role. What factors governed your approach in the first place, and to what extent has it altered in the three productions?*

When Michael Benthall and I first discussed the *Macbeth* production we knew that it would tour extensively from Dublin to Moscow, and so we decided that we would base it on a permanent set which would be easier to travel with. The tragedy anyway is an extraordinarily fast moving one which cannot be held up for elaborate scene changes. From a designer's point of view, the main problem with a permanent set is that one has satisfactorily to locate certain scenes in an interior (the three castles of the play) and certain scenes in an exterior – the heath. Ideally, one would want to clear away all the scenery for the three interpolated scenes on the heath, but as the play has a primitive setting and

Opposite: Michael Annals's designs for *Macbeth* **in action**

145

requires a pretty solidly built basic set this is not practical. What I tried to do was to use on the basic architectural form of the set shapes that one finds in landscapes as one does in architecture. I tried therefore to use shapes that suggested tortured tree outlines, stumps, volcanic rock and so on, which, with lighting, could also suggest an interior as well as an exterior.

When I heard that the production with my sets was to be produced again in London I was anxious that, since a permanent theatre was available for a more or less continuous run, the two sorts of scenery – interior and exterior – should be better located. However, Oliver Neville, who has directed the current production, liked the play as it was before and felt the limitations of a permanent set that had been accepted in the first place brought about fast moving results that were altogether desirable. In the touring version that Michael Benthall is at present rehearsing for America I have added a piece of scenery in the third act which is not used in the London production. This is a sort of cage affair at the back of the set meant to suggest rough battlements put up in a hurry by Macbeth to fence himself in, and I took my cue for it from Macbeth's lines 'They have tied me to a stake, I cannot fly'.

Ideally, one would like to isolate the English scene – the one that has nothing to do with the rest of the play – with a front cloth, but if one were to go on adding in this way production costs would become prohibitive.

Naturally I tried to improve costumes that I was not satisfied with in the first production, and there are a number of small alterations in these. Working with different actors of a different shape and stature also naturally involved certain changes in costume design. I have tried to make the thing as masculine, brutal and barbaric as possible, though in the case of Lady Macbeth I was after something sensual and sexual. The play is essentially a 'northern play', though we decided not to locate it specifically in Scotland with tartans and so forth, which had been done in a fairly recent production, partly because I felt I could invent shapes more suitable than kilts for the play. For the costumes I had tweeds and leather in mind as materials, and in the general design I conceived *Macbeth* as a play in the Grand Manner calling for a certain barbaric splendour.

The effect produced by costumes in red both in *Macbeth* and *Doctor Faustus* has certainly been interesting. A long time ago a very experienced director surprised me by saying 'You'll always get the notices if you use red.' I am sure he is right, and if I had designed the Pope's scene in *Doctor Faustus* or the crowning of Macbeth in blue nobody would have noticed them in the way they have done.

How did you feel about designing Doctor Faustus *for the open stage of the Assembly Hall in Edinburgh?*

I had never worked on an open stage before, and when I heard that the production was to be presented in this way at the Edinburgh Festival I did not feel at all enthusiastic. But when I got there and saw it I was amazed – somehow the magic seemed to happen without one's realising it. One is, for instance, able to introduce actors on to the open stage through the gangways in complete darkness and build up an ensemble such as the Seven Deadly Sins, the Bishops in the Pope's scene or the courtiers in the Emperor's scene, and then flash on the lights so that it produces a gasp from the audience. With an apron stage an audience tends to feel surrounded by the play and is slightly aware of activity going on behind as well as in front, so that there is a greater feeling of participation. I certainly feel that *Doctor Faustus* lost a lot when it came down to London and a different stage.

Would you like to be able to light your own sets?

No. I should hate it.

Couldn't your intentions as a designer be completely misrepresented if not lit in precisely the right way?

By the time you have worked for six weeks with a director he knows pretty well what you are after, especially if the relationship is a happy one. The technical problems of designing are enough in themselves without taking on those of lighting as well.

Of a lot of English designers it can be said that they have an easily recognisable style. Very often, when the curtain goes up, you don't need to look at your programme to see who has designed the set. Do you think that this is something that a young designer should aim for?

No, not aim for. I think that if a designer is an artist of any integrity it is something which happens naturally. I do not think a designer should try to 'imitate' a style. When I have seen it attempted the results have always seemed to me to be disastrous.

It has been very noticeable in recent Shakespeare productions that sets and costumes have quickly been identified with certain painters of certain periods. How do you feel about this?

I think it is lamentable – and boring. Anybody can go to Zwemmer's and get a book for five guineas on some beautiful painter and just copy him. But it is so boring. Of course when one is working on a period piece – as I'm doing at the present – one has to amass a great deal of reference to begin with. But then one has to put it aside and forget it. If one is designing a play that involves ruffs, farthingales or crinolines, one must certainly know all about them. But all books must be put away before pencil is put to paper. *Macbeth* is different, because as far as pictorial reference goes it is prehistoric, so one is not tempted to copy in this way. I suppose one could base one's designs on brass rubbings or something of that kind – but then *Macbeth* has nothing to do with brass rubbings.

Do you think that reference to a particular painter can be justified on the grounds that it imposes an overall style on the designs of a production?

It is the designer's job to impose one anyway.

Is it possible to say how your designs are evolved? The sets come before the costumes presumably?

Naturally one's sets are evolved in discussion with the director, so that one begins with the overall geography of the setting. Materials to be used must be decided on at the outset. Very basic silhouette shapes come before one begins to design clothes for people. I think it is an awful waste of time to design costumes before one knows who is going to wear them and act in them – and it is often quite late on before cast lists are finalised. A lot of actors have a lot of funny shapes and it is as well to know of these before designing for them.

Who do you feel is the greatest influence in theatre design today?

One can only answer this very personally, taking into account influences on one's own work. I would always say Gordon Craig. His life has been a tragic one, as has been said so often before, but his work still remains as a splendid and very stimulating basis for theatre people whether they are actors, designers or directors. There is in his work this marvellous thing of getting back to the words, and also creating three-dimensional, sculptural form. Sculpture in the theatre is something again I feel very strongly about. I think that it is very important and I did study it to a degree in art school. I tend to work from models rather than pictures, and I only paint pictures because they are more convenient to cart around to theatres and wardrobe mistresses. I have found the designs of Leslie Hurry a great influence because of their tremendous theatricality and entertainment. Sets should above all be theatrical. It's the magic that counts.

Do you think a greater number of design exhibitions in theatre foyers and so on would be desirable?

It's a nice idea, but rather silly. Theatre designs cannot be divorced from the words, the music and the lighting. They are part of a whole. Immediately you start to take these things apart they become valueless. A drawing may have a quality of its own but very often what makes a drawing a good design also robs it of any quality outside the theatre. As far as my designs are concerned, my aim is to try to see that an audience going into a theatre has a 'theatrical experience'. It must be an experience that they have not had before, which is why I think it is ludicrous merely to offer copies of well-known painters as set and costume designs.

Do you think that there is a danger here of the sets and costumes becoming a thing in themselves?

I certainly think that a design that swamps a play is a bad design. In Shakespeare at any rate one's first duty is to the words, which one must support and help to explain visually to an audience. At the same time one must take every possible opportunity to allow an audience in the theatre to feast their eyes.

NOVEMBER
1962

Flawed Masterpiece

Charles Marowitz reviews Michael Elliott's revival of Peer Gynt *at the Old Vic.*

Onto a stage shaped like a quonset-hut and rigged with a rising threshold, Michael Elliott, Richard Negri and Richard Pilbrow have devised the clearest production of *Peer Gynt* we shall probably ever see. I immediately include the names of the set and lighting designer because without crisp and cunning inventions this production could never have welded together the elaborate imagery of Ibsen's play. The play itself is a multifarious 19th-century monster stuffed with all the ideas and obsessions Ibsen developed in his later work. An epic inquiry into the nature of identity, much of it anticipates the rise of the New Drama antedating such conventional forerunners as *Ubu Roi* and the plays of Strindberg. In the remorselessness of its logic and in its dogged refusal to settle for facile Christian solutions, it resembles *King Lear*. In suggesting that the quest for self-knowledge and the path of self-destruction are one and in openly declaring that life is too dear a price to pay for birth, it drives home the message of Samuel Beckett with a vengeance.

The play's vastness is intimidating. The mind so boggles at the breadth of the concept that everything else is swept before it. But the flaws, consistent with the whole design, are also massive. The play's symbolism is top-heavy and ultimately, over-explicit. As in many of Ibsen's plays where the symbol outweighs the thing it stands for (*Master Builder*, etc.) the action and dialogue forsakes its own consistency in order to illustrate a purely intellectual notion. Characters like Solveig, for instance, are personified threads in an argument rather than inhabitants of any world peculiar to the play. And indeed, the only way one can accept the world-of-the-play at all is to view it as illustrations of an outlying concept that impinges upon but doesn't always integrate with the action. The central tension is between Peer's single-minded individualism and the murky influence of the troll's world which, if we look beyond the Disney-like depiction of evil, reveals a highly-exotic symbol for the bourgeois.

The role of Peer is an impossibility for any actor as it demands not only that he run the gamut of emotions, but of age as well. In the second act, when Peer is affluent and worldly, Leo McKern comes off best. But as the youthfully-impetuous rustic carrying off the village bride, he is physically and temperamentally unsuited. As Peer in his fierce old age, the character is constantly subverted by a kind of music-hall levity which McKern can never entirely shake off. I will never comprehend the perversity that steers this daemonic and unbeatable clown into heavy roles like Big Daddy and Peer Gynt. Although he is as emotionally resourceful as most straight actors, he suffers from a peculiar limitation of rhythm. Practically everything he does comes out either *stacatto* or *allegro appassionato*. Had he been, let us say Ralph Richardson, we would all be complaining of too much severity and not enough humour. Being Leo McKern, we complain of an excess of lightness which, though it enlivens the play's middle, makes a shambles of its final scenes.

Solveig is played by Dilys Hamlett, an actress who possesses a quality of dramatic imminence which is both tantalising and frustrating. She seems always to be on the brink of an emotion that never quite makes an appearance. She can sustain a pause better than any other actress in England, but when emotion is finally released, only half the flood-gates seem to be open. Her final curtain-song is too well sung, producing a purity of musical utterance which is so effective it supersedes the character. Besides, the play doesn't really end with a resolving lullaby. It ends with a dissonance consisting of the Button Moulder's warning *and* Solveig's song.

On the subject of Adrienne Corri (Anitra) I confess to being helplessly biased. To my hypnotised eye, she possesses the most orotund pelvis this side of the Raymond Revuebar. But I do her a disservice if I suggests that she is all physical endowments. She also has a shrewd comic sense and the kind of feminine magnetism which is all the more compelling for being indigenously sexual.

With Wilfrid Lawson's Button Moulder, once again we find this actor bringing on his own special rhythm which, in every produc-

tion I have ever seen, is at least five times slower than anyone else's. Lawson's dominant quality is of a man making desperate internal efforts to control himself. This produces a peculiarly outstanding performance which asks to be judged in isolation.

A firmer directorial discipline might have repressed the irrepressible Mr McKern, given Dilys Hamlett's Solveig a clearer centrality (sense of belonging) and Catherine Lacey's Aase, a greater degree of contrast which in a short role is always more important than in a long one. But in the mad scenes, in the bland after-dinner chat that opens the second act, and in an overall translucence, Michael Elliott was beautifully on the ball. Ultimately, one leaves the theatre admiring the guts of the man for attempting to capture the wild prolixity of this brilliantly-flawed masterpiece.

1962

Chips And Devotion

John Dexter who first made his reputation at the Royal Court in the late 1950s as the director of Wesker's early naturalistic plays – The Wesker Trilogy *and* The Kitchen *– wrote this account of directing Wesker's play about RAF conscripts and the English class system,* Chips with Everything. *It was to be Wesker's only long-running West End hit.*

I have not yet seen a perfect performance of *Chips With Everything,* I do not suppose I ever shall. The play is elusive. The constant energy and devotion of the cast have made it possible to continue rehearsing throughout 200 performances. Emphasis and tempo have changed; the physical pattern of certain scenes has been altered; the work still seems to grow and fade away just as it did in the early days when even moderate success seemed improbable. Now that the daily, weekly and monthly pontifications are cut out and have faded away, it ought to be possible to have a calm look at the work which has given to Arnold and myself and the boys, security for almost the first time.

How difficult it is to remember the black days of rehearsal. In memory they all seem to have been wonderful. I cannot say I envy any other director facing this play for the first time. I could tell him of the excitement, but if I wrote as well as I know how for the rest of my life, I can never give him the sense of those early days when each morning's work held within itself the possibility of total wreck. For me almost the greatest thrill in the theatre is the challenge of the difficult and unknown, but all I really know of the play, I have been taught by Arnold, Jocelyn Herbert, the designer, and, most of all, by the cast.

The curious love-hate relationship which exists between a drill instructor and his squad must, in some measure, exist between a producer and his cast. I began rehearsing *Chips* with the intention of standing in the same relationship to the boys as did RSM Brittain, or as I remembered feeling towards my instructors in the army, and at the same time keeping amongst them the freedom to experiment and improvise.

The first week of a five-week rehearsal period was divided between drill, drinking and improvisation, a period of truce in which we all took stock of each other and the play. On the first day of the second week, working in three sessions from ten in the morning till eight at night, we blocked in a rough but rigid pattern of movement which, though it has been reshaped a little, stays with us in spirit now, eight months later. Hard angular moves, rhythmic rather than emotional delivery of lines, an insistence on instant response without question, to all direction, produced an

John Dexter's production of Wesker's RAF play at the Royal Court

atmosphere loaded with resentment, but not unlike that of the early stage of primary training and from which we progressed to being able to turn discipline on and off as we needed it. It can be argued that this is the wrong way to direct in the theatre. Perhaps it is. For me, however, it was the only way to direct this particular play. I do not recommend it to another director unless he is as confident and proud of his cast as I was and am. As rehearsals intensified my memory of them becomes confused. In the middle period we came more firmly to grips with the problem of the verbal style to match the visual. Morning, afternoon and evening we struggled with style and reality. No theory written on paper can ease the struggle between these twin devils. Style emerges from reality and reality cannot exist without style.

Recollections are vivid if confused. Ron Lacey in agony with Smiler's running away, Arnold and I seemed powerless to help him find the balance between the reality of the situation and the formal rhythm of the words, a problem he only finally solved for himself 24 hours before the first night. Cuts and more cuts, Arnold's look as another favourite line vanished. George Devine goading and probing at the weekly run-throughs. A vague memory of myself trying to hold on to a few remnants of the confidence with which I began. Sleeping pills at night and pep-up pills in the morning. Changing moves, the effort to find the exact physical space in which a scene could happen most logically. The search for the necessary distance between actor and actor and actor and chair. The joy when for the first time the folk song worked for all of us at the same time. Frank Finlay worried but always in control,

151

taking over the leadership of the company at the end of rehearsals.

These impressions can help no one, least of all a director or actor squaring up to the play for the first time. Whoever you are I wish you luck, if you haven't under your command the cast that I had you will need it. No understanding of our problems will help you with yours. It is, however, the most stimulating play I have ever directed even now when we have read the denigrations of all those critical gentlemen who never step down into the arena. We who have worked on the play know its value, which lies not in its success, but in the work and imagination it brought out of us all, work and imagination of a kind no one had asked of us before. Perhaps we have made a brick to take along to show what our house was like.

Lear – Can It Be Staged?

Peter Brook's 1962 King Lear *production at Stratford-on-Avon with Paul Scofield in the title-role became legendary when it toured both East and West Europe the following year. In this interview with Peter Roberts, Brook discussed his thinking and preparations for the revival.*

'The Lear of Shakespeare cannot be acted,' said Charles Lamb. 'To see Lear acted is to see an old man tottering about the stage with a walking-stick, turned out of doors by his daughters in a rainy night.' Obviously you wouldn't agree with this otherwise you would not be staging it. But do you think there is at least some truth in what Lamb said?

No, none at all. Lamb was talking about the stage of his day and in the way plays were staged in his time. Who said that Shakespeare laid down that you have to see a poor old man tottering with a stick into the storm? I think that's absolute nonsense. I would say that *King Lear* is probably Shakespeare's greatest play and for this reason it's the most difficult. The terrible thing one finds all the time is that it's harder to do masterpieces than anything else. We were complaining of this the other evening at rehearsal and there was James Booth with a skipping rope saying 'Would it be amusing if we did the whole scene skipping?' and I replied 'The tragedy of having to do a play that is so marvellous is that you can't do that kind of thing. Only where you really feel confident that bits are badly written or boring does one have the freedom to invent skipping ropes and so forth.' You know I once did a production of *King John* years ago where we had a medieval newsreel and a man who was the equivalent of the King's newsreelman following the King everywhere. Alas, you can't do this with a masterpiece; it has to be done only one way: the right way. And because of that it's very difficult to find.

We're now coming back more and more to appreciating that not only the later plays of Shakespeare have marvellous things to be found in them but that so also do the lesser roles. *Lear*, for example, has been very much mishandled and mistreated because people haven't recognised the fact that *King Lear* is not a play about King Lear and the others in the way that, from a certain point of view, *Hamlet* is about Hamlet. All the other characters are essential and are marvellous playing parts but they all relate to Hamlet. Hamlet is the pivot of all activity in the play while, in *Lear*, the total structure of the play is the composite meaning of eight or ten independent and eventually equally important strands of narrative. The strands that start in the whole sub-plot about Gloucester eventually become, when they intertwine, the com-

Three views of Brook's *King Lear*: Top, Diana Rigg, Irene Worth and Patience Collier as Lear's daughters. Middle: Brook, right, in rehearsal. Below: Alec McCowen as the Fool and Paul Scofield as Lear

plete play. The result is that one comes up against the fact that the play as written by Shakespeare to be truly revealed on the stage needs not only a capital performance in the part of Lear but equally illuminating acting all the way through. And I think that it is here – rather than in the problem of staging the storm – that the real challenge and the real difficulty of *Lear* lie.

How did you meet this difficulty and this challenge when you directed the play for television in America in 1953?

Oh, that was shredded *Lear*. I cut the whole play down to an hour and 20 minutes and sliced the whole sub-plot out and had the Poor Tom as a real Poor Tom, instead of Edgar in disguise. We even flew out Micheal MacLiammoir specially to play the part.

How many cuts are you making in this new production?

Hardly any. It's a long play and it's a long evening. That's the way it's written. One cuts a play when it becomes too boring or too obscure which often happens with Shakespeare but in this case I've decided against it. I've examined the traditional cuts (you know, around the theatre here there are books, with all the cuts that have been made over the years) and have been interested to find that while lots of them make sense they all lose something. Cutting prevents the actors of smaller parts having the material to build three-dimensional figures and so the net result is the destruction of the real texture of the play.

I've found that there are lots of places where, through filling in the traditional cuts, one suddenly sees – oh the whole fascination of the play. For instance, one finds that most times one sees the play done in the cut version one lumps together Goneril and Regan as two identical women and their husbands, Cornwall and Albany as just two chaps. Yet it is quite amazing the total difference between them. For instance, the Goneril-Regan relationship is a completely Jean Genet one where Goneril is consistently dominant and where Regan is soft and weak: Goneril wears the boots and Regan wears the skirt. Goneril's masculinity continually fires Regan whose squelchy softness of core is very opposed to the steely hardness of her sister. This relationship develops very interestingly through the second part of the play (I'm dividing it into two parts) because one sees that disaster and troubles make Goneril more and more dominant and harder. Regan, on the other hand, completely goes under and in the end creeps ignominiously off the stage poisoned in the stomach like a squashed spider, whereas Goneril takes her leave defiantly. There is, too, a tremendous difference between Albany in all his weakness, tolerance and confusion and Cornwall – impetuous, fiery and sadistic. All this interesting character material comes to light when you *don't* cut.

I'm interested in time and place. Is your production fixed specifically in a certain place at a certain time?

You've touched on the key problem.

Yes, time and place are very fluid in the text, aren't they?

That is the whole problem and one that I have been pondering upon for 12 months. I've been preparing this production for a year and that year has been spent on the particular question. You can't say that *Lear* is timeless which is what the interesting but unfortunate Noguchi experiment at the Palace in 1955 proved. In

his programme note to that production George Devine wrote 'we're trying to show with timeless costumes and timeless sets the timelessness of the play' – an apology which didn't actually touch the core of the problem. Although in a sense it *is* timeless (that's a sort of critic's comment) in actual fact, it is taking place in big, violent and therefore very realistic circumstances with flesh and blood actors in very harsh, cruel and realistic situations. The key problem is – how are they dressed, what do they wear? Looking at the evidence of the play one has got two contradictory necessities; the play has to take place, unless you put it into science-fiction, in the past; yet it cannot take place in any period in the immediate past because any period after William the Conqueror in England has a smell of falseness, simply because every child knows that much history. Even though I've long since forgotten the kings and queens of England I roughly remember the order and I know that 90 per cent of our audiences know that sandwiched between Henry VI and someone else there didn't happen to be a King Lear.

So there is something that is shocked in one's belief if one acts *Lear* Elizabethan or Renaissance, particularly as there is another element that is strong in the play – its pre-Christian nature. The ferocity and horror of the play is destroyed either if, as some unfortunate critics do, you try to tip it into Christianity or if you try to fit it into a Christian era. The imagery of the plays, and gods who are continually invoked are pagan ones. There's Apollo and Jove just as in *Cymbeline*. And, to digress for a minute in this connection, I personally find that with the *Cymbeline* in the repertoire at Stratford at the moment, I am worried in a way that I wasn't with the production Peter Hall did of the play a few years ago. Then I thought he made the intelligent choice of sticking *Cymbeline* into the Druid era because the Druids corresponded with a real streak that goes all through the play. I find that in watching René Allio's costumes which are very strongly of the Middle Ages, that I'm disturbed by a – for me – irritating anachronism that all this pagan and Druid ritual is happening in the Middle Ages. It has a wrong smell.

But to come back to *Lear*. The society is primitive. On the other hand, it is clearly not primitive Stonehenge because if you go back to that you find another falsity. That is that *Lear* is, at the same time, a very sophisticated society. For it is not a society of people that live in the open air under stones. To put the play back to that period is to lose the essential cruelty, which is the cruelty of turning a man outdoors. The people who are indoors feel the difference between the elements and the man-made solid world from which Lear is expelled. If the king is used to being out under Stonehenge the play is shattered. Furthermore the language of the play is not the language of that book of William Golding's where the inhabitants just say 'Og' and 'Gug'. It is the language of high Renaissance. So it seems to me that one has to face the problem that one has to create a pre-Christian society which for present-day audiences has the smell of belonging to an early part of history. At the same time, that early part of history has to be a moment of history where, for those people, they were in as high a state of development as were the Mexican society before Cortez or the high Egyptians.

plays and players
September 1962 2s 6d
THE GINGER MAN
FULL LENGTH PLAY INSIDE

plays and players
October 1962 2s 6d
THE EMPIRE BUILDER
FULL LENGTH PLAY INSIDE

Lenya on Brecht

Brecht on Brecht

In Homer one had exactly the situation that is comparable to *Lear*. The descriptions one has of the palace that Odysseus returns to and finds Penelope and the suitors in is exactly the same world. It's primitive for us because it's a long way away and it's also a world of people of a certain rough and strong physical accomplishment. Yet the description of the furniture, of the beds covered with the best linen, of the perfumes of the bath, of the great copper doors, of the food and drink, show that this was, in that particular cycle of history, a high Renaissance.

Furthermore, accept that *Lear* is barbaric and Renaissance; it's those two contradictory periods. Then we come back to the modern, the timeless school. It is not that the issue of the play is about a king and a fool and cruel daughters. In a way it is so much loftier than any historical setting that the only thing one can equate to it is a modern play such as Beckett might write. Who knows what is the period of *Waiting for Godot?* It is happening today and yet it has its own period in reality. That is also essential to *Lear* because *Lear* for me is the arch example of the theatre of the absurd, from which everything in good modern drama has been drawn.

The aim again of the setting is to produce a degree of simplication that enables the things that matter to be more apparent because the play is hard enough without the added problem that any form of romantic decoration adds. Why does one decorate a bad play? For that purpose – to decorate it. With *Lear*, on the contrary, one has to withdraw everything possible. And this leads us eventually to the conclusion that I've always felt which is that one must plump for deliberate anachronism.

I did this with my first production in this theatre, which was *Love's Labour's Lost*. I felt that, on reading the play, it was closer to the feeling of the world of Watteau – that is to say not a genuine 18th-century world but an 18th-century view of an arcadia which was in the past. Yet when a man came in called Constable Dull it seemed to me that he belonged neither to Elizabethan days nor to the 18th-century, but that he was purely Victorian. He was a Victorian policeman which means that to us Constable Dull means something that couldn't have existed in Shakespeare's mind. There seemed to be only one solution which was boldly to go straight into anachronism on the grounds that if he was true to his character and the others were true to theirs, they would fit into one world in the text.

This in a sense is what we are doing with *Lear*. With Keegan Smith, who runs the wardrobe at Stratford, we've evolved costumes which carry the minimum necessary real statement that each character needs. For instance, King Lear himself has to wear a robe because I think that you can't go round this point. There are certain necessities for an actor as Lear. Even if you take everything else away from him, he has to enter with something that goes down to his feet for a certain regality of the character. He has a robe, therefore, which no one else has. There's no one else in the play who needs that. At the very beginning of the play, then, he has a robe which is very rich and after that he goes into a very simple costume made out of leather. All the other costumes we have simplified down to two essential styles. And the setting has also been immensely simplified. My real aim is to try to give ourselves conditions in which we can in the modern theatre follow what Shakespeare does on the page, which is to put completely different styles and conventions side by side without any feeling of uncomfortable anachronism. One needs to accept the very anachronisms as a strength of this form of theatre and as a pointer to the methods we have to find to stage it.

How have you approached music and sound effects in this production?

I don't think there is any place for music in *Lear* at all. As regards sound effects, the storm is the key problem. If you try to stage it realistically you have to go to the full Reinhardt extent. Yet if you go to the other extreme which is to have the storm taking place in the audience's imagination it cannot work because the essence of drama is conflict and the drama of the storm is Lear's conflict with it. Lear needs the wall of the storm to fight against and this cannot be done if the storm is indicated intellec-tually – i.e. by flying in placards saying 'this is the storm'. That would be giving the conflict of the storm to the minds of the audience whereas it must also be an emotionally charged thing.

After months of working on this problem it suddenly struck us how effective would be a thunder sheet *on view* on the stage. The vibrations of a large sheet of rusty metal have, as anybody knows who has watched a stage manager shaking a thunder sheet, a curiously disturbing quality. The noise is, of course, disturbing but so also is the fact that you see it vibrating. The thunder sheets on view in this production of *Lear*, then, give the King a source of conflict without at the same time being a rather unconvincing attempt to stage it realistically.

How many intervals are you having and where are you placing them?

One interval only – after the blinding of Gloucester.

Over the years you have come more and more to design your own productions as you are doing with this King Lear. *Why?*

Although I have loved working with designers I find that it is terribly important in Shakespeare in particular that I design myself. I find with a designer when you come up against really difficult problems you can never know whether your ideas and his are evolving at the same rate. You come to a portion of the play that you cannot find your way through. At that point the designer finds a solution which seems to fit and which you are bound to accept, with the result that your own thinking on that scene becomes frozen. If you are doing it yourself it means that over a long period of time you eventually evolve your own solution.

Anyway, I doubt whether there is any designer living who would have the patience to work with me. After working for a year on this *King Lear* I scrapped the whole of my original set when the production was postponed. As it happened the new set cost about £5,000 less – so nobody minded.

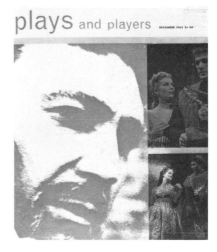

Credits and Discredits for 1962

Best play: Arnold Wesker's *Chips with Everything*.

Best actors: John Gielgud surfacing in *School for Scandal*; Trevor Howard comforting in *Two Stars for Comfort;* Laurence Olivier and Michael Redgrave battling gentlemanly in *Uncle Vanya*; and Paul Scofield growling in *King Lear*.

Best actresses: Elaine Stritch belting in *Sail Away!;* Brenda Bruce buried in *Happy Days*, and Vanessa Redgrave stratfording in *Cymbeline* and just sitting in Trafalgar Square.

The production: Michael Elliott's *Peer Gynt* taking the accent off the Old in Old Vic.

The misproduction: Tony Richardson's *A Midsummer Night's Dream*, which was Greek to everyone. (Runner-up: Volanakis's *Julius Caesar* – ditto).

The design: Sean Kenny's all-singing, all-talking *Blitz!*.

The misdesign: The décor of the New Arts (poppycocteau?).

The disappointment: The Mermaid's O'Casey Festival – the Irish never had troubles like this.

The rivals: Michael Elliott and Peter Hall.

The switch: Bernard Levin of the *Daily Express* to Bernard Levin of the *Daily Mail*.

The word: Lenny Bruce's (whatever it was).

The silences: Marceau and Lord Olivier of Southbank.

The damp squibs: Choice of first play at Olivier's Chichester and choice of first play at Croydon's Ashcroft.

The takeovers: Tony Tanner from Tony Newley; Charlie Clore from Jack ('The Princes') Hylton – or how to succeed in show business without really trying.

Sean Kenny's recreation of 1940's London for Lionel Bart's *Blitz!*

Plays to remember: *The Fire Raisers, Nil Carborundum, Play with a Tiger, Infanticide in the House of Fred Ginger, The Empire Builders,* and for that matter, Osborne's *Under Plain Cover.*

Plays to forget: *Come Back with Diamonds* (they didn't), *The Glad and Sorry Season* (the latter), *The New Men* (they weren't), *Curtmantle* (frying tonight) and, for that matter, Osborne's *The Blood of the Bambergs.*

Plays forgotten . . .

Disasters of the year: *Scapa!* (sunk without trace) and *The Cigarette Girl* (Home is the hunted).

The shipwreck: The (Old) Old Vic's *Tempest* (also sinking without trace).

Miscasting of the year: Joan Greenwood as Ilyena in *Uncle Vanya*.

Glad to see you go: Lord Scarbrough, retiring Lord Chamberlain.

Sorry to see you arrive: Lord Cobbold, the new Lord Chamberlain.

Problem of the year: How to release the Ambassadors from *The Mousetrap*.

Whatever happened to: Michael Benthall, the Revd Timothy Beaumont and his Ikons, Centre 42, Julian Slade, the London Palladium, and for that matter The Royalty.

1963

The year of the Kennedy assassination, the death of Pope John XXIII and the succession of Paul VI was also the year in which Macmillan resigned as British Premier to be succeeded by Alec Douglas-Home. It was also the year of the Great Train Robbery, the Profumo scandal and the year Wilson became leader of the Labour party.

In London the Beeching Report recommended the closing of half the British rail network. The British film industry enjoyed a revival of esteem with the release of This Sporting Life, Billy Liar *and* Tom Jones. *The unveiling of Ionesco's* Exit the King *and Hochhuth's* The Representative *were reminders that dramatic controversy was not confined to Britain, where the Old Vic became the first home of the new National Theatre Company. After a century's campaigning, the new company opened with Olivier's production of* Hamlet *(Peter O'Toole)*

The Rule of the Plot

*John Russell Taylor reviews
Arden's* The Workhouse
Donkey *at Chichester*

We are getting so used these days to plays without plots, or plays, at least, where the elements of plot count for very little, that perhaps we are losing the knack of coming to terms with plot. Certainly much of the mystification which John Arden's latest play seems to have occasioned even in those who most enjoyed it arises from the role of plot in it. For whatever else it has or has not got, it undeniably has plot in plenty. There are at least a dozen principal characters, all of them with important parts in what happens, and the ins and outs of the intrigues in which first one and then another holds the whip-hand are so numerous and intricate that one could fairly safely defy anyone to summarise them adequately after one viewing. So? Well, this is where the knack of dealing with plot comes in. The only sort of plot we are familiar with in the modern theatre is the one-line mechanical conundrum of an Agatha Christie: we *expect* to understand each stage as it is presented to us fully and at once. In the heyday of plot things were otherwise; did anyone expect to catch all of a Drury Lane melodrama like *The Whip*? Or everything that happened in a vintage Edgar Wallace? No more, presumably, than anyone now expects, comfortably settled in for an evening at Covent Garden, to grasp everything that happens in *Don Carlos* or *La Forza del Destino*.

In the opera house we are conditioned to certain Romantic, melodramatic conventions which, in the 'legitimate' theatre, strike us these days as strange and puzzling in the extreme. But these, I suspect, are precisely the conventions we should be bearing in mind with *The Workhouse Donkey;* it is not for nothing, on the one hand, that immediately before he wrote it Arden was adapting Goethe's early romantic drama *Goetz von Berlichingen*, or, on the other, that he subtitled this play originally 'a vulgar melodrama' and explained that by this he meant both a play to music and a melodrama in the more usual English meaning of the term. *The Workhouse Donkey is* melodramatic, it *is* operatic, and the quicker we realise this and accept it, the easier we shall find the play.

Not, I should say at once, that it is difficult to enjoy; in some respects it is almost too easy. As it goes along there are so many quick laughs about local politics, the hanky-panky in the mayor's parlour, the policeman caught with his pants down (literally at one point) that it is easy to ignore the direction in which it is all tending. My main objection to Stuart Burge's production, in fact, is precisely that he takes, and encourages us to take, the easy way out; he treats the play as a patchwork of amusing bits instead of making a clear decision about what sort of play it is, what its real subject is, and then seeking out the style which best brings out the play's over-all pattern.

Basically this seems to be a lack of confidence in the play's ability to work in its own terms. As I have suggested, the plot is so hopelessly involved, and there is so much of it, that we are clearly not intended to take it in detail by detail, turn by turn (which is my excuse for not trying to summarise it here!) but simply to derive from it a general impression of little people scurrying backwards and forwards, grouping and regrouping like ants, while from this intricate pattern emerge two commanding, opposed but finally not so dissimilar figures, Alderman Charlie

Butterthwaite and Colonel Feng, the Chief Constable, with a *tertium quid*, Doctor Blomax, as plotter-in-chief and master of ceremonies. Blomax and the rest are modern, they are without principle, they work entirely by expediency from moment to moment; Butterthwaite and Feng, on the other hand, belong to an earlier age, they are both lost in the present and this is why in the end they are both doomed to defeat.

Butterthwaite is an old-style robber baron of local politics, an anarchic anachronism too awkward to be accommodated in the modern world (just as the workhouse donkey of his song is a big uncomfortable fact which genteel suburbanised civilisation refuses to accept), and we know from the start that before long everyone will have to gang up on him just to make the world comfortable for nonentities. Feng is equally out of place, in that he is a man unswervingly devoted to abstract principle, firm in his determination not to be swayed in any direction and, because he favours no faction, equally uncomfortable to all. He, too, seems left over from an heroic age; he, too, is finally too much of a nuisance not to be eliminated at the last. And so in the end both are sacrificed, made scapegoats – Butterthwaite overtly, decked as a ritual king-victim on May Day, of all days in the year. These two are the firm rocks of the play, the twin bastions round which the others swirl and swarm, and which by sheer weight of numbers are finally overwhelmed.

That is the pattern of the play, and the production should bring it out. But Mr Burge's doesn't. He handles the individual scenes very subtly and sensitively; in fact too subtly and sensitively by half – he spends far too much time bringing out nuances in the inessentials when what is needed is a few incisive strokes of bright colour to indicate what the main focuses of attention should be. The whole thing wants to be removed much further from natural ism (Chichester's apron stage is a hindrance here; if ever a play needed a proscenium as a frame of convention that characters can step in and out of, this is it), to be played much more broadly and swiftly. If it were taken more quickly, too (accepting, that is, that we are never going to follow the plot and not even momentarily encouraging us to try), there might even be time to restore two or three important soliloquies which were removed a couple of days before opening simply – and understandably – so that London playgoers could catch the last train home.

After all this carping and niggling, though, I must in all fairness come back finally to saying that the play is in general superlatively well acted, with a special word for Frank Finlay as Butterthwaite and for Norman Rossington, who hits exactly the right note of music-hall vulgarity as Blomax. Also, the play, even in a demonstrably less than perfect production, is still just about the most exciting – and entertaining – thing to have happened in the theatre for at least 18 months. Go and see it – if you can still manage to get in.

Memento Mori

Martin Esslin reviews Exit the King *at the Royal Court*

In N. F. Simpson's *One Way Pendulum*, Sylvia Groomkirby has a dirty old skull which was given to her by her boy friend. It's supposed to be a 'memento mori'; the trouble is, however, that it doesn't work. It fails to remind her of death. Ionesco's *Exit the King,* on the other hand, is a *memento mori* that does work, a play straight out of one of the oldest dramatic traditions in the world a *dance of death*, a *morality play*, a dramatic ritual from an era when the stage and the altar had not yet parted company. The analogy to Everyman is only too obvious: here as there the chief character is told at the very outset that he is about to die. Here as there the suspense of the play does not lie in any doubt as to that final outcome of the action; but entirely in whether the hero of the play will finally accept the inevitable fact of his dying – and *how* he will accept it.

The hero of Ionesco's play is Bérenger, the same Bérenger who is the chief character in three other plays by Ionesco (*Rhinoceros, The Killer* and *The Pedestrian of the Air*), the proverbial little man, the Chaplinesque waif who somehow survives, and retains his humanity, in the face of the heaviest odds. In this latest play Bérenger is still that same little man, although he sits on a throne and wears a crown and is called King Bérenger I. What Ionesco indicates by this image, and with triumphant success, is the fact that every man, while he lives, is the king of his own world – a world in which he is sovereign and supreme, a world which, when he dies, will die with him. That is why King Bérenger's country, when the play opens, is so obviously falling into decay: the central heating no longer works in the throne-room, the frontiers are receding, there are earthquakes and landslides that make the land as pockmarked and full of holes as a piece of Swiss cheese. The symptoms of King Bérenger's imminent demise, however, go further: when he orders his guard, the last members of a once powerful army, to advance, the guard, although more than willing to obey, can no longer move: for, as each sovereign human being approaches death, his limbs no longer obey him.

When King Bérenger is first told that he will die, he does not give the news a thought; we all know that we shall die some day; we know it intellectually, but not emotionally, for we go on living as though we were immortal. It is the acceptance of the fact of death as more than a mere pale intellectual piece of information, as a living, wholly real and imminent necessity, that forms the real theme of Ionesco's play, and it is this theme which brings the play into such close relationship with medieval Dance of Death drama. There, too, the purpose of the performance was to show that everybody, from the beggar to the king, was about to die, and that the fact of death, whether it came in the next minute or in thirty years' time, should make one live in a different way: more consciously, more deliberately, more responsibly. Ionesco's play is not an allegory; it is, as most plays of the Theatre of the Absurd, a poetic image of the human condition, simpler perhaps, more straightforward than some of Ionescos earlier plays, but also more powerful, more controlled, more classical in form. It is as though Ionesco had absorbed some of the simplicity of line we know from Beckett, some of the ritual quality of Genet. *Exit the King* is a profound and beautiful play.

In George Devine's production Alec Guinness plays King

Bérenger: a better stroke of casting could hardly have been imagined: Guinness has the immense advantage of being both a supreme clown and a supreme tragic actor. His Bérenger is very closely related to Stan Laurel at his most self-deprecatory and bashful, when the corners of his mouth come down on the verge of tears. And yet, Guinness also reminds us of Richard II in the hour of his death, of Hamlet facing the problem of being or non-being. The transitions from Stan Laurel to Hamlet are never forced, are always completely natural; tragicomic acting at the highest peak of perfection.

There is only one other performance in this production which to me seems to come near to this level: Eileen Atkins' servant girl, particularly in the masterly dialogue with the dying King, when she tells him of her hard life and he envies her its very hardness and squalor: there, too, there is simplicity, grotesque foolishness and tragic greatness all in one, encompassed in the little skivvy's plain face with its enormous, sorrowful eyes. Googie Withers and Natasha Parry are Bérenger's two queens (for he, as so many other men in these days, is no monogamist), Peter Bayliss the decaying guardsman, and Graham Crowden the sadistic doctor, scientist and astrologer. They all give excellently controlled and imaginative performances.

Jocelyn Herbert's set and costumes are most beautiful. One might argue that she has accepted the medieval royal setting a little too literally. True enough: Bérenger wears a pair of pyjamas

Alec Guinness as Ionesco's King Bérenger with, left to right, Googie Withers, Natasha Parry and Graham Crowden

and an old pullover underneath his ermine robes – but this is almost the only indication of the fact that his royalty is merely an image. In the Paris performance the throne-room was just a petty bourgeois drawing-room, and the trappings of royalty were quite obviously incongruous and threadbare. On balance, I think, the medieval imagery in this production justifies itself: it emphasises the solemnity, the dignity of the proceedings, while sacrificing a good many laughs in the earlier part of the play.

Donald Watson's translation is excellent. And the musical score for toy instruments, devised and played by Michael Dress, is a brilliant piece of stage music – completely unobtrusive and always exactly right in subtly underlining and creating the mood of the scene. Alec Guinness is not often seen on the London stage; he is even more rarely to be seen in a masterpiece of modern dramatic literature. This performance therefore is a must.

Bolt in Interview

Just as his new and experimentally non-naturalistic play, Gentle Jack, *was about to open (unsuccessfully) at the Queens with Edith Evans, Kenneth Williams and Michael Bryant, Robert Bolt talked to Frank Cox about his earlier work*

In an interview with Plays and Players *three years ago you were reported as saying that with the completion of* A Man For All Seasons *you stood at the cross-roads between experimental form and naturalism. I wonder just how far and in which direction* Gentle Jack *has taken you?*

Well, I don't know quite what I meant by standing at the crossroads – it sounds rather portentous – but ever since I started writing plays I've been unhappy with naturalism, and even in *Flowering Cherry* and *The Tiger and the Horse*, which are fundamentally naturalistic plays, there were timid and perhaps embarrassing steps away from naturalism – do you want me to specify?

By all means . . .

Well, you know, the special effects in *Flowering Cherry*, the confusion between dream and reality, and the big set-speeches which weren't naturalistic. And in *The Tiger and the Horse* people unnaturally conscious of what they stood for and unnaturally articulate about it. But I could see that this wasn't really getting me anywhere very rapidly; the undertow back towards naturalism was much too strong for me, and so I wrote an historical play – largely, I think, as a sort of Dutch courage, because if people are wearing cloaks and funny hats and don't travel on 29 buses as it were, you don't really know the minutiae of their daily lives, you are helped to escape from this tremendous undertow of representation. What I've tried to do in this play is salvage the much more open form, the much more nakedly theatrical form of *A Man for all Seasons* for a contemporary theme and a contemporary setting. You see, it's astonishingly difficult not to write naturalistically unless you simply take over someone else's style lock, stock and barrel. I don't want to do anything on the stage that I don't really understand the reason for – and by 'understand' I don't mean that I could give an exhaustive explanation for – but I want to know, as I do it, why I do it this way rather than that way. The only kind of theatre which I instinctively understood when I started was naturalistic theatre, and to get an instinctive understanding of a non-naturalistic style is, at least I've found, very difficult; I'm far from thinking that I've yet achieved the style I want to. But I do think that this new play is a more bold step away from naturalism than my other two contemporary plays.

Could I take you on now to what I think is one of the basic issues in your writing – the balance in all your plays between the head and the heart? Harold Hobson in the new Penguin edition of A Man For All Seasons *says: 'The play is an intellectual feat of a high order, displaying the intricacies of an acute and cultivated mind'. Would you yourself acknowledge a predominance of the intellect, perhaps at the expense of the emotions, in your plays?*

Well, this is so often said by critics, when they talk about my work, that there must, I suppose, be something in it. Certainly this does seem to me to be a fundamental problem today – the balance between the head and the heart. People theoretically – and only theoretically, I think – opt for one or the other. In the theatre people tend to opt for the heart without apprehending what that entails in terms of loss of shape, loss of intention, and indeed loss of value. This is as it seems to me. And conversely, in the intellectual world at large, particularly in modern philosophy, there seems to be a discounting of emotional values as a subject capable of rational examination – it's an acceptance of a total dichotomy. Now to me life only gets interesting where these two things overlap. A man in a violent temper is not really in a very interesting state of mind – he may be very impressive, he may be very forceful, but there isn't really a great deal to be said about it except that he's in a temper . . . look out! And unless you value passion for its own sake, in a sort of Nietzschean sense, I don't think there's much interest in it. Conversely, a man who is entirely concerned with manipulating intellectual symbols is not finally very interesting unless you are that kind of chess-playing person yourself. Where it gets interesting is where the two things overlap and you have a person struggling to give shape and intention to his emotions, and conversely struggling to keep his mind informed with some kind of emotional investment.

I don't think that audiences find my plays cold or cerebral – mind you, this may be wishful thinking, but they come and they seem to enjoy them as an evening in the theatre, and I don't think they would if they were merely cerebral – but as I say, I'm the last person to be able to judge this. Far more than anything else, what I want to do is give audiences their money's worth in terms of theatre, and theatre to me certainly entails emotion – I don't think there could be anything else to theatre if there isn't emotion – shape and form and intention and all the rest of it can only follow that.

Yes, and your plays certainly do have a remarkable grasp of shape, don't they? – almost unfashionably . . . well, 'neat' is rather derogatory . . .

But I would accept 'neat', you know . . .

You would . . .?

I don't relish it, but I would accept it. What I would prefer, of course, is for you to say that my plays have 'form' – and I am unfashionably fond of form in art – in all art, not that there is any other art that I know anything about really – but in all the arts, what I ask for first is form. Of course, it's a very loose concept in itself, but . . . you see, I may look at an abstract picture and say

plays and players MAY 1983 3s

Tommy Steele as Kipps

plays and players JUNE 1983 3s

that it has no form, and somebody who really knows something about pictures may say, 'You're quite wrong, there's a great deal of form in that picture' – well, I would accept that I'm ignorant; but if a person says, 'Yes, that's right, there's no form, I hate form, I'm against form!', then I'm against this person. I'm in favour of form!

Then how do you react to comparatively formless movements in the theatre, like the Theatre of the Absurd? How do you respond when you watch a Theatre of the Absurd play?

Not well, because it frightens me, and therefore, of course, I'm admitting that there's great power in it, and it clearly rings a very big bell today. People are obviously feeling that form is artificial, that life, in fact, has no form, and they may not be liking this, but they are trying to come to grips with it. One could go on indefinitely about this – in politics, international and domestic; in morality; everywhere you look there is either form falling away from under you or a conscious attack on form, and so the Theatre of the Absurd is obviously very significant indeed. If it were not it wouldn't have attracted, as it has, the brightest talent, so far as I can see, in almost every country. But it does seem to me to be anti-theatre, as it's sometimes called, with anti-heroes, and I am pro-theatre – I want more theatre, not less, and I revere the art-form of the theatre. I would like to strengthen it. Certainly it wants expanding, and I would like, if I could, in some small way to help expand it, and let it grow so that it can cope with the situation we're in now. But I don't think that to attack the form itself can be anything other than a gesture – maybe a very necessary one, certainly a very powerful and disturbing one; but to put it at its extreme it seems to me that the apotheosis of the Absurd would be to bring up the curtain on a dark stage and leave it so, dark and silent, for two hours, and then let the audience go out.

I can see that this might be a very disturbing theatrical experience, and a sensitive audience might well go away in a very chastened and shaken-up state of mind. But the second time it would be slightly less so, and the third time very much less so, and they wouldn't come again – it would be the end of theatre. You see, if you really and truly believe that things are utterly absurd – not more or less absurd, we all obviously think they are that, which is why we struggle to give shape – but if you believe they are utterly absurd, I can't see how meaningfully there could be anything to be said about it, because what you are saying must also be absurd. This is a sort of high-falutin' philosophical argument, but if I truly believed that life was nothing other than absurd I don't see how I could write a play about this.

But doesn't Waiting for Godot *say just this?*

No, on the contrary, I find – as in the plays of Pinter, too – things being said which are not absurd. I find for example in *Waiting for Godot* a kind of a bitterness and a pain and a resentment expressed by this play and by these characters about the absurdity of life which seems to postulate that some reasonable expectation has not been met – otherwise, why the bitterness, why the pain, why the protest? Why not merely a celebration of absurdity, or an acceptance of absurdity? But if there is some reasonable expectation that has not been met, I would rather like to see this tackled directly: what is this reasonable expectation, or how do you claim it to be reasonable? In what ways has it not been met? Is there anything that could be done about it? This is a much more orthodox kind of playwriting than Absurd playwriting.

A question which you're probably tired of being asked is to do with the casts of your plays. When you are writing, particularly now that this is your fourth play, does the prospect of having a specific actor playing one of your roles influence at all the creation of this role?

Well, this play that I'm engaged on now is the first play in which this has in fact been the case. I've always just written and hoped to get the best cast I could. But in this case Dame Edith and Kenneth Williams had both said they would like to appear in a play by me if there were a suitable part, and unquestionably this did influence me in the writing of the parts. I don't mean consciously thinking 'this is something Dame Edith will like to do' or 'this is something Kenneth Williams will like to do', but simply that I always write for actors. I mean I don't have the illusion that I'm writing lines that were spoken by real people in a situation; I'm always conscious in my mind's eye of actors on the stage, lights and so on. And in this case this became that degree more concrete to me inasmuch as I knew the particular styles of those two artists and therefore unconsciously as I wrote I found myself writing lines which were recognisable in the style of those actors.

All your plays are very liberally endowed with stage directions and brackets after lines, explaining how to say a particular line – are you taking a large hand in the actual direction of this play?

Well, I'm certainly co-operating very closely with the director, Noel Willman. He is that rarest of rare birds, an author's director. He is not in any way peddling his own personality. I don't mean by this that he is passive. On the contrary, he is sometimes as strict with me as he is with himself and with the actors. He will point out ruthlessly any theatrical vulgarities or theatrical pedanticisms which I have committed for my own gratification. I mean that his main intention is to find out what I wanted from the actors, from the situation, and, if I'm not asking for technical impossibilities, to get it for me. We've discussed the play in very great detail together, and as you see, I'm here on the premises all the time, so from time to time he asks me to talk to an actor or the actors directly. It's the kind of partnership you can only achieve if the author and the director have great trust in each other, and if the cast has trust in them both. It calls for a certain amount of generosity and tact on all sides, but if it can be done I think it's good. The reason why there is this proliferation of directions is because, as I say, I'm not writing dialogue that was spoken by real people for actors to try to imitate; I'm writing a line to be said by an actor on a stage. And it seems reasonable that the actor should be given every opportunity of knowing exactly what I wanted. What I wanted isn't necessarily the best thing for me to get, and the actor may say, 'No, no, you're quite wrong about that line, I have a better way of doing it,' but I see no harm in his knowing.

So it's unlikely in your case to come to the sort of situation which was reported when Harold Pinter was rehearsing The Lover *and he said, 'We're not quite sure of the author's intention here'!*

That's a delightful story, and very typical of Harold – no, I don't think you'll be likely to hear the author here say that, but I suspect there probably are moments when it's true!

SEPTEMBER

1963

History Revitalised

Peter Roberts reviews Henry VI *and* Edward IV *at Stratford*

The Wars of the Roses, the umbrella title under which Peter Hall has grouped Shakespeare's first historical tetralogy, will soon be occupying the Royal Shakespeare Theatre for an entire day. With the three parts of *Henry VI* divided between morning and afternoon matinées, capped with *Richard III* as the evening offering, theatregoers will be spending some seven and a half hours in the auditorium caught up in an historical marathon they might have been expected to brave with a stout heart and a strong bladder. But those who gathered last month for the first five-hour sprint, when the *Henry VI* plays were run over matinée and evening performances, had a heartening report for the eventual all-the-day-long visitors. Even those wilting souls, who feared their curiosity at seeking Shakespeare's prentice hand at work might be swiftly exhausted by a rag-bag of medieval alarums and excursions carried out by characters with no more character and a good deal less poetry than their place-name titles – even these wilting few appeared to be staggered at the cumulative effect of seeing the three plays at one double sitting. Douglas Seale's two-day version at the Old Vic five or six years ago had pointed the way, but this one-day edition clinches the argument that it is only by seeing the plays together that their integration becomes apparent and only then can a modern audience grasp (in the theatre) Shakespeare's masterly marshalling of the incidents that piled up in the half-century from 1422 to 1472. It wasn't indeed a tangled web of battlefield encounters that Shakespeare wove when first he practised to deceive the Elizabethans with that adroit piece of royal public relations, the Tudor Myth. 'You've never had it so good. Life's better under the Tudors – don't let the Plantagenets or Lancastrians ruin it' might be taken as the plays' message at the purely public relations level. But, of course, the plays are much more than this. They are not Chronicle plays. They are not Miracle plays. They are not History plays. They are an amalgam of all three and, like everything else Shakespeare wrote, they tower above anything else that had been produced at the time in the same field.

In view of this it is really rather surprising that whilst English audiences gladly sit for four nights in a row at *The Ring* to have Wagner's windy deliberations on Teutonic mythology bellowed at them, they have not previously been persuaded to give like attention to their own poet's (by comparison) succinct treatment of English history. There *may* be much in the political outlook of these plays that is unsympathetic to the modern theatregoer. The reactionary view that everybody has his place in society and should jolly well know how to keep it, *may* not find much of an echo today in a democracy which is continually encouraging its members to be one up on their neighbours. And the smug self-

David Warner as Henry VI

esteem of the model citizen, Iden, who hands over Jack Cade to his King ('I seek not to wax great by others' waning . . . Sufficeth that I have maintains my state and sends the poor well pleased from my gate') *may* have a bourgeois complacency that is equally repugnant to the moderns. But – and this is a very big but – this view of history, coloured, distorted and even invented – does make a living experience out of what would otherwise be a colossal dump of dates, battles and rulers. And seeing this living experience through at one sitting does throw an extra dimension of time over even the most superficially drawn characters. For every hour that we watch them they live through a decade and we leave them our feelings bruised by their rude experience of life.

Peter Hall's production and John Barton's edited version of the plays have the three virtues of Faith, Hope and Clarity. The Faith and Hope stem from the belief and optimism in the ability of the original plays to hold a modern audience. John Barton's editing of the plays in consequence is no ham-fisted bowdlerisation but a delicate piece of reconstruction involving some perfectly executed invisible mending in which Shakespeare is deftly patched with Shakespeare and any loose ends that might result from trimming are consequently carefully threaded into the narrative flow. As a result the whole of *Part I, Henry VI* is satisfactorily gone through by the first interval, the only big omissions being Talbot's extraordinary encounter with the Countess of Auvergne and Joan la Pucelle's equally strange encounter with the defecting Duke of Burgundy. And by the time the matinée is over we are well into the fourth act of *Part II, Henry VI* with the double deaths of Suffolk and Beaufort, leaving the evening open for Jack Cade and the following internal dissension in England's sickly kingdom. But of these three virtues, Faith, Hope and Clarity – Clarity is the greatest. Shakespeare was fortunate in that it was for him up to a point ready-made in as far as he could rely on contemporary audiences lapping up the minutiae of royal goings on, such as York's (deleted) family-tree speech in 2 *Henry VI* ('Edward the Third, my lords, had seven sons,' etc). This information was relished just as modern readers of Crawfie devour the under-the-palace-stairs revelation of modern royal nannies. But time has removed Edward III and his progeny from the titillating realms of gossip to the text-book world of history and the process of ready identification has become difficult enough to require the utmost clarity in presentation on the part of the director.

A first impression that this might be achieved through a crude form of labelling ('H V' was thoughtfully embroidered on the drape covering Henry V's coffin) proved to be untrue. The French and English were not dressed in contrasting costumes, like members of opposing football teams, nor were 'country' or 'foreign' accents used as a short cut to identification. True, a map of France was flown down at the back of each French scene, but it contributed to the overall atmosphere and feel of the scene too. True, Peggy Ashcroft as Margaret of Anjou lisped her 'r's – but no actress of her experience saddles herself with anything of that kind if it is to become a liability. No, it wasn't labelling but good company playing that brought about immediate identification – who could confuse Roy Dotrice's Bedford with John Welsh's Gloucester, Nicholas Selby's Beaufort with John Hussey's Suffolk,

Brewster Mason's Warwick with Clifford Rose's Exeter – bickering noblemen though they all are?

The clarity arises also from the very fine integration of direction, design (John Bury) and music (Guy Wolfenden). Mr Bury's sets, coming after the aggressive modernity and nudity of earlier productions in the Royal Shakespeare's repertoire this season, mark a return to a stylised realism; costumed supers shifting the props on an adaptable set with two ingenious lateral walls doing duty as anything from town wall to city gate. The medieval feel is vividly conveyed especially in the leathery costumes giving way in the final analysis to an overall impression of metal – the metal of the swords that dominate the warring of the plays and which is echoed in Guy Wolfenden's musical effects. Indeed, most of the fighting is relegated to musical representation, so that instead of being presented with the ultimately comic spectacle of hordes of sweaty actors convulsed in a succession of Douglas Fairbanks sword fights, the thrust and parry is ominously represented by musical sound – complementing a visual impression of a few silhouetted figures in battle.

The immediate result of this easy grasp of character, place and person is that the plot on a purely superficial narrative level becomes gripping. In an atmosphere of double dealing and intrigue the audience is waiting with not a little fascination to see who will stab who in the back next, and whose is the next head to roll. But it is on the epic level that the production finally makes the grade. The whole gamut of medieval society rises up out of the text writhing agonisingly in the grip of something that is bigger than itself. The Father who has killed his Son and the Son who has killed his Father are mere pawns in their country's strife. Henry, the bookish king, is in the grip of a situation he is temperamentally unable to control. And the bickering Lancastrians and Plantagenets in the delusion of gaining their own ends are mere agents for the working out of the ancestral curse, consequent upon the slaughter of the Lord's Anointed, Richard II.

When plays are performed so rarely as these, there is little opportunity to compare performances. One does, however, remember Barbara Jefford at the Old Vic as being a more immediately dynamic Margaret of Anjou than Peggy Ashcroft – but, if memory serves, nothing like as varied in performance. The extraordinary thing about Ashcroft's performance is its development. The young bride brushing aside with a girlish gesture the embarrassment of her dowry-less arrival in England; the foreign queen tentatively sitting at a remote corner of her husband's council chamber; the dominating partner fighting his battles; the stricken mother deprived of her own child – all these facets are there and they seem to grow inevitably one from the other. Henry VI, played by David Warner as slender, gangling youth, is a finely executed study but Mr Warner will have to make more of his later scenes, particularly the soliloquy on the Yorkshire battlefield, to deserve the almost hysterical praise he has received. Roy Dotrice's lady-killer Edward IV is a beautiful foil to this hesitant Henry and Ian Holm's embryo Richard III shows every promise of existing outside the long shadow cast by the Olivier Richard. The most underpraised performance has been Janet Suzman's tough performance in Shakespeare's unchivalrous portrait of Joan of Arc.

171

But one could go on indefinitely about performances, as indeed about the production. The important thing about these *Henry VIs* is that they are certain to bring about as fundamental a reappraisal of the plays in performance as Tillyard has brought about for them in the study.

OCTOBER
1963

Anti-Climax

Peter Roberts reviews Richard III *at Stratford-on-Avon*

Rarely has a first night audience assembled in such a corporate spirit of confidence as the history-happy group which waited last month for the lights to go up on the Stratford *Richard III*. This production was to complete John Barton and Peter Hall's extraordinarily successful *Wars of the Roses* cycle and all that seemed necessary and appropriate was to applaud the Royal Shakespeare Company to the winning post on the last and presumably easiest lap of the trilogy. The two earlier *Henry VI* productions had taken the company over the uphill climb of the unfamiliar plays so triumphantly that the final jog home amongst the dearly beloved villainies of Richard Crookback seemed an inevitable walk-over. Yet the chance of crowning the chronicle of the first half century of the Wars with a final piercing account of their closing 25 years was frustratingly muffed. And the frustration was all the more keenly felt because the production only narrowly missed its mark due to a number of minor set-backs, some of them temporary.

Wrenched from its context as the summing up of all that had gone before in the cycle, *Richard III* becomes, admittedly, an easier play to win over an audience with. Alone, it is less a play about England and the implications of her return to (a Tudor) salvation and more a dark comedy about a merry hunch-backed villain whose sardonic humour has been played with varying degrees of success and psychological motivation. The fact that Ian Holm's Richard at Stratford is not only physically smaller than any of the Richards we have seen, but is also drawn on a scale that subordinates the character to the overall pattern of the four plays of the cycle is a measure of its rightness. Commentators have foolishly invoked the Olivier Richard in order to take a stick to Holm's – but the Olivier Richard, brilliant though it was, belonged to a different sort of production, a production where Richard's opponents were mere puppets and not powerful retributive forces. Now Holm's Richard, besides being smaller and conceived with less of a flourish, is also more a person and less a part. Twisted in mind as well as in body, his devilish behaviour compensates not only for his unattractive appearance to women but also, if I interpret Mr Holm aright, for his impotence in dealing with them as bedfellows. He can deceive himself about his limitations as long as he is successful in his grotesque wooing of Anne Neville, but begins to crumple when she proves, not unnaturally, a barren bride. By the time he is manoeuvring to secure himself a second wife by exactly the same means of flattery he had gained his first, Richard is a desperate man whose self-deception and self-esteem are vanishing and whose impetus and grasp are consequently sinking into a decline. The twitches, grimaces and growing wildness with which Mr Holm hints at this

Opposite: Eric Porter as Richmond and Ian Holm as Richard III

interpretation are nicely managed without any recourse to an orgy of delirium tremens which sometimes passes for great acting in paranoiac roles. Even so, on the opening night, Mr Holm's grasp of the part was not uniformly secure and three-quarters through the verse seemed to be carrying him instead of the other way round. But he recovered his grip towards the end and his final encounter with Richmond was truly horrifying.

But Holm's grasp of the title role was not the only thing that was imperfectly sustained on the opening night. Many of Peter Hall's scenes were beautifully staged. Many more were not. Among the more successful was the wooing of Anne Neville over the coffin of Henry VI. Usually the improbability, not to say absurdity, of this scene is glossed over with an uneasy naturalism. Mr Hall boldly takes the bull by the horns, exposing the bleeding corpse over which the two converse, thereby making out of the grotesqueness of the encounter its very strength. Among the less successful scenes were those with the two cocky little Princes. Precociousness in stage children, heaven knows, is difficult enough to bear in prose, but in blank verse it becomes insupportable.

Worse, because it goes on for much longer, is the metallic crunch of army boots that sets in on the production as Richard assumes power. Its introduction is clearly intended to suggest that under Richard England became a police state of the kind that this century has also known well. But this point could have been made less insistently and the audience might have been credited with enough gumption to work out modern parallels for themselves. As it is, the relentless crunch of army boots, with all its modern associations of two World Wars, shatters the beautiful medieval feel that John Bury's sets and costumes had so finely achieved. And by the time we see them in *Richard III* these sets and costumes have acquired a cumulative hypnotic effect arising from associations we have of them with characters in the earlier plays. A sensitive spectator had no need of Shakespeare's ghost parade to be reminded of the generation of courtiers, now dead, who had used these same chairs and tables and died in this same Tower. Their shadows lurked in every corner – at least when the crunching of modern martial feet allowed the imagination free rein.

When on the few occasions the production seemed to be slipping apart and the interest level in the audience noticeably declined, Peggy Ashcroft as Margaret, sole survivor from the first *Henry VI* play, put the pieces together again and sent the excitement shooting up to fever pitch. Dishevelled, with gnarled hands and shapeless body, she is the physical and spiritual ruin of Henry's young bride and later his strong-willed warrior. Reduced here to the role of a cursing Cassandra foretelling the doom of all in sight, the part makes tremendous technical demands on an actress and it is fascinating, when possible, to stand outside Ashcroft's performance and watch her at work. A brief curse in the theatre can be dramatic but it is difficult to make pages of them sound interesting, let alone spine-chilling. The effectiveness of Ashcroft's variations in pitch, tone, speed, rhythm and pace have to be heard to be believed. Though I still have a minor reservation about the plumminess of the Ashcroft vowels (why does she say 'they where' when she means 'they were'?) I have nothing but the highest praise for her performance in these plays. It is the work of a great actress in the prime of her powers and only a fool will allow himself to miss it.

It would be nice to be able to write as enthusiastically about the rest of the company, but on the first night the company seemed tired. It had, after all, just completed a mammoth production we shall be talking about years hence.

1963 Awards

Chosen by the London Theatre critics
Best new play: *Next Time I'll Sing To You* by James Saunders
Best performance: Alec Guinness as Ionesco's King Bérenger
Best production: *The Wars of the Roses*

This month Plays and Players sees in the New Year by making the first of its annual awards for the Best New Play, Best Performance and Best Production seen in the year that is over. Thirteen of London's theatre critics have been invited to cast their votes for these awards, and though some have not found it easy to boil down the experience of twelve months' theatregoing into what are necessarily three very simple categories the voting has been conclusive. Two new plays,

four performances and two productions quickly established themselves as standing out from the rest of the theatre of the year. Rolf Hochhuth's *The Representative* was given two votes as against one each for other plays, but the Best Play Award goes to James Saunders' *Next Time I'll Sing to You*, voted for by three critics. Michael Redgrave and Rosemary Harris were both given two votes for their performances in *Uncle Vanya* at the National Theatre, but Alec Guinness as King Bérenger in *Exit the King* gained a third, conclusive vote for the Best Performance Award. As David Warner's performance as Henry VI in *The Wars of the Roses*, given two votes, has been especially praised, a Best New Actor Award is being given this year. Two votes went to Olivier's production of *Uncle Vanya*, four to Joan Littlewood's *Oh What a Lovely War* and a conclusive five to Peter Hall's *The Wars of the Roses*.

Above: Hochhuth's *The Representative* with, right, Alec McCowen. Below: Michael Redgrave

1964

The year Lyndon Johnson was returned as US President, the British Electorate gave the Labour Party and Prime Minister Wilson a majority of four, Khrushchev resigned and power passed in Russia to Brezhnev and Kosygin. Cassius Clay became the World Heavyweight Boxing Champion.

In Britain the BBC opened a second TV channel, BBC2. Five new Universities were founded. The Windmill Theatre which boasted that it never closed, closed. Topless dresses were seen on the streets of London. Theatrical highlights were the opening of Osborne's Inadmissible Evidence *and Peter Shaffer's* The Royal Hunt of the Sun.

1964

Private Experiment – in Public

Peter Brook's RSC season at the LAMDA theatre of surrealistic vaudeville inspired by Artaud and undertaken with Charles Marowitz laid the foundations for the Marat/Sade. Simon Trussler went to interview Brook.

Mr Brook, what is your attitude as a director towards Artaud's theories?

I believe that to make the first attempt by a permanent company at very experimental work, we have to define for ourselves why experiment is needed. I feel that in our theatre it is needed more by the director and the actor than by the writer. The reason for this is largely practical – the writer shares the privileges of almost all other artists, and to make experiments all he needs is the wish to experiment, imagination and very cheap materials – pencil and paper for the writers, sketchbook and pencil for the painter, or piano and a pair of hands for the composer. The writer of plays is largely in the same position of absolute freedom – if he wishes to make an experiment he can sit at home and turn the theatre of his mind into a semi-realised form on a scrap of paper that he can then discard. Now of course for this to become concrete, that writer should be working with actors and directors and his vision should take concrete form.

This is the ideal situation. Actually, at this moment there are in existence in England, in France, in America, a lot of texts by writers who have gone a considerable way in tackling problems *on paper*, which they have partially resolved from their end, but which no theatre company in the world is yet truly qualified to resolve from *their* end. Let's take for an example Genet: he is very much an *avant-garde* experimental writer, but he's not as utterly and completely way-out as a writer like Vautier, who has reduced language to monosyllables and has written plays that are like ballets and symphonies – just the making of sound patterns. Now Genet has evolved over the years a very complex dramatic technique which calls upon all the resources of many different and often conflicting theatre traditions, from the Japanese theatre to naturalism – and there are aspects of all these in that particular many-levelled form of writing.

This kind of synthesis is very far from Artaud's belief that the whole Western idea of theatre was wrong, and that we should return to the Oriental concepts . . .?

I don't believe that there is a possible theatre today that is *not* a theatre of synthesis. To me the direction of the theatre and the direction that I want to explore is one that in one way or another has always interested me – something that I was exploring a long time ago, in *Salome,* and in different forms in *Titus Andronicus* and in *Lord of the Flies.* It is a field in which ritual and what one calls outside reality completely overlap: and this is the world of Genet. He is a symbolic and poetic writer, yet in *The Screens* he is writing a play that is at the same time an epic about the Algerian war. He creates (in the same way that John Arden or Samuel Beckett created) a stage image – a structure of stage behaviour and attitudes whose meanings can be read off continually in different and complementary and contradictory ways. *Hamlet,* too, is more than anything else a stage *construction,* which can be read and re-read in performance and always yield new meanings, yet never in itself changing – which is, I think, the essence of a structure and the essence of a ritual.

There are very few actors anywhere in the world qualified to understand how, within a virtually naturalistic framework which passes at times into what one can call an epic framework, there

can suddenly take place an Artaud-like ceremony. Few actors exist who can take that in their stride, and certainly no group of actors each one understanding what the others are doing and being able to respond in shifting styles.

All this would rather suggest that you will have to exert as director a very firm control over this experiment. Is this in fact so?

Well, no, because Charles Marowitz and I have felt for a long time that we wanted first of all to create a group, then experiment with the group, so that as a unit they could acquire the same freedom towards different styles (through firsthand experience) that the writer can enjoy sitting at home. Consequently the first step is to create this unit, by giving the group experiences and exercises that blend it together and make it supple, ready to respond to certain challenges. Now we've got eight weeks of preparation and in this time one cannot tackle a really demanding play like *The Screens*, and to tackle any less demanding play isn't at the moment our function. I feel that there should certainly be in London a theatre doing what the last Stratford season did at the Arts, presenting plays like *Afore Night Come* and *The Empire Builders* and so on, but those aren't our terms of reference. We want to create a *common language*, creating certain possibilities for both actors and directors, working and gathering experience *at the same time*. For this we are using a whole lot of very varied material – some of it worked up by ourselves, some pulled out of

Cruelty in the making: Charles Marowitz, seated, and Peter Brook

Cruelty in action at LAMDA, above, with
masks; opposite, with Glenda Jackson

its context and we are experimenting in many different directions
at once. Actually, these directions are related, to us, but I think a
member of the audience will take away conflicting impressions – a
bit of science fiction, a bit of *Hamlet*, a bit of movement, a bit of
prose patter, a bit of Jarry, a bit of Artaud.

*You do after all describe the programme as a surrealist vaude-
ville . . .*

Yes; but we also want to make out of the evening a programme
which conforms to certain inherent rules – though these have to
be *read*, they aren't explicit. I mean, we could come forward and
say, 'You are now going to see an experiment on such-and-such
lines . . .' and once or twice we *are* going to do just that. But we
hope it will be more interesting to the audience to get this out of
the juxtapositions; and so why one can call this a surrealist revue
is because we are putting together fragments into a collage. I'd
say the real images are mobile ones, we're hanging pieces of
different shapes and sizes on to a lot of different wires, though
they are all literally hung from the same ceiling. That's what will
swing past the audience!

*Within this framework, then, the actors are going to have
considerable freedom of approach?*

Well, I'd like to start in a negative way by saying what I'm *not*
doing. There have been a number of attempts to make the actor
completely flexible, and he's given a variety of work in different
styles for this purpose – so that if he plays with a mask in

eighteenth-century costume, every part of his body takes on the appropriate stylistic qualities.

Now we are putting the actor in situations where, for instance, he has to take his first impulse and turn it maybe into pure sound like an Artaud cry, maybe into formal gesture, maybe into a leap, maybe (as in *The Screens* itself) into rushing up to a sheet of white paper and attacking it with paint. What we are *trying* to bring about is for the actor, in making his choice, to make it as an independent, responsible creative artist. Instead of turning his impulses into one of the many forms that are already there (so that his choice fits into the form that he has learnt to appreciate and assimilate), here his responsibility is to transcend his first naturalistic impulse, and then he has to manifest the best expressive choice, in a way that he can afterwards defend as being to the limit of his consciousness. Funnily enough, what the actor first wants to do in an improvisation is only superficially his first idea: when he realises this, in a Zen-like way he can find an even quicker expression, one in which he is operating as an *artist*, not in accordance with his trained reflexes.

To relate this to one other thing: I think it's our job today to discover how we can make any contemporary theatre event as bold and dense as an Elizabethan event could be, facing the fact that the blank-verse device which the Elizabethans used no longer fits, and that we have to find something else. We're exploring what can take the place of blank-verse in the theatre: that is really the simplest summing-up of what we are doing.

Artaud believed that this boldness and density could only be achieved by a complete involvement of the audience in a total theatrical spectacle. One recalls his vision of a theatre in which the audience was surrounded on all sides by the action. Are you going to explore this kind of solution?

Yes: all I can say is that what we want to do in the course of the evening is to reopen the question from *all* the points of view that strike us at the moment. Some attempts have been made. In one respect I've been experimenting myself a number of years to try to bring *musique concrète* into the theatre. And there are the attempts to use still or moving projections – mostly, to me, disastrous attempts! But they have all been trying to find a twentieth century language that can expand the single moment, so that more can be packed densely into it. The element of staging exists purely in relation to reopening these questions.

By *asking* the questions, we hope to weld the group of actors into a special sort of fighting force. Our main hope in this particular experiment is that it will have the right sort of provocative *professional* effect – and this is different to what Artaud was doing. His aim was infinitely larger, and would relate to something that we can't attempt to get at once, which was to have that effect on *life*.

But would you accept this as an ultimate *aim?*

I think that everything has to develop organically in its own way, and I can't believe that in 1964 organic development in the direction we are taking will end exactly where Artaud left off. Actually, I think that the nearest thing to an Artaud theatre we have had was the Brecht theatre – its achievement was certainly often quite different from Brecht's own analyses of it. What he

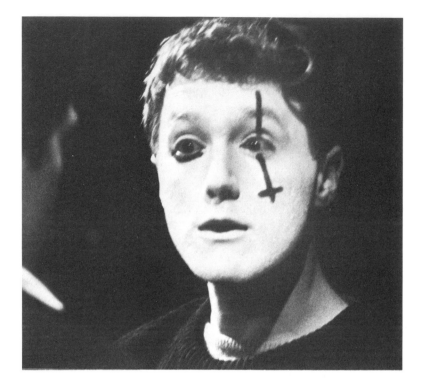

Experimental make-up for the *Theatre of Cruelty* season

was actually doing in his best work as a director was creating forms and rituals, and in his most remarkable work you can read off many levels of meaning. Like any great realistic work on life, there is obviously a strong social level: but Brecht, by being both writer and director, could also create a completely formal structure; which had as complete an existence as a play of Shakespeare's has on the printed page. The contradiction that was thrown up at Edinburgh between the Committed Theatre and the Theatre of the Absurd is a false one, based on the minor figures of both sides: but the proper theatre represents the true creative area where the two become one and the same thing.

Although Brecht and Artaud are approaching the thing from different theoretical angles, in practice they meet?

I wouldn't say they *meet*, but I'd say they are closer than one can easily imagine. Incidentally, we are doing the only play that Artaud ever wrote, *The Spurt of Blood*, which lasts three minutes. His only piece of dialogue . . .

I did read the scenario for his Conquest of Mexico. *This you feel is outside the scope of your experiment?*

To do that, perhaps, one would need the subsidy of the National Theatre and the stage of Drury Lane!

But isn't that what one feels a lot of the time with Artaud's theoretical writings, that they are so totally divorced from any conceivable theatrical reality?

Yes – well, Artaud *was* a madman. But this carries with it all forms of lucidity. So he was more lucid and also *righter* on more theatre subjects than a lot of saner people.

This – some of our best-loved critics notwithstanding – is a very bad play. But it is a fascinating human document. Why is it a bad play? Above all because it fails to lay the indispensable foundation for any drama in this, the realistic, convention: it fails to establish a credible central character. We are told Bill Maitland is a solicitor. It is hardly possible to believe that he could ever have managed to pursue this profession for one year, let alone for a couple of decades. We see him receive four clients. In each case he deals with them by letting them tell him their story (to which he quite obviously pays no attention whatever) after which, far from dispensing any advice or taking any action, he bundles them out of his office. Admittedly, we are shown Bill Maitland in the final phase of his breakdown. But even in the sorry state he is in, if he had ever exercised the profession, he would at least have acquired the *routine*, the mask, of professional competence; it would have become second nature to him to act *like* a solicitor even while his mind was a complete blank.

Secondly: this purports to be a play about a man in the process of breaking down. To make that process moving or interesting we ought to be given a glimpse of what that man was like *before* he broke down; or rather, we shan't be very moved about his downfall, unless we felt that there *was* a '*noble mind*' to be '*o'erthrown*'. Here we get nothing of the sort. We are made to understand that Bill Maitland has always been the same randy, incompetent, ranting and thoroughly unsympathetic character he is in the hour of his breakdown. He insists that he has never been very good at the law, that his only virtue was a certain quickness of mind, that he has always relied on other people. He was, in short, *bound* to come to a bad end; and now he *is* coming to a bad end. Incredibly late in the day in view of his incompetence – see above; yet one is merely compelled to ask: what of it? No sympathy having been aroused, there is very little to be sorry about.

Thirdly: no credible relationships between the hero – or anti-hero – and the other characters emerge. We see Bill Maitland being left, one by one, by his secretary, chief clerk, telephonist, articled clerk, his daughter and his mistress. They all leave him within twenty-four hours, and yet they must have known all along what he was like; nothing whatever happens to precipitate this deluge of desertions. The secretary at least informs him that she is pregnant (not by him) and that she wants to give up work. There at least is a motivation. But his chief clerk seems to have known for many years that he was suborning witnesses and seducing his office staff. Why should he leave the very same day that Maitland's attractive and intelligent mistress decides to walk out (in whose infatuation for him it is quite impossible to believe; she would not have been able to stand that stupid emotional ranter for five minutes, if she is as charming and sensible a girl as Sheila Allen makes her, let alone for the long period that is here suggested).

Certainly not a good play then. Of course it has its moments of effective rhetoric, the famous vituperative eloquence that carried other plays by the same author, notably the historically and psychologically puerile and moreover ill-constructed *Luther*, to box office success. John Osborne can probably claim to be the

Fascinating Document

Martin Esslin reviews Inadmissible Evidence *at the Royal Court*

Inadmissible Evidence in rehearsal: right,
Nicol Williamson as Maitland, opposite,
Sheila Allen, director Anthony Page, Nicol
Williamson and author John Osborne

finest writer of letters signed 'Disgusted' of all time; he can
complain about dirty trains and the deplorable habit of British
drivers of having mascots in the rear windows of their cars, with a
fiery sweep of a Cicero indicting Catilina. The speech in which
Bill Maitland sums up his disgust with, and envy of, present-day
teenagers, when his daughter visits him (she can't get a single
word in edgeways, poor girl) contains material for several hundred
letters to the local press, ammunition for battalions of
'Disgusteds'.

A bad play, but a fascinating human document. What is it all
about? That it is not about a middle-aged solicitor having a
nervous breakdown, is evident enough. It is an outburst of disgust
and guilt. That is also evident enough. Disgust with present-day
life in this country? It seems so. It has even been suggested that
Bill Maitland might be a symbol for present-day Britain: mediocre, incompetent, lazy, about to break down . . . after all, Archie
Rice in *The Entertainer* was fulfilling a similar function, and so
was Jimmy Porter's father-in-law in *Look Back in Anger*. There is
something in this view, certainly, but it cannot hold water at closer
examination: there are so many elements that won't fit in; the
randiness above all, the seductions and marital quarrels make it
clear that Maitland cannot stand for a collective concept, not even
for a way of life. Although he is not an individual in the sense of
being a credible human being, he is a mouthpiece for an individual's disgust. He is as angry as Jimmy Porter ever was, as despicable
as Archie Rice, as blindly rebellious as Osborne's Luther (not
history's – who knew perfectly well what he was for and against).
All these characters are channels through which this self-same
torrent of abuse, disgust and anger rages (the same disgust that
pervades John Osborne's angry outbursts in the newspapers as
well).

And what are all these characters so angry about, so disgusted
with? The state of England clearly – the Sunday papers and their

readers, the complacent people in their little cars with mascots, the greyness of the skies, the shoddiness of life in general, the class system – or rather upper class accents (poor Jones, Bill Maitland's apprentice, gets a packet of abuse; what for? Poor fellow he seems to have been to Oxbridge. No other reprehensible trait is adduced, except that he runs a scooter and wants to get married, yet he is treated by Maitland (and presented by Osborne) as a dead loss, barely human – just because he speaks with that accent!). Already in the case of Jimmy Porter there was some bewilderment at the shallowness of this *critique* of England. It was rightly said that Jimmy Porter was angry without knowing quite clearly what he was angry about. With Archie Rice Osborne succeeded in raising the angry character to the status of a valid symbol. With Bill Maitland we are back to blind anger without a target that would, at first sight at least, deserve such emotional intensity.

Bill Maitland raves and rants at the state of England – but the audience is left in no doubt that in fact he is not disgusted with the people in the Mini-cars so much as with *himself. His anger at England is merely an outward projection of his self-disgust:* his disgust about being a mediocre intellect, a man, who (unlike his mistress's father) is incapable of conceptual thought, his inability to achieve sexual fulfilment, which leads him to try again and again with ever new objects of desire; his guilt which is merely the reverse side of the puritanism he still carries within his subconscious because he is not strong minded and intelligent enough to exorcise it by conscious thought, his dependence on other people, his awareness of the fact that being unable to love he cannot really be loved by others and will therefore always be in imminent danger of being 'disowned' (as his own phrase puts it that goes through the play like a *leitmotiv*). This self-disgust is the dynamo – for it is of tremendous intensity and force – that drives the torrent of anger which gives the play its wild eloquence, its semblance of poetic force. And yet – impotent disgust, unallied with intellectual perception and analysis that might lead to positive action rather than mere ineffectual vituperation, is on the whole an unedifying spectacle. It certainly cannot produce *catharsis* in Aristotle's sense, nor *insight* in Brecht's.

The performance, under Anthony Page's direction, is wholly admirable. The dream sequence with which the play opens (and which is quite unnecessary, no more than a fairly patent device to enable the hero to state his name and professional and marital status directly) is rightly haunting with the dream-judge's eyes shining eerily in the dark. Clare Kelly, who plays the three ladies

185

seeking divorce (why these three characters should be played by the same actress never becomes clear) differentiates them cleverly and is most touching in the first episode. John Quentin is excellent as the apprentice solicitor and very moving as the client in trouble for homosexuality (again there is no possible explanation why these parts should be doubled; otherwise – why are the various mistresses not played by the same actress? That at least would be consistent). And the story he has to tell is sensitively written; it merely does not fit into this play.

Ann Beach is splendid as always; Arthur Lowe a real solicitor's chief clerk, a thousand times more credible than his employer. Lois Dane portrays the telephone girl with complete conviction. And Sheila Allen as the mistress is far too beautiful, intelligent and sensible ever to have got mixed-up with Bill Maitland.

Nicol Williamson is the anti-hero. He gives a memorable performance, eloquent, varied, full of imaginative touches. A mammoth achievement. My only quibble is that he does not, he cannot look like a credible solicitor. In fact, to me he looks much more like an actor.

Skeleton at a Feast?

Hay Fever *at the Old Vic is reviewed by Hugh Leonard*

A horrifying evening. And straight off let me say that *Hay Fever* is a gem in its wholly limitable way, that Noël Coward directs it in the manner of one who has seen a hundred previous productions and has welded the best from each into a stylish unit, and that the Old Vic cast was not only stellar but, by and large, highly talented. Yet I hope that the newly deified Mr Coward, who sat at the back of the dress circle looking like the 13th Caesar, was as repelled by his second-night audience as I was. But one mustn't be unreasonable; it is not the business of writers of comedies to look gift hysteria in the mouth, and it is a maxim among authors that there is no such thing as an undeserved laugh.

In the case of *Hay Fever*, the audience roared like a demented Silavent from rise to fall of curtain. A race seemed to be in progress: one sat with ears a-quiver, waiting for the intake of breath which heralded an actor's imminent dive in search of a laugh – sometimes like a seal going after a mackerel – and the trick was to beat him to the punchline with a premature guffaw. Even throwaway lines were greeted with howls of mirth; the slightest item of stage business drew rounds of applause; while Edith Evans' song, rendered *à la* Louis Armstrong and calculated to cause confusion at nearby Waterloo Station, was received with a rapture usually reserved for such demi-gods as Malcolm Sargent and Godfrey Winn. In fact, never in the course of theatrical history has so little been applauded by so many for so long.

If I seem like a skeleton at a feast, the reason is that *Hay Fever* simply isn't *that* funny. The audience, I will swear, laughed from start to finish because of an acute awareness that they were sitting in the National Theatre, the putative home of definitive drama, watching a play, which they have been told repeatedly across the years is the last word in hilarity, enacted by a glossy cast, comprised of two stars and several meteorites. This self-consciousness is a cross which the National Theatre will have to bear as best they can; the horror of becoming fashionable is that the virtues and vices of a play are distorted by the fog of adoration and self-congratulation which befouls the auditorium. If the company can work in this atmosphere, then more luck to them; certainly it is fascinating, in a grisly sense, to see a mausoleum in the making.

Hay Fever concerns itself with a family of four non-conformists (who dress for dinner, however), each one of whom is counterbalanced by a weekend guest from the world outside. From an acting viewpoint, the visitors came out of the proceedings more creditably than the home team. There was Maggie Smith, for instance, as the *femme fatale* whose femininity grows less fatal as the weekend wears on. Miss Smith possesses an angularity which is temperamental no less than physical; she seems to *belong* to the 1920s. Her timing is impeccable. For the most part, she regards her ill-mannered hosts with a deadpan balefulness, but her right hand is the giveaway: it wields her cigarette-holder and handbag like a rapier and a mace, respectively, seemingly owing not the slightest allegiance to the parent body. This was a superb performance. I liked, too, Robert Lang's diplomat, game for anything and wandering to and fro, body inclined gently forward as if in anticipation of something nice just around the next corner. Lynn Redgrave's flapper lacked technique, but was dead right from an instinctive point of view. Miss Redgrave's desperate bid to snatch a tea-cake by stealth was for me one of the high-lights of the evening.

The character of Judith Bliss, we infer, is that of a retired actress of great charm and considerable sex appeal. Edith Evans managed the actress part of it without a bit of difficulty, but was just about as sexy as old boots. Lest I be suspected of being a shoe fetishist, let me clarify: Dame Edith was miscast; when she addressed another character, it was in the tones of Catherine the Great calling for Potemkin; while everyone else was making a soufflé, Dame Edith was cooking cabbage. A surprisingly bad performance, abetted by the approval of an irresponsible audience.

I doubt if *Hay Fever* will survive. Too much of it is a send-up of bad plays of the 1920s; and if the melodramas which it holds up to ridicule are, in time, forgotten, then *Hay Fever* must, of necessity, lose its yardstick. But this was a careful and scrupulous production, beautifully costumed, and with a miracle of perspective visible through the french windows. Mr Coward has the distinction of having created an entire era which possibly never really existed, but is the more fascinating for that reason. I find myself envisaging a play with the same basic situation as that of *Hay Fever*, but set in the 1960s. The pairings-off would be a good deal less innocuous than as indulged in by Mr Coward's characters, and the party games considerably more lethal. But it occurs to me that this later play has already been written. It is called *Who's Afraid of Virginia Woolf?*

1964 Awards

voted for by the London Theatre critics

Best new play: *Inadmissible Evidence* by John Osborne
Best performance by an actor: Nicol Williamson in *Inadmissible Evidence*
Best performance by an actress: Uta Hagen in *Who's afraid of Virginia Woolf?*
Best production: Peter Brook's *Marat/Sade*
Best designer: Michael Annals for *Royal Hunt of the Sun*
Most promising newcomer: Jennifer Hilary

Plays and Players again this year begins the New Year by compiling an Honours List for the one that is over. Twelve of London's theatre critics have voted for what most impressed them in 1964 – the play, the performances, the production, the set and the most promising newcomer.

In many ways 1964 was a lively year – it was a year in which Theatre of Cruelty replaced Theatre of the Absurd as the number one talking point. And it was a year in which English philistinism became unusually vociferous in the theatre with the Aldwych 'dirt plays row' making the front page of the dailies.

The public was treated, in the words of Penelope Gilliatt, to 'the unlovely sight of a powerful pantomime king and a hawker of theatre tickets knifing talented and serious men in the back.' After the storm the public quietly showed its support for talented and serious men by packing the Aldwych – and the National Theatre and the Royal Court.

By and large, though, the critics looking back over the year didn't find it a good one for new plays. But they cast six votes for John Osborne's *Inadmissible Evidence* as Best Play of the year – with three going to Edward Albee's *Who's Afraid of Virginia Woolf?* and one each to Peter Shaffer's *Royal Hunt of the Sun*, John Arden's *Armstrong's Last Goodnight* and James Saunders' *A Scent of Flowers*.

The award for the Best Performance (Actor) was the most closely voted for. Nicol Williamson's performance in *Inadmissible Evidence* received five votes – only one more than the four which went to Olivier's Othello. Robert Stephens came up a close third with three votes for his Atahuallpa in *Royal Hunt of the Sun*. No less than eight different actresses were voted for in the Best Performance (Actress) award which went to Uta Hagen for her performance as Martha in *Who's Afraid of Virginia Woolf?* – with four votes.

The best production was easily decided upon with Peter Brook's *Marat/Sade* collecting ten of the 12 votes. Finally, in a field where the critics agreed there was talent, Michael Annals was voted best designer for his set for *Royal Hunt of the Sun* and Jennifer Hilary was thought to be the Most Promising Newcomer (five votes) with Karin Fernald a close second (four votes).

Performance of the year: Uta Hagen as Martha in *Who's Afraid of Virginia Woolf?* with, above, Arthur Hill and, below, Richard Easton, Arthur Hill and Beverlee McKinsey

1965

The year in which Winston Churchill died and Edward Heath became leader of the Conservative Party in Britain was also the year in which Rhodesia under Ian Smith made its Unilateral Declaration of Independence.

Natural Gas was discovered in the North Sea and London's newest tallest building, the Post Office Tower, was opened.

The mid-sixties bulge in admired new plays continued with the premières of John Arden's Armstrong's Last Goodnight, *Frank Marcus's* The Killing of Sister George, *Osborne's* A Patriot for Me, *Bill Naughton's* Spring and Port Wine, *Pinter's* The Homecoming *and Wesker's* The Four Seasons.

All in the Text

The Royal Hunt of the Sun is reviewed by Martin Esslin

It is quite a good experiment, this: to see a play one missed and to compare the impression given by critics and word-of-mouth repute with one's own reaction. And in this case the test was made more interesting by the transfer from the wide open spaces of the arena stage at Chichester to the more conventional boards of the Old Vic. How much, in fact, did Peter Shaffer's play owe its reputation as a stunning sight, a kind of wide-screen spectacular largely dependent on fantastic costumes and cunningly choreographed movement in the round, to the magic of an open stage?

I personally have no doubt that in fact *The Royal Hunt of the Sun*, greatly though it benefits from excellent design and choreography, is above all a *first rate text:* witty, wise and well written; if it owes much to its being *total theatre* (mime, dance, chanting, ritual) it is the basic conception, the text, which evokes these effects; and the visual effects would be nothing without the text. In other words: to ascribe the success of a play to these elements would be legitimate only if they had been grafted on to a text that lacked and did not evoke them, so that the imagination of a designer or director had to make up for deficiencies in the imagination of the author. (This argument has been very widely – and stupidly – used in connection with Peter Brook's *Marat/Sade* where it is equally inapplicable, for the author of that play is a painter who thinks in visual terms.) And certainly it was Peter Shaffer's imagination that demanded the visual effect of *The Royal Hunt of the Sun*. As Peter Roberts pointed out in his review of the Chichester production this is, in many ways, a Shavian play, very similar in feeling and intellectual atmosphere to *St Joan*. But whereas Shaw's imagination remained largely verbal, here we have a most fruitful combination of Shavian argument and keenness of intellect with the full panoply of Brechtian epic technique: the narrator who introduces his own alter ego as a young boy – a typically Brechtian split-image device, and most effective; the abandonment of naturalistic scenery; the use of mime inspired by Chinese and Indian theatre; the highly effective use of masks; the stress on ritual; the meticulous dating of key scenes which reminds the audience that they are watching an account of history, valid only as a manifestation of past social conditions; all these Brechtian devices are most ingeniously and perceptively employed and Peter Shaffer joins Bolt, Arden and the John Whiting of *The Devils* in the select group of British dramatists who have genuinely benefited from the conception of epic, i.e. narrative, techniques in drama.

The advantages of such techniques for this particular type of subject, the large-scale exploration of a major historical event, are only too obvious. Indeed, it would be well-nigh impossible to do such a subject justice in a more conventionally realistic style. For even if it were treated in a multitude of realistic scenes rather than in the more rigorous structure of a well-made play, the issues involved could not be brought to life without the element of reflection, the juxtaposition of past and present, that the epic convention allows the playwright.

The Royal Hunt of the Sun is by no means perfect: while the two central characters are strong and fully worked out, there is a certain paleness in the characterisation of Pizarro's men, with the consequence that, up to the point at which Pizarro and the Inca

Atahuallpa enter their full confrontation, there are some thin stretches of exposition; even the narrator, Martin Ruiz, in his fascinating double aspect as boy and wise old man, remains somewhat schematic – a brilliant device rather than a completely realised human being. But once the two protagonists are fully engaged all this is forgotten: the play becomes a confrontation of two philosophical concepts, two political systems, and at one and the same time a poignant love story as well as a bitter religious parable. When, in the end, the Inca consents to die for his friend and conqueror, this is an act of supreme sacrifice to a beloved person *and* a daring religious test. And Pizarro's tragedy lies as much in his grief at having killed the one human being he could love as in the shattering of his one chance to gain a religious faith that would bring him escape from the inevitable extinction of time and mortality. That last scene is a truly great and memorable theatrical moment.

The performance is excellent throughout. The first fruits of working together as a permanent company are clearly discernible in the way some of the smaller parts are acted. Michael Turner, for example, does wonders with the small and somewhat pallidly written part of de Soto – a remarkable ensemble performance; or Derek Jacobi as Felippillo, the young comedian of *Hay Fever* utterly transformed into an inscrutable savage with a face straight out of a museum of pre-Colombian archaeology; Robert Lang as the old Martin Ruiz consolidates his claim to be regarded as one of the most skilful character actors now active.

For the two principals, Colin Blakely as Pizarro and Robert Stephens as the Inca, no praise could be too high. How easily Atahuallpa could become a conventional lay-figure, a dressed-up dummy on a float in the Lord Mayor's Show! To infuse human feeling, historical credibility into a character so remote from our experience, so stylised and hieratic, without making him banal or merely declamatory is an achievement of a genuinely creative imagination which, moreover, demands most unusual technical resources of voice, agility and sheer physique: with this performance Robert Stephens establishes his claim to be regarded as one of our major actors, not far off in status from his own director, Sir Laurence himself. Colin Blakely's achievement matches his partner's: behind the gnarled old soldier's rough exterior he suggests, with the subtlest of means, great depths of sensitivity, delicacy, torment – the soul of a poet. A brilliant creation. Set and costumes by Michael Annals and John Dexter's and Desmond O'Donovan's joint production have already received their well-deserved share of praise. They remain fully effective on the Old Vic's stage. All in all, a production of which the National Theatre, and the nation, can be justly proud. It should remain in the repertoire for a very long time.

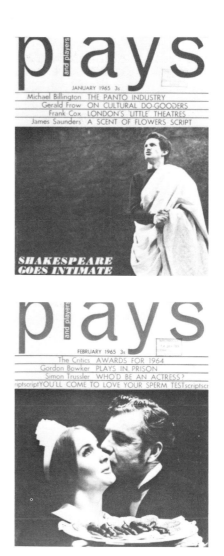

Two Jews at Stratford

Clifford Williams talks to Frank Cox about his productions of The Merchant of Venice *and* The Jew of Malta

Clifford Williams's highly praised production of *The Jew of Malta* opens as the second item of the Royal Shakespeare Company's Stratford season, and barely sixteen hours later is followed by a new production of *The Merchant of Venice*. As well as the influence of Clifford Williams as director, the two productions will have the same designer, Ralph Koltai, the same composer, Guy Woolfenden, and the same leading actor, playing within twenty-four hours the arduous roles of Barabas and Shylock, Eric Porter. Moreover, the two plays will be seen in conjunction throughout the season, sometimes as matinée and evening performances, always placed within easy reach for the visitor to Stratford. What is the significance of this linking of the plays, and what justification is there for such a fusing of two differing works? Between rehearsals in a sunny but as yet uncrowded Stratford, Clifford Williams discussed his attitude to this production:

Clifford Williams's production of *The Jew of Malta* designed by Ralph Koltai

Let me say from the start that originally there was never any intention of making a joint project. When we decided last year to do *The Jew* there were no plans to link it with *The Merchant* and it was only after the success of *The Jew* in London that its inclusion in the Stratford season seemed to tie it up in some ways with the projected *Merchant* revival. One small point – non-Shakespeare plays have always done notoriously badly here; people would apparently rather see a Shakespeare play that they don't even know, than a non-Shakespeare, whatever it might be. However, when it came to the prospect of doing *The Jew* here and also *Merchant* the more justification there seemed to be for recognising at least the basic links between the plays. At first these were pretty self-evident. Both plays were written by contemporaries, both had a Jew hero-villain in the central role, and in both cases the Jew received his 'comeuppance' at the hands of Christians.

But when you consider that Shakespeare had certainly seen Marlowe's play – it was remarkably popular, and there was an approximately seven years gap between the composition of the two, during which it's inconceivable that Shakespeare wouldn't have come across it – then an infinite number of bigger and more important correspondences became clear. Shakespeare cribs lines from Marlowe – Shylock's 'I am not well' for example is an echo of Barabas's 'Me no be well'. He also cribs situations – in both plays the Jew's daughter turns away from her father, and this unhinges him; Barabas's spate of killing and violence stems directly from Abigail's desertion, as does Shylock's determination to exact the forfeiture follow from Tubal's news of Jessica's betrayal. Interestingly both plays have a balcony scene and in both cases the action is that of the daughter lowering jewels to someone on the ground – Abigail to Barabas, Jessica to Lorenzo. In fact, it's no exaggeration to say that Shakespeare plagiarised Marlowe's work piecemeal, and yet the plays are still undeniably different, and naturally so. Give a common subject to Arden and to Wesker and you'll get two very different plays.

That's why it's just as well that there was no long term plan to join the two. If there had been, there would have been a temptation for instance to have one dual purpose set, which would have lessened the force of both works. What we're looking at is not the similarities between them but the differences. When Eric Porter and I began discussing the two parts we visualised the scene in a restaurant with Barabas taking Shylock out to dinner. The contrast between them is easily imagined – Shylock would be the small man, the ordinary man, fanatically zealous in the matter of Jewish food, despised for his appearance, easily spat on, whereas Barabas, though still not liked by the other customers, would command a certain awe. He'd be a spruce, immaculate, a carnation in his button-hole, not too fussy about eating pork if it suited him, liable to make a noise and throw his big-business weight about. The attitude of fellow customers would be markedly different towards him, because when it comes down to it he's got more money, more cars, more ability than any of them. Barabas sits like a king on top of them all – there's no scorn thrown at him. But there's no point in labouring these contrasts at the expense of the plays themselves. The important thing is to recognise both plays for their own special worth, and the links between them are only a small part of that task.

For one thing *The Merchant* has peculiar difficulties for the director today, in as much as it's so well known that every aspect of it has been explored already. It's impossible to find one's own slant on the play without someone observing 'Oh yes, that was done in '54!'. Unlike *Hamlet*, a work so diverse that new ideas of presenting it are limitless, with *The Merchant* there is only a certain amount of digging possible. So what we're trying to do is brainwash ourselves into approaching the play as new, rather than using some single quality in it to illuminate the whole. The result won't necessarily be so revolutionary as a revaluation, but it may lead to a rebalancing of the play, simply by not stressing one particular aspect of it.

And once we acknowledge for ourselves the danger of trying to force the two works into a false mould in order to fit some neat

intellectual pattern, then valuable things emerge from the comparison. Barabas, for instance, the big extrovert who by ignoring little details and failing to obey his own rules brings about his own farcical ruin, helps us to understand Shylock, the ordinary man who finds inside himself the ability to become monstrous. When Shylock comes into that courtroom with his knife, he's fully prepared to carve a chunk of flesh from Antonio's chest, and it takes cold water shock treatment from Portia to jerk him out of this state of mind. But whereas Barabas learns nothing – when he frizzles, all he's aware of is that he's frizzling – Shylock does learn something. At the end of the court-scene he's beginning to glimpse that somewhere he's gone totally off the track. His line 'I am not well' is no gesture of pathos but a dawning of self-realisation.

What we call the trial scene, by the way, is no trial at all. It's more a private hearing in chambers, because Shylock's case is cut and dried. The Duke says as much in his first speech to the Jew, and Portia grants the justice of his claim from the start. In particular, Antonio himself recognises the validity of Shylock's case. Here we come up against the whole economic basis of the plot, which it's important to get into perspective. Borrowing money was an integral part of business transactions and merchants like Antonio would commonly find themselves without ready cash, because whatever money they made would be pumped straight back into new ventures. And because the means to borrow was so vital to the businessman, so the lender was protected right up to the hilt by a system of strict usage, in order that lending could continue. This was established practice throughout the sixteenth century, and it was not uncommon for bargains of the sort struck by Antonio with Shylock to be honoured in the strongest terms. Loss of a hand upon non payment by a certain day was a standard procedure and wholly in accordance with the law of *ius strictum*. Portia's appeal, upon which the issue entirely hinges, bows to this law but cites the new opposing law, use of equity, which protects the borrower by urging give and take, or mercy. The clash is that of the old order with the new, and the tragedy is one of change, for with the Renaissance use of equity became accepted on equal footing with strict usage. What happened to Antonio wouldn't happen to Antonio's son half a century later.

But the most fascinating thing of all is the treatment which Shylock receives at the end of the scene. The lines are exact and unequivocal. Everyone has been carrying on about the two claims, Portia for mercy and Shylock for justice, and Shylock has finally been forced to submit by the literal application of his own argument, an extreme form of *ius strictum*. Now he is obliged to kneel before the Duke and beg for himself the equity which he has been so willing to withhold from Antonio. By the letter of the law his life is forfeit. But the Duke grants him life straight away. As for the half of his goods which the state may confiscate, it is returned on condition that he behaves himself in future. Then Portia invites Antonio's verdict, and Antonio urges the court's permission to put his half of the fine in trust for Shylock's daughter and his son-in-law. This is a time when Jews are forbidden by law to leave their wealth as inheritance to their children. Shylock is stunned and unable to comprehend this compassion, but Antonio has earlier expressed his sympathy for Shylock the businessman, so this bounty is not so incredible. Shylock leaves the court not bent on hanging himself as many a production would suggest, but perhaps with some prospect of rehabilitation from the animal-like state in which he finds himself at the climax of the scene, knife in hand.

The comparison with *The Jew* is unavoidable here, for where Marlowe is perhaps more tuned to present day attitudes with his invitation to us to laugh at the desperate wickedness of the world, Shakespeare's conclusion is one of magnificent banality – that we might do no worse than try to love each other. The last thing I want to suggest is that we're making a deliberate parallel between the two plays or demonstrating that one is better than the other, or more relevant, but correspondences do exist and the plays, though totally different, are yet very close. They show a similar concern with the awful fragmentation of society which, if anything, is worse today than ever before.

Eric Porter, right, as Barabas, the Jew of Malta

Harold Pinter's new full-length play is, as always, at once surprising and inevitable-seeming. It is surprising because in his radio play *The Dwarfs* and in his last three television plays he has seemed to be more and more involved in the progressive fragmentation of human personality and the endless ambiguity of our perceptions. Inevitable because, if he was not to work himself into a complete impasse (drama, like life, depends to a large extent on our readiness to assume, rightly or wrongly, that there is one 'real' reality beyond our infinitely fragmented and distorted perceptions of it), he had sooner or later to put the Humpty-Dumpty of human personality together again. This he began to do in *Tea Party*: the man whose perceptions of the life around him become so confused and ambiguous that he can no longer fit them together into any coherent (even if totally incorrect) picture is, after all, going *mad* – it is not necessarily that in a game of ping-pong he goes to hit two balls because two, or an infinite number of balls are or may be coming at him, but simply that for more or less complex reasons connected with his own mental situation he sees two balls when in fact, 'really', there is only one.

His situation at the end of the play, when he retires into a sort of cataleptic trance in which he cannot see, hear or move, might almost be symbolic of a dramatist's situation when he sees so many mutually exclusive possibilities coexistent in any character or situation that he has to stop even trying to fit them into one coherent dramatic pattern. Such might easily have been Pinter's situation, but at the end of *Tea Party*, significantly, we (and he) are on the outside, looking in: the battle between objective and subjective viewpoints (the party as it really is intercut with the party as he sees it) is ultimately resolved in favour of the objective, and reality is reintegrated with the unfortunate Sisson as odd man out because he has contracted out. So, with a bit of hindsight, it was to be expected that *The Homecoming* would mark the real beginning of a new, 'objective' phase in Pinter's work, and that in

A Pinter Power Struggle

The Homecoming *at the Aldwych reviewed by John Russell Taylor*

Michael Bryant, Terence Rigby and Ian Holm
in *The Homecoming*

fact is just what it does. Compared with what has gone immediately before it is a work of dazzling directness and simplicity. True, it may not be as simple as it seems. The question has been raised: when Teddy, the bright boy of the family, comes home allegedly from America with a woman he alleges to be his wife and talking about three children and a good job teaching philosophy at a university, is he telling the truth? Several critics have assumed, perhaps correctly, or perhaps as a result of knowing too summarily what they expect of Pinter, that there must be a lot more in it than meets the eye.

Is there any truth in Teddy's story, or is it just a convenient fantasy in which he may even believe himself? He shows, for example, a general unwillingness to engage in philosophical chit-chat with his fast-talking brother, on the grounds that the question posed is outside his own field – a reaction which might be thought suspicious, though actually this sort of niggling intellectual demarcation-dispute seems to me more suggestive of a real academic than an impostor. His wife drifts off into reverie whenever she might be embarking on some precise details of their life in America, and so on. So maybe it is all fantasy: I don't know, and I really don't care. It is not a question which the play goes out of its way to raise – in fact I don't think there is any real hint in the play that we should take what is said on the matter at anything but its face value – and even if there is a mystery here it is certain that the secret of the play does not lie in our providing a neat crossword-puzzle solution.

No, the point is that Teddy and his wife come home, and by doing so intensify conflicts which already exist in the household and add one or two of their own. The homecoming is a test of strength for Teddy: having got away from his terrible family and built up his own life, his own family, he comes back to meet his past on its own ground, and finds that nothing has changed. For all his education, his prosperity, his other, settled life, within the charmed circle of the family he is still unable to act: his civilised irony has no effect on anyone; he is a liberal humanist preparing to sit down in protest while the storm-troopers move in and kick him out of the way or, worse still, regard him as too insignificant even to be worth moving.

If the play is about anything other than the interplay of six characters it seems to me that it is about the battle between intellect and instinct, between thought and action. Teddy is the thinker of the family: Max, his ex-butcher father, is a tremendously lively, active, vicious old bastard, consumed with love and hate, but particularly hate; his older brother, Lenny, is brutal, fast-talking, a coarser, more savage version of Mick in *The Caretaker* without Mick's saving grace of not seeming to believe more than half of what he says; his younger brother, Joey, is an unsuccessful boxer, all brawn, very little brain, and hardly a vestige of amiability to go with his stupidity.

Teddy's Uncle Sam is the only one who might occasionally think before he speaks or acts, but this seems to be the principal reason why he says little and does less – and is disregarded by everyone. And as for Teddy's wife, Ruth, well, she is a quintessential Pinter woman, one who thinks with her body and manages better that way than most men do with their brains. She was, we gather, a 'model' (no doubt in the shadier sense of the term) before she married Teddy; she has allowed herself to be made over by him for so long – just as a cat will attach itself, or apparently attach itself, to a new owner – but now she is ready without a second thought to do what her body tells her and go back on the game, managed by and in her spare moments supplying the needs of her husband's family, and thinking with cool confidence only of what conditions she can impose to make the contract best suit her.

Around Ruth and her fate the action of the play crystallises: it is a straight struggle for power without appeal to any authority outside the wills of those involved. There is no moral framework by which what happens can be judged, morality being invoked hardly at all by anyone, and where it is only according to the speaker's whim of the moment – the dead mother of the family may be referred to as a whore or an angel from one breath to the next, but it is all a manner of speaking, and does not presuppose subscription to any hierarchy in which whores are inferior to angels, or indeed noticeably different. In the battle for power naturally the body wins over the mind: the weapons of Teddy and Sam are too feeble to wound Max, Lenny or Joey. But then the man, even when ruled entirely by his body, by instinct, is no

match for the woman who makes no practical distinction between body and mind: it is Ruth finally who dominates Max, Lenny and Joey just as they have dominated Teddy and Sam. And in the part of Ruth, Vivien Merchant is, as ever in Pinter roles, superb: she has just the right feline brand of calculated sensuality, the insidious, inescapable presence and, naturally, a flawless understanding of just how the lines should be pointed to make their maximum effect. Michael Bryant as Teddy and Paul Rogers as Max are both also excellent, one cast to type and the other, very successfully, against type. Only Ian Holm as Lenny seems to be working hard at the role and overdoing it slightly – not because he actually is hamming it, but because one is constantly aware that he has to *play* the part all the way, rather than to a certain extent just being it. However, it is a small reproach against one of the best overall productions the Royal Shakespeare Company has given us in a long time, and one of their most striking new plays ever.

Dramatic Milestone

Michael Billington reviews The Killing of Sister George *at the Duke of York's*

Confronted by a new play, a critic naturally searches for the appropriate descriptive label. But with Frank Marcus's *The Killing of Sister George*, such tactics won't work. Already our daily press have ransacked the available categories and come up empty-handed. Such is the originality of Mr Marcus's play that it eludes instant definition. Neither black farce nor blue comedy, it can best be called a highly personal and heady blend of satire, knock-about and tragedy.

The satirical strand is the most facile element in the play but that is not surprising when you consider that Mr Marcus has chosen a sitting target – the BBC ('One of the great comic institutions of our time,' according to Malcolm Muggeridge). Sister George is, in fact, the district-nurse heroine of one of those deathless, daily radio serials. But, though the programme may be immortal, the character is not and, with the decline of her popularity ratings, she faces contrived extinction. Predictably, Mr Marcus shows us the extent to which the actress identifies herself with the six-year-old part so that even in her Devonshire Street flat she lapses into Mummerset dialect and offers comforting clichés all round. Much more deadly and precise is his portrayal of the visiting BBC lady executive, who takes tea and dispenses sympathy with that chill Portland Place politesse. In this role, Lally Bowers coolly and elegantly typifies all those in 'admin at BH'.

The farce and tragedy alternate in the home life of the actress herself – a tweedy, cigar-smoking, brown-stockinged Lesbian. Concurrent with the death of Sister George, runs the break-up of her 'marriage' to a child-like, apparently vulnerable blonde. At first, this ménage provokes laughter. While the dolls belong to 'Childie', the bread-winner explains to her BBC guest, the horse-brasses are hers. And when a tea-party à trois is menaced by 'George' throwing the home-made cake at her partner, the BBC high-up placatingly coos – 'Now, now girls.' Gradually, however, the poignancy of the set-up emerges. There is a model scene in the Second Act when, by the light of a cold September dawn, the jealous fear of the older woman that she may lose her sexual power over her highly-feminine mate is compassionately shown. Comparably, there is the unembittered regret of the younger woman for the way her life has gone. 'I might have had babies,' she factually remarks. The writing here shows both insight and tenderness.

Neither evasive nor sensationalist, *The Killing of Sister George* is a dramatic milestone. At last a homosexual relationship has been greeted with simple acceptance by the author, the characters and the audience. The play's frequent bursts of robust levity mercifully deprive it of the aura that normally surrounds any sort of sexual irregularity. And instead of adopting a moral attitude towards his subject, Mr Marcus is content to reveal the tragicomic facts about the sexual non-conformist.

Since the play's run in Bristol, where I happened to see it at a matinée, the writing, acting and direction have visibly improved. All three now concentrate on bringing out the tragic potential of the theme earlier on so that there is no danger of one feeling that a diverting comedy is violently changing its mood. After one or two recent traveller's tales about plays emasculated during their pre-London tour, it is good to report on one that has been palpably strengthened. Beryl Reid's Sister George is a commendably unsentimentalised creation, as full of viciousness and asperity as of quiet desperation. The butch, like the fey, are usually objects of caricature on stage but Miss Reid avoids any such pitfall. As her gauche lover, Eileen Atkins could not conceivably be bettered. Pale, watchful and frightened, Miss Atkins acts with an unemphatic honesty that one remembers for days afterwards. Individually superb, Miss Reid and Miss Atkins also subtly suggest all the shared experience of a near-marital relationship. For this, and for the general control of mood and tempo, Val May's direction must take due credit.

I find it hard to review Mr Osborne's new play in the wake of Mary McCarthy, who has set out so lucidly all I'd have wished to say about it (and, incidentally, about *Luther*, the most inert of his earlier plays). Like her, I was distressed by the anonymous flatness, and above all by the apparent aimlessness of the exercise. It wasn't badly written – Osborne knows how to deliver even clichés with a certain sharpness – but it felt every minute of its three-and-a-quarter-odd hours, at the end of which I personally emerged having felt, and learnt, next to nothing. The play starts, as a matter of fact, rather well and with everything in its favour. The Hapsburg atmosphere is darkly pregnant. A handsome young subaltern of the Seventh Galician Infantry Regiment at Lemberg (not Lemburg, incidentally, as flashed vastly and inaccurately on the Royal Court front-drop) is about to fight a dawn sabre-duel with a fellow-officer, Von Kupfer, who has insulted him by implying that he is not only Jewish, but pansy to boot. The handsome boy, seconded by a tall saturnine fellow called Redl, is

A Bit of a Drag

John Holmstrom reviews A Patriot for Me *at the Royal Court*

A Patriot for Me with, right, George Devine in drag and, opposite, Jill Bennett and Maximilian Schell

killed by Von Kupfer in the duel. About an hour later (playing time) Redl turns out to be queer, and about two hours later so does Von Kupfer. In between, so does most of the Austro-Hungarian officer class, some of whose paragons are seen frolicking at a drag ball *chez* the Baron von Epp. Redl, shadowed by the Russian military intelligence and blackmailed by them when they pin down his private foibles, betrays top secrets to them for money (the Austrians later – after 1914, for all this is documentary fact – blamed Redl for their ignominious showing against the Russians). His own side find out, and order him to shoot himself, which he does. The Russian intelligence men are shown as the curtain falls turning their attention to one Dr Schoepfer, of whom we know nothing except that he had earlier delivered an address on sexual deviation. Whether the doctor was himself deviant, and if so what conceivable use he was going to be to the Russians (strategic formulae weeded out of queer Hapsburg generals on the psychiatric couch?) – don't ask me.

Osborne's handling of his material seems misguided in many ways. Firstly, only the most blinkered innocent could come to *A Patriot for Me* unaware that it was about a homosexual; yet the long first act of the play – culminating in Redl acknowledging his nature, bedding a soldier and being beaten up and robbed by his cronies – leads up to this with laborious, antiquated evasiveness, dropping heavy hints and trembling with suppressed excitement as if some really frightful shock were in store for us. Then, having got over this milestone and set Redl on his right road, we might reasonably have expected some deeper insight into him, some development into either a tragic or didactic hero. But in fact our gentleman, who so far has been strong, silent and tortured,

dwindles more and more into the shadows. He advances smoothly up the ladder of success, reaching the top of his own army's Intelligence Service; he hovers aloofly on the fringes of the homosexual and heterosexual *beaux mondes*; he retreats from an amorous countess, toys forlornly with a succession of young men none of whom (understandably) seem much attached to him and all of whom want to go off and get married. He is also shown to be as arrogant, brutal and anti-semitic as most of his fellow-militarists. Osborne's aim here presumably was to show him as an unwhitewashed man of his times and background, not a flawless martyr, but the point deserved closer scrutiny – so many perse-cuted minorities are only too eager to persecute others. (I remem-ber a hideously self-righteous homosexual in a radio interview, waxing furious about pederasts: 'Hanging's too good for them,' he lisped).

On the whole, though, Osborne has done little to present a 'real' person, either in the psychological or documentary sense. The character seems to invite the wooden, bleakly distinguished playing it gets from Maximilian Schell. The factual Redl, one gathers, was a plump, pink, bristly person with not a grain of craggy romanticism; and his factual colleagues, dammit, were Austrians, not the heel-clicking ramrod-backed stage Prussians we see at the Royal Court. One inaccurate cliché has been superim-posed on another to present – what? A flat reconstruction of a real-life melodrama? A plea for more thorough screening of homosexuals in positions of trust? A pathetic study of the futility of homosexual passion? An exposé of what Gay Vienna really meant? Surely not. Osborne is too intelligent and humane to cherish such petty aims.

The drag ball is fun for a few minutes, after which it becomes repetitious, obvious and over-full of girlish giggles. But it gives a splendid opportunity to George Devine as the robed and tiara'd Baron(ess) von Epp, snapping like a bossy old salmon and forcing us to admire his tough determination that standards shall be maintained, in or out of camp.

1965 Awards

voted for by the London Theatre critics

Best new play: *The Killing of Sister George* by Frank Marcus
Best musical: *Hello Dolly!*
Best performance by an actor: Paul Scofield as Timon of Athens
Best performance by an actress: Claudia McNeil in *The Amen Corner*
Most promising newcomer: Eileen Atkins
Best productions: Peter Hall's for the RSC
Best designer: Lila Di Nobili for *Love For Love*

Twelve of London's theatre critics vote for the play, musical, performances, production and set they most admired in 1965. The Best New Play category in fact brought the most decisive voting with Frank Marcus's *The Killing of Sister George* collecting seven of the twelve votes. A poor year for musicals had two critics casting No Vote for Best Musical and one qualifying his *Hello, Dolly!* vote with 'for want of a better'. *Dolly!* in fact took six votes against two for the nearest runner-up – Leatherhead's *The Matchgirls*.

Voting for the best performance by an actor was spread over no less than nine performances – Paul Scofield's Timon of Athens gaining the award with three votes. Voting for the best performance by an actress was also spread widely, with seven actresses included. The three votes cast for Claudia McNeil in *The Amen Corner* gained her this award. Eileen Atkins collected votes in both Best Actress and Most Promising Newcomer categories and gained the latter award, since no one actor polled a majority vote. By pooling votes for his Hamlet and The Homecoming productions, Peter Hall is nominated as responsible for the best productions and Lila Di Nobili's sets for the National Theatre's *Love For Love* gained a majority vote in the design category.

Peter Hall's production of Pinter's *The Homecoming* with Michael Bryant, Vivien Merchant, Terence Rigby and Paul Rogers

1966

In Britain's General Election Wilson and the Labour Party were returned with a majority of 97. In India Mrs Indira Gandhi succeeded to power on the death of Shastri. In Australia the resignation of Sir Robert Menzies saw the arrival of Harold Holt.

In Britain it was the year of the Aberfan mining disaster. The Severn Bridge was completed and England won the World Cup. The Times, *which passed into the hands of Lord Thomson, carried news on the front page for the first time. David Mercer's* Belcher's Luck *and Charles Dyer's* Staircase *were both premièred by the RSC. At the Royal Court another new British playwright was sent into international orbit with the controversial première of Edward Bond's* Saved.

A Brave Try

John Russell Taylor at the Royal Court where, following the death of George Devine the theatre was under the artistic control of a triumvirate – William Gaskill, Iain Cuthbertson and Keith Johnstone

Well, general opinion seems to have labelled the Royal Court a disaster area now that the other two productions in its first repertory of three under the new régime have been unveiled. I'm not sure that I altogether agree, but I see what they mean. I liked *Shelley* more than most people. I think – maybe my childish pleasure in being told something interesting in the theatre pulled me through, and maybe in feeling that way I was reacting in the way intended by Ann Jellicoe. Anyway, I found it an agreeable and by no means boring evening in the theatre, if not on the other hand a particularly electrifying one. That I cannot say as much for N. F. Simpson's new play *The Cresta Run* does not surprise me, since Simpson has always been the one dramatist in the whole British new wave whose charms are completely lost on me; what does surprise me rather is that so many other critics who have hitherto found his works hysterically funny or intellectually profound (or both) did not do so this time, since I cannot see any vital difference between this play and what came before. As for *Saved*, I'm afraid I must take that most tiresome way out, the pseudo-judicious middle way: I didn't think it as good as the author and his small band of fanatical supporters think it, but then I didn't, either, think it as bad as almost everybody else did. So obviously this has not been a triumphant comeback for the Royal Court, but I can't see that it has been any less than a brave try, and that at least is something.

Simpson, I find, is one of those writers it is impossible to argue about. You either find him funny or you don't, and there is no possibility to compromise. I have toyed from time to time with the idea that he doesn't really mean to be funny, that he is more interested in the nonsense logic of humour, the way jokes work, than in actually telling jokes in such a way as to make us laugh. This at least would explain why all his jokes go on and on, piling on detail with such strenuous assiduity that they are continuing with unflinching determination minutes after the laugh has come and gone. A lot of his humour depends on portentous statements of the obvious and everyday as though it is somehow extraordinary and open to question. There is a classic demonstration in the new play: the would-be member of the Secret Service has to fill out an enormous form for club membership, and perusing the contents his superiors come across the suspicious fact that he claims to have had *two* parents. Not only that, but he further asserts that he had *four* grandparents. Strange (scattering of uneasy laughter). And so on through a couple more generations, until we arrive at the quite amusing thought that if we believe him he must have had 17½ million direct ancestors at the time of the Norman Conquest, though the population of Britain was only about 1½ million (big laugh). But then, where were the other 16 million? Out of the country, perhaps? Could they all have been on holiday abroad? What if they were perhaps not British at all; what would that mean in relation to an application for admission to a Secret Service club? And so on and so on long after the joke has been battered to death and buried beneath a heap of inert verbiage.

On the other hand, if you think all that sounds funny, this may be your play. It has a little more plot than most Simpson, which may or may not be an advantage, and such plot as it has concerns the currently inescapable entertainment subject, spying. A Secret

Saved at the Royal Court: above, John Castle and Barbara Ferris, below left, Richard Butler, Barbara Ferris and Gwen Nelson, below right, John Castle and Gwen Nelson

Service chief arrives at the door of an ordinary suburban home at dead of night to hand over to the occupiers a Secret (it later transpires that he has had a dreadful urge to divulge state secrets to strangers since early childhood), and the rest of the play is taken up by various attempts on the part of the chief and those approached to clarify the situation. A lot of the humour, which concerns itself with such matters as flocks of Russian ostriches fitted with monocles and released from submarines to spy on the coast of Yorkshire, is too painfully strenuous and fourth-form to pass muster even as absurd, let alone Absurd; most of the cast (Avril Elgar as the sceptical housewife being an honourable exception) overplay with wild extravagance, as though all too painfully aware of how feeble their material is, and how funny they are meant to be with it. This has impelled one or two critics to blame Keith Johnstone's production for the play's failure, but in all generosity it is difficult to see how anything could have saved it.

At least agreement seems to have been pretty general on *The Cresta Run*, but *Saved* has revived things a bit by being 'controversial' – i.e., about two critics liked it, the rest hated it with quite extraordinary vehemence, and before we knew where we were it had spawned letters to the papers, television controversy, and even a Sunday-night teach-in presided over by Kenneth Tynan. Despite all of which, it is not really as curious, or radical, or alarming, or good, or bad, as everyone says. To capsulate, it is by *Infanticide in the House of Fred Ginger* out of *Say Nothing*: a pleasant, ordinary young man goes to bed with an apparently pleasant, ordinary young woman, moves into her home as lodger, and rapidly finds that he has walked into a madhouse. The girl's father and mother hate each other and haven't spoken to each other for years, and the girl herself, it emerges, is a grade-A bitch who, having got what she wanted from the boy, turns on him with utter savagery and pours scorn and derision on his doggily devoted head. She has a baby (by someone else) which she loathes, and before long it is conveniently stoned to death by thugs. Its father (at least, she says he is) is on the fringe of the group, and unaccountably carries the can back for them. The girl stays devoted to him while he is in prison, but when he comes out he doesn't want to know, and repulses her as brutally as she is still repulsing the first young man. The play ends with young man number one deciding, not before time, to move out of his grim home-from-home, but then after all staying on, and the curtain comes down on a picture of emotional deadlock and concerted misery. (Well, the author says it comes down on a gesture of hope, but how he makes that out escapes me.)

The bits of the play that work – rather well, some of them – are those closest to *Say Nothing*: the earlier scenes in which Len drifts into involvement with his pick-up's strange family are quite holding, and the further exploration of his relationships with the parents in the second act throws up a couple of good scenes, notably that in which he nearly seduces the mother, or she nearly seduces him, while he darns a hole in her stocking. The parts which are closer to *Infanticide in the House of Fred Ginger* (also directed by William Gaskill – a curious coincidence, or is it?) are a very different matter. The scene which has caused most com-

The baby-stoning in *Saved*

plaint, of course, is that in which a group of wild young men rub the baby's face in its own excrement and then stone it to death. To begin with, I can't really see how anybody could be seriously offended by something so feebly written and inertly directed: I know Mr Bond thinks he has something to say about arbitrary and unmotivated violence in modern society, but there are limits to the arbitrariness permissible in drama – actions may not have, and often don't have, reasonable reasons, but they must surely have some sort of reason, some emotional build-up at least.

Perhaps Mr Bond is saying that nowadays teenage tearaways congratulate each other on having run down and killed children just for fun, and simply suggest, in a fairly matter-of-fact sort of way, that they should stone babies to death before casually suiting the action to the word. But I find it difficult to believe, and the way he writes these scenes does not make belief any easier. Oh, I don't doubt that such things happen from time to time, but in quite this way? And if the answer to that is that the play is not meant to be realistic, then surely it is more than ever up to the author to create a compelling imaginative substitute for life as we think we know it. Perhaps what the play needs, in fact, is not less violence but more, some sort of real sadistic kick which might urge us, however shamefacedly, to identify with these characters and share their emotions instead of coolly watching the actors going through the motions of violence. But anyway, if the play is about anything it is not really about this, and though 'good taste' can hardly be invoked any more as a criterion, relevance I suppose can. It is in the scenes of gloomily obsessive family life that Mr Bond shows, intermittently as yet, some real quality as a writer, and it would be a pity if all the fuss about the weaker sections of his play were to divert him from the areas where his genuine talent lies.

207

Matinee Fare, Superlatively Crafted

John Russell Taylor reviews A Song at Twilight *at the Queens*

Times have certainly changed in the theatre. Who would have thought, even ten years ago, that the time would come when one could settle for a nice evening's theatre in the plush comfort of the Queen's Theatre, and find oneself witnessing Lilli Palmer, of all people, saying to Noël Coward, of all people, in a new play by Noël Coward, of all possible playwrights, 'You have been a homosexual all your life!'. And yet here we are, and that is precisely what is happening. A longish, slowish first act – a trifle too slow in parts, actually, though sustained with all Mr Coward's old cunning – introduces us to an elderly and pernickety writer, busy building himself into an irreproachable grand old man of letters, and his younger, German-born wife, who is helping him in the construction work. He is expecting a visit from a once quite well-known actress who was also, years ago, his mistress. When she arrives she is not, needless to say, the strident, ageing creature Latymer half-hopes, half-fears to meet, but glamorous, ageless Lilli Palmer. What, exactly, does she want? Mystery. Over a long and admirably sustained dinner-table duologue they spar and needle each other, until finally she asks Latymer if she may print his love letters to her in her forthcoming autobiography. He, stuffily on his dignity, delivers a priggish and moralistic refusal, but still does not quite believe that this is the only reason she came. Nor is it. She is just about to leave when she drops her bombshell: never mind about the letters to her, she must now decide what to do with the other love-letters in her possession, those addressed by Latymer to his former male secretary and companion, the one real love of his life.

A thumping good first act curtain, you see. For all the disdain we affect to feel for the 'well-made play', when a past master is manipulating the form, and manipulating it with conviction, it really does work: one would defy anyone held in his seat that long to walk out on the play during the interval. And now, once the ball has been set well and truly rolling, it rolls on happily to the end, with Latymer gradually having every shred of his moral pretension and carefully preserved reputation stripped from him, first by the relentless Carlotta and then, even worse, by his long-suffering ex-secretary wife, who turns out to have known all the time. Ingenious, and yet at the same time not unsubtle in its character-drawing and the issues it raises: in a sense the part that Coward has written for himself (if he did originally write it for himself) is the slightest, often almost non-existent while one or other or both of the women talk, and yet, unobtrusively, Latymer's case, his side of things, is written in too.

He hardly says anything about the dead man, and makes no attempt to defend his own later callousness towards him (his disingenuousness in his memoirs he does defend on grounds of expediency which are comprehensible if not particularly admirable), and yet we are left finally with an image of a completely hopeless, impossible passion for a hopeless, impossible person, such as could be resolved only, if at all, in hatred and bitterness. In other words, whatever the ever-ready, over-ready simplifications of Carlotta on how he ought to have behaved, we are left feeling that after all he has at least experienced something really and deeply, and reacted humanly if not very well towards it, while she, for all her intelligence and wit, has never grappled with the realities of passion at all, and is therefore not in such an impregnable position as at first she seems to point the moral.

So the play, as well as being superlatively crafted matinée entertainment – which it is – does sometimes cut unexpectedly deep, rather as did Rattigan's *Man and Boy*, a play which *A Song at Twilight* resembles in some obvious and a number of less obvious ways. Oh, it is not exactly a masterpiece of character penetration or anything of the sort, not even the deepest play Mr Coward, that light entertainer par excellence, has ever produced. But there is decidedly more to it than a lot of our more modish and modern critics have allowed. Perhaps Mr Coward has trodden on too many toes in his unflattering comments on the work of some of our younger dramatists (much as many of them admire him), and now that he has chosen to avail himself of one of the new freedoms they have helped to win for the West End theatre – that of discussing homosexuality openly – no doubt the temptation to be superior about the result was almost irresistible.

Nevertheless, the play works with almost complete confidence on its own chosen level, and the satisfactions it offers, if of a slightly old-fashioned variety, are none the worse for it and anyway undoubtedly genuine. It is admirably acted by Mr Coward and Irene Worth, who hits exactly the right tone as the wife, a rôle which only just skirts the edge of caricature and could easily be pushed over by an off-key performance. Lilli Palmer seemed at the beginning of the run a trifle less secure, especially in the early scenes, where she is required to assume a rather vulgar, extrovert manner foreign to her nature as an actress. But I should imagine this will right itself when she has played herself into the part for a week or so. And meanwhile the play remains London's obvious first choice if you want to take Aunt Edna out to a good strong evening's theatre and enjoy yourself into the bargain.

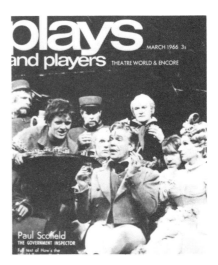

Whatever one's reaction to *US*, the Royal Shakespeare Company's semi-documentary Vietnam programme, there is no denying that it is a major theatrical landmark. Using all the resources at the theatre's disposal, it launches a ferocious, frontal assault on the massive indifference of most of us to the war now being fought. As far as I know, this is something without precedent on the English stage. What little documentary drama we have seen has generally been concerned with the reconstruction of a past event: *US* involves us in a current happening. I can only report that the application of so much artistic skill to a theme of such magnitude as the Vietnam war produced an event that penetrated my memory and troubled my conscience for days after I had seen it.

The evening is divided into two parts, dissimilar in tone yet organically connected. Beginning with an act of Buddhist self-immolation, the first half traces the history of Vietnam, shows the impact of American intervention in the conflict between North and South and finally plunges us into the blazing, cacophonous hell of a bombing raid. The mood ranges from one of militant frenzy, in the demonstration of how American troops can be

209

transformed into Cong-hating automata, to one of tranquil solemnity, out of respect for the American Quaker, Norman Morrison, who burnt himself to death on the steps of the Pentagon because he could not reconcile himself to a world in which napalm was used to destroy innocent people. The second half deals with our reactions to the war. A mythical English martyr, matches and petrol can at the ready, is confronted by a young Left-wing female with the futility of his protest. Her initial scepticism gradually fades; and she ends the play with a scorching and unforgettable indictment of the passionate non-involvement of the English in anything happening outside their shores. In this half, the dilemma that confronts anyone disturbed by recent world events is conveyed with clarity and simple eloquence. To protest about something one can never hope to influence may salve one's conscience but achieves nothing; yet not to protest is implicitly to condone whatever governmental decisions are taken. No solutions are offered by *US:* but the problem is there for all to see.

The chief virtue of *US* is that it forces one to redefine one's own attitude to the Vietnam war. What worries me about it (as it has worried others) is its selective use of fact. It is, of course, nonsense to say that it is anti-American. As Denis Cannan has pointed out, it is no more anti-American than are the numerous American citizens who are openly or quietly critical of official Government policy. At the same time, *US* distorts the truth by its suggestion that Hanoi is constantly offering an olive-branch, repeatedly flung back in its face by Washington. It is also a culpable sin of omission to ignore the Vietcong atrocities.

Factually, *US* is incomplete; and its value as 'balanced comment' (which is how it is recommended to us in the programme) is thereby weakened. But that does not make its attack on our apathy any less salutary nor does it prevent its being an overwhelming theatrical experience. Peter Brook's production incorporates many different theatrical styles and he shows himself a master of each of them. The history of Vietnam is presented in a series of tableaux, using devices one associates with Chinese theatre (rippling blue silk for water and so forth); basic facts are supplied by a girl with a hand-mike at the side of the stage; and the whole thing has the heady carnival exuberance one associates with the best American musicals. By contrast, a Saigon news-conference is presented in a vein of quiet realism so that one can almost feel the air-conditioner working as the American officers drawl out the latest information to a blasé, faintly sceptical press corps. The only part of the production that does not work is the now-famous end to the first half when the actors grope their way, as victims of a bombing raid, towards the auditorium exit. On my second visit, I was glad to see that they had taken the paper-bags off their heads and thereby removed the Christmas-charade element; but the device is neither a true test of the audience's humanity nor a stunning theatrical *coup* – half the people in the theatre can't see what is happening anyway.

Although *US* is a group effort, I think it only fair to mention one or two individuals. Obviously one must stress Peter Brook's genius for creating spectacular and sometimes beautiful effects. Amongst the cast, Glenda Jackson dominates the second half. As Miss Jackson, pallid and square-shouldered, delivers her final harangue against cosy English isolationism, the combination of her words and her presence leaves an unforgettable imprint on the mind. Briefly, one must also praise Richard Peaslee's strikingly tuneful score. After this, I need hardly add that *US* cannot be neglected by anyone who takes a serious interest in the theatre and its relation to the world we live in. If you miss it, you will live to regret it. At least, I fervently hope you will.

During the last few years the hard-pressed journalists who are paid to chart our cultural pulse beat, have consumed handy theatrical labels at a spanking rate. Having worked through 'Kitchen Sink Drama', 'Theatre of the Absurd', 'Black Comedy', 'Theatre of Cruelty' and 'The Happening' they are now busy pasting the label 'Documentary Theatre' on any slightly unusual piece of work. But documentary theatre is no forced hothouse product of the mid-sixties. Its origins are to be found in the years following the first World War. Before 1914 drama (and life?) was largely conceived of as 'character in action'. But the cataclysm of the Great War and the social collapse of a supposedly stable Europe made artists aware that there were greater forces at work in society, than the mere clash of personalities. Dramatic emphasis shifted from the character to the event. Germany in her post-war misery, sought in her theatre to examine the maelstrom that had engulfed her. In Russia, too, the Revolution of 1917 had generated a similar mass of creative theatrical energy, far removed from the world of Chekhov. This theatre in Russia and Germany which devoured the turmoil of the age as its subject matter, eagerly embraced the latest technological developments to create theatre of a mechanical complexity which in recent years we have seen fit to lavish only on works as insubstantial as *Blitz!*

In England such a politically and socially questioning theatre was not to appear until the very end of the twenties when it was pioneered by the Communists and other Left-wing groups. Perhaps a delayed shock reaction to the Great War, this didactic theatre of prospect arose when it became increasingly clear how 'A land fit for heroes' was treating several million of them. This theatre really found its feet when it imported from the States the technique of the Living Newspaper which had been pioneered by a group of Federal Theatre actors and directors (including Jo Losey) as both a product and a reflection of the Depression. In England we have never entirely lost the tradition of the Living Newspaper. When the second World War came a Major Michael MacOwan happily experimented with Living Newspaper techniques in his work with the Abca Play Unit which was financed by the War Office as a teaching medium for the troops. With the end of the war this unexpected Government subsidy for experimental theatre naturally ceased but intermittently the experiments continued. There was Ewan MacColl's *Uranium* 235, which treated in a documentary extravaganza form with the scientists' attempts to discover the secrets of matter culminating in the production of the atomic bomb, which was in the repertoire of Theatre Workshop for a number of years. There were a few scattered Living Newspaper productions and the English Stage Company's attempt at an improvised documentary – *Eleven Men Dead at Hola Camp.*

Documentary Theatre

David Wright on the background to a fashionable label

Then in April, 1963, Joan Littlewood's production of *Oh, What a Lovely War* sparked off a whole new interest in the genre. One of those who was enormously stimulated by this extraordinary work created by Joan Littlewood and her talented company as a corporate production, was Peter Cheeseman, director of the Victoria Theatre, Stoke-on-Trent. During the last two years he has created with his company three musical documentaries at Stoke and I spoke to him recently about these.

'I've always been interested in the techniques ever since I saw a Living Newspaper production at the Merseyside Unity Theatre many years ago, but the actual impetus came when Alan Ayckbourn, our resident dramatist, left the company. With no playwright, I felt the company must become its own dramatist. Our first documentary – *The Jolly Potters* – was based on the early history of the potteries, as I felt we should use local subject matter of interest to the community. I also wanted to create a form of theatre which would be fluid, and flexible enough to allow each member of the company to utilise any special talents that he might have. At the moment, revue and pantomime are usually considered to provide this freedom, but to me they are spent theatrical forms. We have now staged three of these documentaries and although we never get more than four weeks rehearsal, research will start about a year ahead. An important side effect of this work is that actors involved return to conventional scripts with a new sanity. All too often actors are either contemptuous of a script or, if it happens to be a classic, over-reverential. But when he has had to create a text, then he starts to achieve some sense of proportion, of creative maturity.' I went on to point out that although the three topics he had dealt with in the documentaries were certainly of local interest, they were all historical pieces and perhaps of no great contemporary interest. Cheeseman countered, 'I find that by using historical subjects, one can comment with greater freedom on contemporary situations. Look at the work of John Arden, for instance. *The Knotty* – our last documentary – told the story of a now defunct railway system but its real subject was the impact of science on a community. The difficulties of dealing with contemporary subjects in a documentary manner in the theatre are enormous . . .' And the greatest of these difficulties is perhaps the Lord Chamberlain, whose powers of political censorship are far more disturbing than his sexual prudery. *In the Case of J Robert Oppenheimer*, recently at the Hampstead Theatre Club, was refused a licence for public performance. *US* apparently had great troubles with the Lord Chamberlain and I myself remember the extreme intractability of the gentlemen at St James's, over a documentary script I had devised, which was only finally overcome by the descent en masse of Lord Gardiner, Lord Willis and the present Minister of Health to dispute those worthies' decisions!

Although there are running in London at the moment two basically 'documentary' productions with several more promised, it would be a mistake to think there is a cohesive documentary theatre movement. Much of the most interesting work in this field is undertaken by amateur groups often unaware of other experiments along the same lines. The work ranges from a splendidly wry look at our last twenty-five years of social history – *Out of the*

Ashes – which was staged by a youth theatre group at the Belgrade Theatre, Coventry, last year, to a group of historians at York University who have prepared a documentary on the ferment caused by the French revolution among English radicals. There has been the enormously exciting works created by Charles Parker for the Centre 42 Festivals which blended actors, folk singers and a dance group with recorded actuality tapes and multiple projection, but as yet nobody has built on this work. Such works as these, produced as a result of corporate intelligence brought to bear on documentary material, with all their rawness upon them I find more exciting than the scripted documentaries such as Kipphardt's *Oppenheimer* or even Weiss's *The Investigation* where the material is often contained and deadened by a conventional dramatic form. In any medium the best documentaries are those which are open-ended and ultimately, personal statements. The actual script may not be the product of an author, but in the selection, editing, assembly and treatment of the material the artist is revealed. The theatre documentary that threatens with the premise, 'That's just how it was; we haven't invented a thing!' is a bad documentary because it presumes a God-like prescience. One of the great strengths of Peter Brook's *US* was that it attempted no answers and is ultimately built on a bewilderment and frustrated perplexity as great as the audience's. And again like *US*, the good documentary is a hand-tailored product. *US* succeeds because it was created by, and for, a given group of actors, for a specific audience, in a specific theatre, at a specific time. And thus in one way *US* is more about the Aldwych audience than Vietnam.

As a further example I might instance *In White America*. Two years ago I saw in New York this very modest documentary dealing with the negroes' position in American society. Tailored for a liberal Manhattan audience it was an enormous success and the press notices suggested a work somewhere in the Aeschylus-Shakespeare-Brecht league. Transferred last year to London, it raised not a ripple. In the context of the theatre documentary, the concept of the universality of art needs a long, hard look.

Documentary theatre is now fashionably 'in'. The Hampstead Theatre Club is in the middle of a documentary season. Peter Brook has created a furore with his 'documentary' happening. The Oxford Playhouse promises us a documentary in the New Year on the Kennedy assassination by the American lawyer Mark Lane. The long-awaited documentary on the Cuba crisis by the National Theatre is still long-awaited. For the scripted documentary one cannot pretend that the future looks particularly bright – the forces of reaction are far from defeated. But for the corporate documentary the future looks even bleaker. It will be safely contained by the Lord Chamberlain and the inflexibility of the English production system. No commercial management will consider any such project (Wot, no script!), the reps cannot afford the long rehearsal period required and unfortunately one cannot assume that the RSC is going to give itself over to a policy of continuous and expensive experiment. And yet this is exactly what *must* happen, if the lessons learnt during the preparation of works as diverse as *US*, Charles Parker's *The Maker and the Tool* and *Oh, What a Lovely War* are to be assimilated and extended.

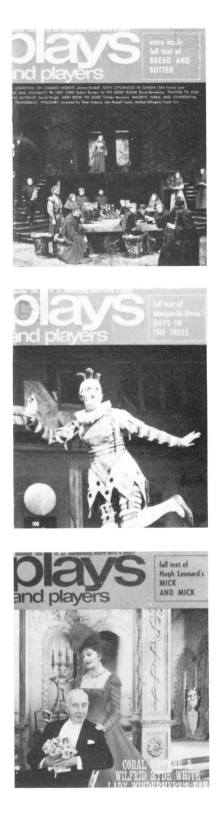

1966 Awards

voted for by the London Theatre critics

Best new play: *Loot* by Joe Orton

Best new musical: *Jorrocks* by Beverley Cross and David Heneker

Best performance by an actor: Paul Scofield in *The Government Inspector* and *Staircase*

Best performance by an actress: Vanessa Redgrave in *The Prime of Miss Jean Brodie*

Most promising actor: Ian McKellan

Most promising actress: Vickery Turner

Best production: Peter Brooks' *US*

Best designer: Josef Svoboda for *The Storm*

Best actor and actress: above, Paul Scofield in rehearsal for *The Government Inspector* with director Peter Hall and fellow actor Paul Rogers; below, a portrait shot of Vanessa Redgrave

As 1967 gets under way, a last look at 1966. Twelve of London's theatre critics vote for the play, musical, performances, production and set that most impressed them in the year that is over. In the Best New Play category, voting split closely between David Halliwell's *Little Malcolm and his Struggle Against the Eunuchs* and Joe Orton's *Loot*. The award in fact goes to Joe Orton who polled four votes to Halliwell's three. Nobody thought 1966 much of a year for new musicals but that didn't stop *Jorrocks* and *Funny Girl* each collecting four votes apiece. A casting vote from Plays and Players' editor, and *Jorrocks* emerged as Best Musical. Most decisive voting was in the field of Best Actor with Paul Scofield picking up nine of the 12 votes either for *The Government Inspector* or *Staircase*. In the Best Actress category Vanessa Redgrave collected six winning votes for her performance in *The Prime of Miss Jean Brodie* with four votes going to Peggy Ashcroft in *Days in the Trees* and two to Irene Worth in the *Coward Trilogy*. Vickery Turner was voted most promising newcomer amongst the actresses and Ian McKellen amongst the actors. Five votes for Peter Brook's production of *US* made it production of the year, and seven for Josef Svoboda's sets for *The Storm* made it design of the year.

1967

The year of the bloodless coup *in Greece that sent King Constantine II to exile in Rome was also the year that 'Che' Guevara was killed in Bolivia and Dr Christian Barnard performed the first heart transplant in Cape Town.*

In Britain the introduction of colour TV and the popularity of the Galsworthy TV adaptation of The Forsyte Saga *emptied churches at transmission time on Sunday evenings or caused service times to be adjusted. The Abortion Act legalised the termination of unwanted pregnancies and the Sexual Offences Act legalised homosexual acts between consenting adults in private. Jeremy Thorpe succeeded Jo Grimmond as leader of the Liberal Party.*

Tom Stoppard's Rosencrantz and Guildenstern Are Dead *and Peter Terson's* Zigger Zagger *signalled the arrival of still more durable dramatic talents.*

A Case of Vice Triumphant

Tom Stoppard at Otway's The Soldier's Fortune, *Royal Court.*

By virtue of its rowdy randy excess of energy over matter (the matter being the consummation of a soldier's desire for a magistrate's wife) this play – first performed in London in 1680 and seldom since – classes itself simply as a 'Restoration comedy', all musical beds and poxy nosegays; but there is more to it than that. A vein of bitter melancholy recurrently breaks through and is expressed in the genuine grievance of a redcoat returned from the wars, denied spoils or position and thrown back into a seamy civvy street where the grafter and the sycophant have prospered in his absence. It is also a time of shifting political winds, only a year or two since the Popish plot and the first Whig Parliament which was the reaction to it, twenty-two since the death of

Cromwell; and Otway saves some of his scorn for the respectable citizen who has shuffled into line with the weathercock (for comparison's sake, note that exactly the same number of years have now passed since the death of Hitler). There are many men whose pasts do not bear scrutiny, and Otway feels this keenly enough to bring in three gratuitous walk-ons for his soldier hero to dismember (effectively done at the Court, with the trio freezing in tableau, black clothes against white background), and this is some of his best stuff: one of them was 'my father's footman not long since, and has pimped for me oftener than he prayed for himself; that good quality recommended him to a nobleman's service, which, together with flattering, fawning, lying, spying and informing, has raised him to an employment of trust and reputation'; another was 'a committee man' whose father was 'as obscure as his mother was public', who helped Charles I to the block, sat in the Rump Parliament and did well enough for himself to secure his pardon on the accession of Charles II . . . 'Tis as unreasonable to expect a man of sense to be preferred as 'tis to think . . . a priest religious, a fair woman chaste, or a pardoned rebel loyal', and there is much talk of preferment or the lack of it, together with a plangent nostalgia for the 'glorious days' of a soldier's campaigns.

The Royal Court's excellent programme notes give us the key to all this. Otway himself went with his regiment to the Flemish

Arthur Lowe as Sir Davy Dunce in *The Soldier's Fortune* with, above, Wallas Eaton as Sir Jolly Jumble and, opposite, Maurice Roeves as Beaugard

war in 1678, but before the summer was out an unexpected peace treaty brought him home again no better off than before, and *The Soldier's Fortune*, his eighth play, was his outlet for the resentment he felt against the treatment of the disbanded troops. He himself was part of the glut on the preferment market, and one hears his voice within the first few minutes . . . 'Of all strumpets, fortune's the basest. 'Twas fortune made me a soldier, a rogue in red, the grievance of the nation; fortune made the peace just when we were on the brink of war; then fortune disbanded us, and lost us two months' pay . . .' Well, another war will come along – 'there's a gentleman on the other side of the water that may make work for us all one day' – but in the meantime, patience; and the actor (Maurice Roëves) gives the speech a fine bitterness: 'Complain to a great man that you want preferment, that you have forsaken considerable advantages abroad, in obedience to public edicts; all you shall get of him is this – "You must have patience".'

So it is a very personal and cynical view of the world that Otway brings to his hero Beaugard, and in his terms the main plot might be stated like this: an honourable, ill-used, 'sympathetic' officer returns from the war to court his old love who is now unhappily married to Sir Davy Dunce, 'an old, greasy, untoward, ill-natured, slovenly, tobacco-taking cuckold, . . . a horse-load of diseases, a beastly, unsavoury, old, groaning, grunting, wheezing wretch that smells of the grave he's going to . . .'; and virtue triumphs in that Beaugard, with the help of a go-between pimp, has it away with Lady Dunce leaving Sir Davy, characterised as cruel and corrupt, belittled and compliant. This apparently went down very well in 1680, but today, even within the context of the period's supposed cynicism of love and marriage, it's quite a lot to take, and in fact, whether through aforethought or the vagaries of casting, the production at the Court goes right against this grain.

This is chiefly because Arthur Lowe brings to the part of Sir Davy a lightness of touch, a felicity, an innocence and a charm which is lacking everywhere else; conversely, Beaugard and his pal Courtine come over as a couple of bums on the make.

Furthermore, Lady Dunce – for all Sheila Hancock's delicious sense of the ridiculous and her way of making lines hilarious through sheer delivery – is a hard case, for her description of her husband, quoted above, is manifestly unkind. Perhaps Otway thought as little of the wife as of the husband, but the emphasis has certainly shifted, for so endearing is our Dunce that at the end vice has triumphed. But no doubt one should be grateful for what one has got – in this case, three funny period performances from Mr Lowe, Miss Hancock, and Wallas Eaton as Jumble the palsied pimp – and stop trying to impose moral terms on clockwork dancers.

There is also some by-plot and sub-plot, and the latter includes several very modern and effective duologues between Courtine and Sylvia, who can only communicate on the level of mutual insult – but this I'm afraid, goes for nothing. Still, there is lots of fun in the lines, quite a bit in Peter Gill's direction, and one long moment of brilliance in Mr Lowe's negligent awe at being invited to dine with the Lord Mayor. John Gunter's designs almost manage to make a virtue of economy, and would probably have succeeded better if the acting had made a better front for them; unfortunately the cast, as they say of bad cricket teams, has a very long tail.

1967

Not a Job for Vagabonds

Peter Cheeseman in 1987 was still with the Victoria Theatre in new premises in the round. He first became director in 1962 when it opened but had been locked out of his own theatre when he gave this interview to Peter Roberts in 1967.

A palace revolution that makes the headlines invariably proves a hornets' nest in the hands of any investigator attempting to chart its eruption and throw light on its injustice. The deposition last month of Peter Cheeseman, for four years director of the Victoria Theatre, Stoke-on-Trent, is no exception. The fact that Mr Cheeseman found himself locked out of a theatre he has brought from obscurity to national attention was in itself guaranteed to bring his dismissal prominent attention in both local and national papers. Press for details, however, and you find yourself caught up in an explosive and complex situation reaching back over many months. At this stage you soon decide that to invite the participants of the Stoke drama to give their version of the theatrical goings-on will result merely in unproductive mud-slinging.

What immediately strikes the outsider, of course, is the supreme irony of the situation. Most people working in regional theatre appear to do so as a means of graduating as quickly as possible to London's West End or national ensembles. But Cheeseman, who won't accept offers to come to Town because he just wants to stay working in the Potteries, is the one who is being shown the door. Although the issue is the first cultural matter to draw blood locally (it pushed China off the front pages of the local papers and brought out students to picket the theatre) Cheeseman is nonetheless to be sent packing at the end of March, unless rescued by the joint actions of the local authority and the Arts Council.

In the long run the details of the squabble and the personalities involved are dwarfed by the underlying passionate belief in the importance of a particular sort of regional theatre. When I spoke to Peter Cheeseman, therefore, we decided to keep off the well beaten track of the circumstances of the current row and talk about the sort of theatre he believes in.

The interview took place in London. Now 34, he looked a trifle stockier than I remembered him on his home ground, but his manner was equally as animated. His transport caff chuckle and uninhibited flow of ideas sent an appreciable ripple through the SW1 tearooms where Belgravia matrons were pecking at afternoon gâteau. In the course of the dialogue Cheeseman got through two cups of black coffee and his restless hands reduced a massive rock cake to a sand of crumbs. The conversation was on these lines.

You're not a Potteries man yourself, are you?

No, in fact I didn't used to feel I belonged to any particular region. I've had 48 homes and been to 10 schools. I was an adolescent in Liverpool, a university student in Sheffield and spent three years in Scotland with the Royal Air Force.

How, then, did you come to anchor at Stoke?

After leaving the Derby Playhouse I joined Stephen Joseph's Studio Theatre Company which was at that time touring. It was looking for a permanent home and when arrangements fell through for it to settle in Newcastle-under-Lyme we discovered this disused cinema in Stoke-on-Trent and turned it into a theatre-in-the-round. It now runs with a £20,000 annual grant – £15,000 from the Arts Council and just over £5,000 from local authority grants.

Have your ideas about regional theatre evolved solely through working at Stoke or do they go back to earlier experiences?

The principles of group theatre I came across through the Liverpool Unity Theatre and through working with the Merseyside WEA Players. Then books like Peter Cotes's *No Star Nonsense*, J. B. Priestley's *Theatre Outlook* and, in particular, Harold Clurman's *The Fervent Years* impressed me. I was specially struck by Clurman's account of his attempts to express the 'American-ness' of the life in the community he was working with. Something quite different which very much affected me at that time was a trip I made to Paris – my only one abroad. Visiting the theatres there (and indeed those in the West End on the way through London) I was troubled by the sense that the audiences were audiences of visitors. You felt the foyers were full of people who were strangers to one another and somehow all this seemed to me to be fundamentally wrong.

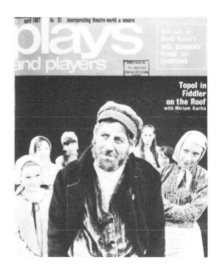

Didn't you find the prospect of settling down in Stoke a daunting one? It must present about the grimmest piece of 19th century industrial landscape you can find in Britain.

That's precisely what I found so challenging about it. I remember the shock of coming upon it the first time and seeing the slag heaps, the belching factory chimneys and the desolate stretches of waste ground between the towns. I felt I had to stay there and make sense of it all. I don't believe it's any good turning one's back on the realities of 20th-century industrial life and escaping to the countryside. You've got to live with what's there and make sense of it.

Actually there were two things about Stoke that made it a particularly exciting place. One was that there was no current

habit of theatregoing and hence no prejudice about what theatre is supposed to mean. Newcomers didn't turn up their noses at theatre-in-the-round in the way that audiences conditioned by proscenium arch theatre might have done. That was one thing. Another was the fact that Stoke is a curiously egalitarian community. It stems from the fact that the pottery industry is still not grouped in large units like, for instance, steel. It's made up of small family businesses and there's still a sense of personal involvement as well as craftsmanship about. What this means is an almost complete absence of the well-to-do middle-class who make up the bulk of regional audiences elsewhere. The two things together meant that one could start absolutely from scratch.

The most talked-of feature of the work at Stoke has been the succession of documentary musicals based on local material. Was that part of a deliberate policy to create a special regional drama instead of using the theatre as a sort of cultural out-post for feeding in metropolitan entertainment?

Well it's not quite as simple as that. Obviously *The Jolly Potters, The Staffordshire Rebels, The Knotty* and the Arnold Bennett programme we had in the pipeline for his centenary this year were all on local themes. But it is important to say that for plays to reflect a certain area they don't necessarily have to be set in that district. A play that takes place in the Sahara could have as much to say to Stoke audiences as one set in the Six Towns. As far as metropolitan entertainment is concerned, one must recognise that it includes much that is valuable but that it is not the only path on which one can travel. The important missing link seems to me to be in folk theatre and the oral tradition, a sphere in which some very important work has been done by Charles Parker, for instance, both in his brilliant radio ballads and with amateurs in Birmingham. When the industrial revolution came along it completely smashed the village community and what the mass of people are being sold now is the culture of the aristocracy and the educated middle class of the 18th and 19th centuries. It's a rich tradition but it's not the only tradition.

How have these documentary musicals evolved?

Well, the company was brought into existence by Stephen Joseph 10 years ago with a basic twofold aim: to explore the potentialities of theatre-in-the-round and the work of new dramatists. When we opened the Victoria I took over the main responsibility for the company's work, and I felt it was up to me to use Joseph's two bases to form a creative relationship with the community in which we had now settled. The company could only do that if it had an identity, and you only get that if actors stay long enough together. Any change in personnel had to be organic so that when actors did respond to the inbuilt restlessness of our profession and wanted to move on I made sure that things were organised so that their departures could be staggered. This meant that the company identity could not be really lost. The result is a very real continuity through the many changes of four years. There is, for instance, no long break at the end of each season. Everyone goes away for a fortnight's holiday and comes back again. Nobody leaves then. We didn't, however, begin with the idea that the company should write its own material. We had always had dramatists working as actors or executives with the company, like Alan Ayckbourn, or in close association with it, like Alan Plater. When Ayckbourn left for the London production of his *Mr Whatnot* we were without a writer actually on the staff, and it was then that I felt the company should try to create its own material, and the first result was *The Jolly Potters*. Since then we've gradually streamlined what was an uncertain process so that now the research for a programme like the one on Arnold Bennett is completed in nearly 12 months by my wife and Peter Terson and then gradually worked out over the last few months, with myself, and then the last few weeks with a number of the company while a small-cast play is rehearsed, then in a four-week rehearsal period turned into a show by all of us. One of the results of the work on the documentaries is their effect on the work of the associated dramatists, and also on our approach to classics (our programme is now equally divided between new plays and classics). Peter Terson, our resident dramatist, has just created with us a play with music – *Jock-on-the-Go* – which is a direct response in style to our work on the documentaries. And, as a result, for the first time since Alan Ayckbourn's *Mr Whatnot*, we are getting large audiences for a new play. Normally the new plays get the small houses, the classics the big ones, though the documentaries always do well.

What do you mean when you talk about a creative relationship with the community?

What I don't mean is the sort of coffee mornings when the audience comes round to gape at the actors. It's for the actors to serve the community usefully by giving demonstrations, helping amateur groups, visiting schools to make the examination texts come alive as theatre – that sort of thing. What I would like to see above all is the theatre accepted as a necessary and useful part of the community – as useful and as necessary as the doctor and the shop on the corner. It shouldn't be just a luxury item for a minority with special tastes.

Do you think regional theatre will grow as a result of its usefulness?

I don't think the problem of getting new audiences is a managerial one. It's not an outside public relations job of selling the theatre. It's an artistic problem that's to be solved by the actor, the writer and the director in their contact with the community. It's a matter of finding a style and an approach to subject matter that will enable the artist to attract and make contact with the entire community without any loss of integrity or lowering of standards. I believe that this is possible. Above all, it's a matter of making friends, of winning the trust and respect of the community you live in. To do this, you've got to stay put. It's not a job for vagabonds any more.

The Feast of the Fiddler

Frank Marcus reviews Fiddler on the Roof

I am fairly immune to ethnic whimsy: leprechauns, pearlies, and Yiddisher mommas seeking favour in my eyes tend to meet a hard unblinking gaze. *Fiddler on the Roof* disposes systematically of just about every cliché in the Jewish calendar: Friday night, marriage brokers, a wedding, pogroms – it's all there. In New York, where this show has played to full houses for the past three years, whole families pay annual visits to see it again and again. It's almost become another ritual feast. To a large proportion of them, this fanciful picture of their grandparents' lives (Russia, 1905) has an irresistible personal appeal.

It is not, of course, a true picture; nor does it try to be. The stories of Sholem Aleichem – and in particular his play *Tevye, The Milkman*, on which this show is based – are charming, ingenuous chronicles and anecdotes about life under the Tsars. They are full of wry submissive ghetto humour. On the other side of the coin, there's the desperate hope for the Messiah expressed in mysticism, as depicted in the play *The Dybbuk*. Modest, undemanding plays, usually with interpolated songs, deriving from this tradition, could, until fairly recently, be seen in the Yiddish theatres of the East End. *Fiddler On The Roof* is fundamentally just a glossier version of these melodramas. By a similar distension, a play by the Viennese Nestroy has, after several mutations, turned into *Hello, Dolly!* Obviously, folklore has found expression in musicals. Did someone say Robin Hood? Skip it.

By a miracle, this potentially nauseating material has become a work of art. The miracle's name is Jerome Robbins. Robbins is one of the most creative directors of our time. His gift is for lyricism and his medium is movement (this includes the movement of objects and of light). Choreography is too restricted a word to describe it. He has the knack of getting to the core, to the poetry, of his subject. *On The Town* made me nostalgic for New York long before I visited that marvellous place; *West Side Story* conveyed the same, almost physical, reality, so that when I trod the rock-like steaming pavements – sorry, sidewalks – I felt I'd been there before. He constantly transcends his trite material. This brings me to his blind spot: he lacks judgment. In *Fiddler On The Roof*, he spreads his genius evenly over the whole work, the good parts as well as the bad. The curtain call is as much a work of art as the climactic wedding scene – and it shouldn't be! A foolish and fortuitous dream scene – which, incidentally, introduces an incongruous element of voodoo – is blown up with full choreographic effects. Lastly, and most seriously, the musical ends with Tevye, deprived of his home and three of his five daughters, pushing the handcart containing his belongings (on a revolve, too!), wandering on. This is a piece of blatant plagiarism; Robbins, who recently directed *Mother Courage*, should not have permitted it. When, oh when, will he create the Great American Musical?

Taken individually, most of the components of the show are unremarkable. On the credit side are Boris Aronson's Chagallian settings, including beautifully-painted backcloths full of vivid yellow, green and orange. The lighting, by Richard Pilbrow, is also most imaginative and expertly handled. But the music (Jerry Bock) has no surprises: it is predictably derivative from traditional sources. There are only two or three tuneful numbers, of which

Three views of _The Fiddler_ with Topol as Tevye and Miriam Karlin as Golde

'If I Were a Rich Man' is the best. The lyrics (Sheldon Harnick) are clever in the accepted Broadway idiom. The book, by Joseph Stein, is workmanlike rather than inspired. The episodes are shrewdly selected, but the dialogue – except for a generous sprinkling of Jewish jokes – is often woefully prosaic and unsubtle. This is particularly noticeable in the farewell scene between father and daughter, enacted on a remote railway station in the midst of cornfields. This should have had a Chekhovian poignancy, but didn't. Still, in most cases the stodgy narrative passages are saved in the nick of time by the entrance of the dancers, now stamping,

Fiddler on the Roof directed and
choreographed by Jerome Robbins

with arms extended, now swirling into view, forming and re-
forming chains, and binding the show together like a bouquet.
The dancing here is almost as good as in New York – which is
high praise indeed; the singing, alas, isn't. But the acting is better
here.

Tevye is a whale of a part. Henpecked, good-natured, and
warm-hearted, he submits the many problems that befall him to a
method of Talmudic reasoning ('On the one hand . . . on the
other hand'), which usually ensures that his decisions, when
reached, are overtaken by events. Thus his eldest daughter
marries the poor young tailor, instead of the rich old butcher, the
second one follows the revolutionary idealistic student into political exile to Siberia, and the third one – and here the father
practically tears off his beard – marries out of the faith. Understandably impervious to her father's advice ('A bird can love a
fish, but where would they make their home?'), she is disowned
by her family – cue for handkerchiefs, ladies. Tevye expresses his
complaints and unburdens his troubles in direct colloquies with
God, whom he addresses as a quirky, unreasonable, but unfortunately omnipotent boss. Who can blame him? Whereas in New
York Tevye's every word is given the weight of prophetic utterance, the Israeli actor Topol rightly stands detached and pokes
(very gentle) fun at this simple bewildered man. Lacking the
mature sonority of his American counterpart, he more than
compensates with his intelligence and humour. An excellent
performance.

Miriam Karlin is the mother: a part which does not allow her to stretch her considerable talent. This actress has had a 'line' in Yiddisher mommas for quite some time; indeed, I cannot forbear to remind her that almost fifteen years ago, in the midst of the Great Smog, she appeared briefly as *my* mother! What more can I say, except, 'Come home, mum, all is forgiven'? Of the smaller parts, Sandor Eles turns Perchik, the student, into a credible flesh-and-blood character. Like Miss Karlin, he is much better than the part. Paul Whitsun-Jones is amiable as the ill-used butcher. The Russians are portrayed like British colonial administrators: ineffectual, kindly, and confused, indulging in meaningless acts of violence. The truth was different.

On the one hand, a pretty extensive catalogue of negatives; on the other hand, the overall impression of a work of art. Perhaps I ought to be thankful for not-so-small mercies, and show gratitude? Which reminds me of a story – do you know it? Well, one day Moishe and Shloime went to the circus. On comes an acrobat, who proceeds to balance five chairs on top of each other, climbs to the top, stands on his head – and plays the violin. Upside down. Moishe watches for a minute, turns sadly to his friend and says: 'He's no Heifetz!'

Can it be – I sometimes wonder – that drama critics are the last people who ought to be reviewing drama? So much drama these days, after all, seems to be directed, perhaps from painful necessity, at people who do not normally go to the theatre. Of course, to those who for some reason or other have decided to go to one particular show without having a large and constant background of reference and comparison, things come as a bright new excitement which very probably strike the inured theatregoer, and inevitably the critic, as very familiar and immediately recognisable. But is this critic's reaction necessarily the fair and proper one, the one which best carries out the old school-room injunction: decide what the writer is trying to do and then judge how well he has done it?

These thoughts struck me forcibly seeing *Rosencrantz and Guildenstern are Dead* at the National Theatre. Apart from the scattering of critics, the audience seemed to be very much the average sort of National Theatre audience. They must be, I imagine, people who go to the theatre as a special event, and rely on the National to provide it: you can be pretty sure that there you will get a substantial, well-written play, probably classic, with a stellar cast; you are not likely, or have not up to now been likely, to be affronted with anything too difficult or 'modern'. Now this, I think, is a very good and favourable setting for Tom Stoppard's play. Five minutes at the outside will establish for the critic exactly what sort of play it is and where it is likely to lead (or not lead). As soon as the lights go up on the solitary couple playing some interminable coin-tossing game in which every coin, in defiance of all the laws of probability, comes up heads, we know immediately that we are in that pale region of Theatre of the Absurd where knockabout and arid philosophical speculation mix

The Road to Dusty Death

John Russell Taylor reviews Rosencrantz and Guildenstern are Dead *at the Old Vic*

or alternate while the awaited never comes, the characters hover on the point of action without ever actually acting, and our little stage is bounded by the dread unknown world of happenings.

This much the critic at once divines, and thereafter his main interest is to see just how well and inventively the dramatist spins his slender thread unbroken through an evening's theatre. But for the audience around me it was quite otherwise. In the first long interval (for some reason there are two twenty-minute intervals in a performance lasting overall two hours and fifty minutes, which seems to say the least of it over-generous) speculation was rife on all sides. People were asking each other with every show of excitement What it was All About. Some said that it had taken them a long time, but they thought they were beginning to get the hang of it now. By the second interval a lot more had got the hang of it, or resolved that even if they didn't understand it, at least a lot of it was jolly funny along the way. Only one dissenting voice did I hear: the man immediately behind me said loudly: 'Of course, I tend to turn and run a mile at the first hint of anything *clever!*'

Yes, well, Mr Stoppard's play is undoubtedly clever. The idea is simple. In *Hamlet* Rosencrantz and Guildenstern are a couple of characters so unimportant that Olivier could remove them from his film without any noticeable difficulty and with almost no one regretting their departure. They are the perennial 'attendant lords', 'friends to the duke' and what-have-you who lurk on the sidelines of drama ready to receive confidences from the principals, carry out commissions and do any minor dirty work that happens to be going. But what are their private lives like? Do they have any? Mr Stoppard thinks not. They live, suspended in existential doubt, on the fringes of life. They never know what's happening, who is who and what is what. Occasionally they witness puzzling snatches of big events going on around them, but their attempts to interpret them are limited and half-hearted. They recognise, in spite of themselves, that life, like laughter, is always in the next room. In the end they go so far as to make a choice of another, but it is only death that they choose, a death which will at last define and give shape to their pointless, shapeless lives.

Is that all? Yes, really, when you come down to it, that is all. A fine subject for a gnomic one-acter, but a longish three-act play is something different. There is no denying the ingenuity with which Mr Stoppard spins out his material, or the skill with which he works in such fragments of *Hamlet* as concern his own non-heroes. His play is written in brisk, informal prose, suitable for those waiting in the wings, while Shakespeare's verse marks off the brief incursions of a larger life into the colourless, mystifying existence of Rosencrantz and Guildenstern. A lot of Mr Stoppard's dialogue is agile and funny, and beautifully played by John Stride and Edward Petherbridge, who make the most of their dramatist's characterisation of the couple as a sort of Holmes/Watson double act, one dashing ahead (if in no direction he wishes to travel) and the other lagging doggedly behind. Derek Goldby's direction is varied in pace and texture, introducing (metaphorically and literally) as much light and shade as possible into the text. Desmond Heeley's Victorian-Jacobean costumes and mouldering Fonthillgothick sets are stunningly glamorous. In short, everything is done to make the most of the play and bring out its best.

The result is, undeniably, a quite interesting, unusual evening in the theatre. It suffers, like so much Theatre of the Absurd, from the law of diminishing returns: more and more energy is devoted to saying less and less, until finally the observation on the characters and, more broadly, on life which the play offers seems a very small mouse to emerge from such an imposing mountain. Or to a theatregoer used to this sort of play it seems so. We recognise the pattern and procedure at once, and from then on the play can hold few surprises except conceivably in what it says. But, as I say, to audiences for whom the dramatist's procedures themselves are novel and exciting, the ultimate effect will no doubt be very different. If *Hay Fever, The Master Builder* and *Much Ado About Nothing* are usually your mark in the theatre, you will find *Rosencrantz and Guildenstern are Dead* an intriguing and probably an enjoyable experience. If you know your way round Beckett and early Pinter, not to mention a shoal of minor followers, you will be likely to find the road Rosencrantz and Guildenstern follow to dusty death all too familiar and uneventful to be worth travelling for a whole evening.

OCTOBER
1967

Terson's Yobs

Benedict Nightingale reviews
Zigger Zagger *at the Jeannetta Cochrane*

Zigger Zagger is quite an achievement: it works as a piece of theatre, and it palpably works as a piece of youth theatre. A whole battalion of NYT seemed to be on the stage, row on row of them, swaying, singing, bawling, waving rattles, and all with perfect timing, like a Nuremberg rally of dwarfs and pubescents. I've stood in the Kop at Everton myself, at the time when the bottle-throwing and rowdyism was supposed to be particularly desperate; but the cheerful, ragged blustering and cursing I witnessed there had little in common with the disciplined ferocity at the Jeannetta Cochrane. Sitting in the stalls, you felt rather like Ibsen's Master Builder, old, vulnerable, and about to be overrun by a storming new generation.

This piece confirms the growing reputation of its author, Peter Terson, the shock-headed, fuzzy-haired games teacher from Newcastle-on-Tyne. For one thing, he writes about youth, and potentially delinquent youth at that, in the most unpatronising way possible. The middle-class is inclined to talk dismissively of 'yobs', meaning roughly the pimply male adolescents who, though generally quite inarticulate, prove capable of occasional excruciating vowel sounds and look capable of all kinds of petty violence, from pushing old ladies off buses to ripping the ears off small boys' teddy bears. That's the yob's public image; and Nigel Humphries, mooching sullenly about in a black leather jacket and plunging from major to minor with adenoidal insensitivity, seems to confirm its truth. But Terson won't let the matter rest here. His ear is in the dance hall, his nose in the gymnasium, his eye firmly on his chosen subject: he *knows* it isn't as simple as that, and, in his natural, unaffected style, suggests that 'yobs' have much the same affections, hopes and fears as captains of men.

Humphries plays Harry Philton: a performance at once thoughtful, questioning and technically assured. Harry is a horrible failure in school, the sort of boy who makes teachers write to the Minister of Education begging him not to raise the leaving age to 16. Not a bully or a thief or a wild homosexual; just totally uninterested in (as they tell him) taking anything out or putting anything in. 'I taught him fractions and eventually got him to grasp decimals,' moans the maths master, 'but by the time he knew the decimals he'd forgotten the fractions.' His real absorption is the local soccer team, the Reds. He has what journalists call football fever; and Terson is prepared to defend the exhilaration he finds in the game against the dry headmasters, the didactic youth officers, the pundits, abstracters and generalisers. He, Terson, suspects all those who theorise about youth and all those who construct theories of not theorising about youth. That betokens a lack of respect for the individual, and Terson is pressingly aware of individual character; it means that the observing eye is wavering from the subject in question. But Peter Terson is far from being the kind of messy romantic who thinks we should let life spill where it wants and worship what we find of it: he is prepared to make some grudging obeisance to society. His Harry rips up bus seats, scraps with the police and appears regularly before the beaks, not because he's bitter or vicious, but because of the fever: life itself engenders an excitement which finds momentary expression in watching a game which, in turn, lifts that excitement to a pitch that can't be stilled at the honk of a policeman's whistle. Society doesn't offer much in the way of 'creative outlets', so poor, inarticulate Harry becomes, in his clumsy, doggy way, mildly asocial; and yet, at the same time, a sense of dissatisfaction and responsibility begins to grow. Should he follow Zigger Zagger, the Reds' cheerleader, a Pan-ish tearaway who believes in living now and paying never – or his sister and brother-in-law, respectable, steady and moderate in all things? It's a conflict, loner versus in-group, at the centre of all Terson's work, *The Mighty Reservoy* (successful recently in London), *A Night to Make the Angels Weep* (seen there, unnoticed, two years ago) and *All Honour Mr Todd* (successful at Stoke-on-Trent). And when Harry decides to join Them, and becomes an apprentice, it isn't because Terson has unfairly manhandled the scales to weigh against football and fever. Zigger Zagger has a lithe, animal appeal, especially in Anthony May's performance; and Michael Croft's direction ensures that we don't miss the excitement of the field and terrace.

No, if anything, he is less than fair to the faction that wins, the good traders and suburbanites. They water plastic flowers, plant stone gnomes, quote the *Readers' Digest*, admire Peter Scott ducks. The Laughing Cavalier, and every neo-Pooterism in the bourgeois concordance. The faults of the play are bits of pat caricature, like these, a tendency towards overstatement and verbosity, and Brechtian songs that flop drably out of the informal bustle of scenes. The virtues are the bustle, the sense of life, the observation, the obvious intelligence of the author and the quite remorseless energy of the bounding demons onstage.

1967 Awards

voted for by the London Theatre critics

Best new play: *Rosencrantz and Guildenstern Are Dead* by Tom Stoppard
Best new musical: *Fiddler on the Roof*
Best performance by an actor: Laurence Olivier in *Dance of Death*
Best performance by an actress: Irene Worth in *Heartbreak House*
Most promising actor: John Shepherd in *The Restoration of Arnold Middleton*
Most promising actress: Estelle Kohler as Juliet
Best production: Michael Croft's *Zigger Zugger* (National Youth Theatre)
Best designer: Ralph Koltai for *Little Murders* and *As You Like It*

Two winning performances: Olivier's the Captain, left, and, above, with Robert Stephens and Geraldine McEwan in *The Dance of Death* for the National Theatre; and, overleaf Shepherd's Arnold Middleton in David Storey's Royal Court play

229

As 1968 begins, a backward glance at 1967. The London theatre critics vote for the play, musical, performances, production and set that most impressed them in the year that is over. Only in the best production category was the voting inconclusive and an editorial casting vote required. This went to Michael Croft's production of *Zigger Zagger* with the National Youth Theatre rather than to Derek Goldby's *Rosencrantz and Guildenstern are Dead* and the production by Joseph Chaikin and Jacques Levy of *America Hurrah!* which also collected two votes apiece from the critics. All three were truly remarkable productions but it was felt that Croft's was, perhaps, the most remarkable for having been achieved with amateur actors. *Rosencrantz and Guildenstern are Dead,* however, was voted the Best Play of the year with Tom Stoppard receiving eight of the 13 votes. *Fiddler on the Roof* with ten votes emerged as the year's Best New Musical. Laurence Olivier and Irene Worth were voted Actor and Actress of the year for their performances in *Dance of Death* and *Heartbreak House* with eight votes each. The most promising performances from an actor and actress were felt to be John Shepherd's in *The Restoration of Arnold Middleton* and Estelle Kohler as Juliet at Stratford-on-Avon with six votes for Shepherd and four for Kohler. Ralph Koltai, who collected votes for his sets of *Little Murders* at the Aldwych and *As You Like It* at the Old Vic, was the Designer of the Year.

1968

The year of the Sorbonne riots in Paris leading to the return of an increased Gaullist majority in France was also the year Nixon became President of the USA. Martin Luther King was assassinated in Tennessee and Robert Kennedy was killed in Los Angeles.

London Bridge was sold to the States for £2.4 million and London theatre continued to attract the international spotlight with new plays ranging from Peter Luke's Hadrian The Seventh *to Osborne's* The Hotel in Amsterdam. *The Lord Chamberlain's censorship of stage plays in Britain came to an end in time for the London presentation of the rock musical,* Hair.

Peter Brook

talking to Frank Cox about Seneca's Oedipus *which he directed at the Old Vic for the National Theatre*

Peter Brook agreed to talk about his production of *Oedipus* a couple of weeks before its opening at the Old Vic. We met in the National Theatre office-huts at the back of Waterloo after a long day of rehearsal. Geoffrey Reeves, working with Brook on this, his first venture at the NT, was also present. I asked, with apology for the inevitability of the question, how Brook's celebrated declaration of antipathy to Classical drama a few years back squared with this present project.

BROOK: I've never been interested in the second-hand experience. To take a simple example, it's always a great or fairly great composer writing music for a play, because when you are watching a play you learn the language of that particular evening, and then when the music comes in you are asked to make a mental adjustment – this is a different experience, a second-hand one. The language of another culture must be a secondary language and so in some way removed from us. When the knife goes into the stomach it is the knife of the House of Atreus entering the gilded stomach of Clytemnestra . . . it's spurious, ridiculously superficial and unimportant but it happens . . . we put up a barrier; nobody welcomes the direct experience in the theatre, so the barrier is entertained. And so, in revulsion from this we go to the immediate, to Vietnam, say. There's a ridiculous paradox in the reaction to a play like *The Royal Hunt of the Sun*, for instance – that has, unmistakably, the theme of genocide, yet the audience, to a lady, says, 'Isn't it lovely!' In *US* we deal with genocide in Vietnam, but if you go back twenty-five years to Auschwitz – well, it would be possible, I think, to stage *Arturo Ui* so that it would seem 'lovely' from this distance. When we were doing *US* we tried thinking back to *Oh What a Lovely War* and the first thing that happened was that the face lit up at the recollection; the first response is that it was 'lovely', and it's only after that that you remember it was, say, disturbing or depressing. The topical is powerful, the immediate effect of the topical is *intense*. With something as remote as Oedipus it has the insulation of the Classic – it happened so long ago that all the barriers are up.

REEVES: There was a moment last night at the Festival Hall – a Stockhausen concert – and after the music one of the musicians was moving off the platform and he bumped into a cymbal and made a crash, and the audience cheered, you remember?

BROOK: That's right, it was after a part of the performance, and the audience was affected by the music. If it had happened before the concert they would probably just have laughed and then stopped, but as it was there was the beginnings of a real elation, a great roar, before they realised that it was inconceivable, and then it froze. It was a powerful piece and the barriers were, for the moment, lowered.

We were working for an audience all the time; not always the audience that wants the kind of theatrical experience that audiences tend to want. Of course we hope that the audience will buy what we're offering – we'd be very depressed if they didn't buy it at all – but we're making something that has a use.

I've been quoted as saying that I'm more easily bored by Shakespeare than by any other author. Certainly I don't support the fallacy that even in a bad performance of Shakespeare his brilliance will carry it through. For me, the worse the performance, the worse he seems. And what I loathed about the Classics was reading the Greeks in the sort of version we have to read them in, because all I got from them was the crust of Gilbert Murray and vases.

REEVES: One thing about this play is that the amount of information in a speech is much greater than in a modern work. You have to make the effort of peeling the onion to get to the material.

BROOK: And it's only if you get to the material that you're on to something. If you only touch an electric wire on the outside you don't get a shock.

REEVES: The line here is terribly narrow. This is a play that can only please entirely or not at all. For instance it's possible to play *Hamlet* for a schools' matinée, just playing the thriller aspect, and you're still doing the play some justice. Then in the evening, to a different audience, you can go deeper, using the same text. But this is like the second act of *US*, where there was no opportunity of putting your foot down.

BROOK: It's full of fantastic levels of meaning which are sometimes not possible to present. The very nature of the theatrical experience is submerged most of the time, because few people want to ask questions. You can't blame audiences – they go to the theatre as a critic does, to a bit of this, a bit of that, and one night they find themselves at a Greek play. Brecht describes it as a social utility, this need just to go to the theatre. And the last people to know why they are going are theatre people themselves. When you ask why anybody has chosen to do a Classical play you get swept away rapidly into the realms of 'what good parts, aren't they?' and Heritage and the British Museum!

What in particular is Seneca's Oedipus *about then, I asked.*

BROOK: This play, which to all appearances is as Classical as any, seems to present the stuff of the material *most* directly. It comes straight from its time with extraordinary directness – it's as if a document were to be found in Rome which gave us the story of the Gospel at first hand without using the familiar words. It's not historical in the terms that Greek drama is – not full of references to mythologic lore. Rather in the way that *Prometheus* can communicate today through the notion of Man chained to a rock, without one's having a knowledge of the legend itself, so there's a chance that the specific quality of the Oedipus story will come over on its own. If you like, in the way that *Godot* made an impact in San Quentin! In a way, because *Oedipus* seems so related to the theme of evasion, we're really going straight on from the Vietnam thing!

In the poor Miller-Loeb translation which I read the Chorus passages drag on at some length, extolling Bacchus and considering the Icarus legend with little apparent connection with the central problems of the play, but rather as showpieces for Seneca's stoic philosophising and flamboyant powers of rhetoric. How, I asked, did this fit into Brook's view of the 'directness' of the writing?

BROOK: The Choruses have been reworked to some extent in this adaptation, which has been done by Ted Hughes. The translation was the work of a BBC man, David Anthony Turner, who sent it to the Third Programme . . .

REEVES: Which, incredibly, turned it down, despite the fact that,

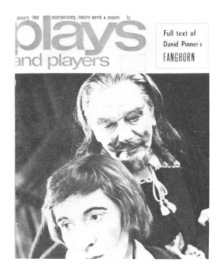

January 1968 incorporating theatre world & encore

plays
and players

Full text of
David Pinner's
FANGHORN

february 1968   incorporating theatre world & encore   4s

plays
and players

Full text of
CLIMB THE
GREASED POLE
by Vincent Longhi

as far back as in 1927 Eliot described the play as 'broadcast drama'. So he then sent it to Tynan.

BROOK: Turner's translation is a singular achievement – he's put it back into almost Hemingway prose, revealing that a hard, crisp play is there, giving the key to how it could be approached, and it's this version that Hughes has used to produce our present text. The central image is the interest, and the only thing that sustains the play is the word. Without the word there is nothing. But we haven't come round full circle – Beckett talks about the theatre as 'specific tensions'.

REEVES: He shows Winnie, an ordinary woman facing the ordinary problems of waking up and getting up, but he puts her up to her waist in sand.

BROOK: Probably very few lines of Beckett would mean anything at all, pulled out of context, yet it's those lines that support the plays. Seneca was not writing for the stage; his plays were declaimed, so include descriptions of action that would be impossible to create in naturalistic terms. For instance, there is a blood-curdling sacrifice of a white bull and a heifer, related by Tiresias and his daughter, Manto, in picturesque detail.

I asked how about problems in staging?

BROOK: The violent action in the play – it recalls the violence of Artaud – can only be presented through words spoken publicly. Declamation and rhetoric can have many meanings. Tiresias and Manto can only stand on the stage, but they allow a torrent of physical action to present itself through public speaking. It's similar to the Noh theatre, where the actor chants for twenty-five minutes and you're aware of the action unfolding. Well, we are declaiming.

REEVES: But it's not like a poetry reading.

BROOK: I suppose someone will say, 'They're trying a new gimmick now, everyone standing still!' But it's not different from the movement in, say, the *Marat/Sade*, there's just as much action, but through the word.

No, it's true there's little differentiation of character in Seneca's text, but the trap would be in trying to remedy this. If we try to bring action or character to it, we destroy it. Instead there are other qualities to be examined, technical wonders like the point at which he puts into an unbroken sequence two straight cinematic cuts; as brutal as a Godard jump-cut, the scene and the circumstances simply change twice to suit the flow of the action, within a single speech.

It's interesting that, just at the moment, there seems to be a revival of interest in Seneca on the Continent too – Barrault does the *Medea*, Roger Blin the *Thyestes* – because the original impact of the man's writing managed to influence at the same time two opposite extremes – the French Classics, like Racine, and, in contrast, the Elizabethans, to whom we're swinging right back in the current theatre.

Lawrence wrote eight plays, and all of them, even the disconcertingly lush and grandiloquent Old Testament epic, *David*, deserve attention. Their historical importance is pretty obvious: where else in our early twentieth century drama do we find any comparably intelligent attempt to deal with personal relationships onstage? Shaw? Too facetious, too glibly cynical. Galsworthy, then? Thin and predictable; didactic, too. Lawrence doesn't seek to impose any preconceived meaning on his plays. Rather, they are in the fullest sense of that overworked adjective, exploratory. All his energy goes into observing human conflict, comprehending and trying to explain it, as much (you feel) for his own peace of mind as for his audience's pleasure. And even if he does fight shy of social conclusions, his worst plays invariably penetrate closer to the heart of things than Galsworthy's best. Indeed, any purported conclusion or 'message' would probably seem pat, inappropriate, given the doubts and wonderings and complexities that emerge from the investigation. The plays are impressive for their refusal to pin down characters for approval, parody or condemnation. There are no villains and no heroes, no fools and certainly no wise men: only a number of people, usually rather self-righteous and invariably maladroit, trying to sort out the problems they continue to create for one another. There is continual action, reaction and re-reaction: they are the least static plays one could imagine.

In short, they are tremendously alive; and Peter Gill's triple production at the Royal Court has captured both new subtlety and new vigour. The three plays he's chosen are all set in Nottinghamshire mining country. The wives draw hot water in long ladles from the heavy black stove, and the miners sprawl over the kitchen table in their pit-dirt. The cottage is warm, neat, respectable and comfortable in a maroon-brocaded, heavy-furnitured, stolid, mahoganied sort of way. Labour troubles may loom outside, but it is far from being the stark place that Galsworthy, too remote and sheltered to avoid middle-class sensationalism, visualised in *Strife*.

Lawrence knows his miners, and their voices too: 'whoam' for home and 'dunna' for don't, words like 'sluthering' and 'chunterer', proverb and counter-proverb.

'Marriage is like a mousetrap for either man or woman. You've soon come to the end of the cheese.'

'Ay, but ha'f a loaf is better than no bread.'

The language is straightforward and resilient; even the clichés have a freshness. It all adds up to a sense of place rare in British drama and considerably greater than in those plays in which Lawrence elects to do his human excavation outside Notts, whether in England, Italy or ancient Israel. I don't think Peter Gill and his associates could have chosen better than *A Collier's Friday Night*, *The Daughter-in-Law* and *The Widowing of Mrs Holroyd*.

These plays have other characteristics in common, too. Their older women tend to be formidable, dominant; their young women have some of the same strength, and intelligence to boot. Neither wives nor mothers have much respect for pitmen and butties, and their husbands and sons are well aware of it. That is why they, the men, are so often so inarticulately angry. That is why they strike the table, like Holroyd, and bellow 'What? What?'

On the Coal Face

Benedict Nightingale reviews the D. H. Lawrence season at the Royal Court

Victor Henry, Michael Coles and Judy Parfitt in *The Daughter-in-Law* directed by Peter Gill

at the mere whiff of an insult. 'I'm not a fool!' they reiterate, knowing quite well that they are, at least by comparison. It is only brute force that gives them any advantage over their women, and the more they use it or threaten to use it the more the women despise them, and the more essentially emasculated the men become in turn. Even the cleverer men don't escape. Most of them have been effectively castrated by their mothers. It is a sad, sad business.

Again and again one's reminded of *Sons and Lovers*, the problems of the Morels and of the Lawrences themselves: and in play after play Lawrence puts these problems in a different perspective, views them in a fresh light. This isn't to imply that the plays are the least repetitive. I, and I think the whole audience with me, was held by them to the point of, childishly, wishing they wouldn't end. They would be better described as complementary. If you've seen one, you're likely to appreciate the next one the more for it. Best, really, to insist on seeing all three.

A Collier's Friday Night is the earliest (1906) and the simplest. Mother lives only for her children, the daughter a pert school-teacher, the son a university student and an embryo D. H. Lawrence. She's uncomfortably jealous of her boy's girlfriend and barely on snarling terms with her husband, a grumbling old crosspatch who shambles truculently around the house, a palpable gate-crasher determined to prove that he's really the host. It may be that Lawrence's dislike of his own father did in fact affect his judgment for the first (and I think, only) time in his playwright's career. The stage directions include implacable phrases like 'in a tone of brutal authority' and 'he speaks disagreeably'; but John Barrett's performance has the dignity to correct any imbalance, win him the guarded sympathy his situation merits. And this is achieved without any evident distortion: whatever the stage directions, however Lawrence may huff and puff on the periphery, the lines are judicious and true. The man isn't altogether at fault; it is clearly the Mrs Morels who make the Morels what they are.

Nothing much happens, true, but, so intrinsically interesting is the situation, so deftly is it treated, it hardly matters. The other two plays bring more plot to approximately the same framework. In *The Daughter-in-Law* (1912) mother still has her emotional hooks firmly fixed in her sons, one a gay scallywag of a bachelor, the other, Luther, unhappily married to a young woman cleverer than himself. Luther is an amiable man, capable of a slow, deep anger that builds up impressively in Michael Coles's performance – a difficult part since he must be both the over coddled child and the harried, resentful husband; a mouse in the process of becoming a Morel. Surprisingly, this is the most mellow, and perhaps the best, of the three plays. Certainly, it's the only one in which anything approaching a reconciliation takes place. I say 'anything approaching', because Lawrence doesn't understate the marital conflict or suggest that it won't recur again later. Indeed, he actually seems to find some hope in the intensity of it – even in the dramatically startling incident in which Luther, enraged, thrusts £90 worth of his wife's possessions into the fire. This marriage, he suggests, ought to endure.

The Widowing of Mrs Holroyd (1914) is a much bleaker piece of work, for all the ebullience of its first act. It begins with Holroyd, tipsy as usual, bringing home a couple of frowsy ladies he's met in the pub (though it should be said that Lawrence, characteristically, treats even them with a certain wry sympathy). It ends with him dead, suffocated in the pit, lying in his grime on the cottage floor, while the wife, who couldn't bear him alive, laments his passing in words that are painful and unnerving to hear, every one the authentic language of intolerable stress: 'Oh my dear, I can't bear it my dear – you shouldn't have done it. The children's father – my dear . . .' Between the two events, we have witnessed their relationship crumble apart. And so strong is her contempt for him, and so angrily does he respond to it, that there is really no alternative but that one or the other should die. Divorce, mooted by a young admirer of Mrs Holroyd, would be a kind of fraud: one can't believe that emotions so intense could be subject to a merely judicial solution. One can't imagine the Holroyds content with any separating.

The simple fact is that, like all Lawrence's married couples, they are unable to leave each other alone. The men cling to the bitches, the women to the bastards: somehow, in spite of themselves, they have to do so. Nothing else matters much. The choice, then, is a necessarily fraught and instable *modus vivendi*, as in *The Daughter-in-Law* or a battle to the death, as in *Mrs Holroyd*. There is no third way.

Thus the trilogy offers one a better understanding of Lawrence's own upbringing. We have the family situation simply stated for

what it is in the *Collier;* and then we get, in effect, two different attempts to explain the nature of his parents' early relationship. Indeed, the trilogy should help the reader to a better appreciation of Lawrence as a novelist. It is genuinely seminal. But there are half-a-dozen more immediate, less discreet reasons for going to the Royal Court. Anne Dyson, solid, strong, formidably rigorous, as the older mother in all three plays; Judy Parfitt, afire with repressed passions, part coquette, part embryo tragic heroine, as the younger wife in the last two; Michael Coles (again) sullen and ferocious as Holroyd in the last of all. The acting generally has an emotional togetherness – to borrow a phrase from Lawrence himself – rare on the British stage. There are no passengers; and that, in itself, is a sort of triumph.

1968

Ich Bin Ein Berliner

Frank Marcus reviews Cabaret *at the Palace*

The framework of the musical *Cabaret* is a stroke of genius. A *conferencier*, or Master of Ceremonies, bids the audience welcome with a song sung in three languages: 'Wilkommen, Bienvenu, welcome'. The setting is a glittering, garish night-spot in the Berlin of 1929–1930. There are table telephones to encourage illicit assignations, a ladies' orchestra, and the Kit Kat Girls, clad in leather pants, transparent aprons, long suspenders and, occasionally, wild and outrageously tasteless headgear, striking suggestive poses and looking like illustrations from a fetishists' catalogue. The MC resembles a ventriloquist's doll designed by Georg Grosz: tiny and white-faced, with rouged cheeks, wearing a waistcoat of pink silk with sparkling adornments, and carrying a cane. He moves sinuously, leers exaggeratedly, and sings vibrantly and beguilingly of the pleasures of sexual unorthodoxy. He is freakish, mesmeric, and slightly sinister: the presiding deity at an orgy. As a symbol of his time, he is more than valid: he is unforgettable. In one number, he extols the joys of living in a *ménage à trois*, practically tying himself in knots with two girls. It is a song of irresistible gaiety. In another number, he partners a gorilla in a *tutu*. In yet another, the girls embody different international currencies and the MC *plays* them: they have miniature drums in their bra and a tiny gong dangling from their crotch. And once he goes into drag and joins the chorus line.

The conception and treatment of these cabaret scenes is immensely subtle. The decadence of pre-Hitler Berlin was not a mortal disease, or even a symptom of one, but a last heroic act of defiance. Sex is the most personal and private expression of individuality and the open derisive flouting of accepted social mores is always an act of anarchism. The political cabarets were high on Hitler's black list, but they continued their subversive function right through the 'thirties. Small gestures of insolence assumed revolutionary proportions. There was a comedian, well-known for his liberal sympathies, who walked on to the stage with his right arm extended in the Hitler salute. The audience gasped. Then he turned his palm upwards and observed genially: 'It's raining'. You may think this very mild, but the story spread through Berlin like wildfire. I was too young to experience the

Three scenes from the first London *Cabaret*
with Judi Dench as Sally Bowles

Berlin of Isherwood, but I have a precise appreciation of its tone. My home was full of gramophone records of the period, of bound volumes of *Stachelschwein* and other literary journals, of books by Tucholsky, and of the plays of Brecht and his circle. Above all – like recollections of carnival during Lent – there were the reminiscences of my parents of the glamorous golden days before Hitler, many of them concerning the great artists of the *Kabarett*.

But this musical is more than a recreation or a pastiche. It hides behind a cunning alibi – 'it's not *our* decadence, folks, it's that of Berlin' – but it doesn't fool me. New York, with its violence in the streets and its despairing passion about Vietnam, is extraordinarily similar in atmosphere to Berlin during the last days of the Weimar republic. And, as so often happens, a corroding society has brought a flowering of the arts. The extreme explorations of the artists of Greenwich Village, and their escape into drugged fantasy, makes old Berlin seem like a Boy Scouts' outing. This added dimension – a tribute of one decadent city to another – gives *Cabaret* its poignancy. It implies that decadence is an expression of freedom, and I believe this to be true.

The menace of Nazism is treated with similar subtlety. The waiters sing a seemingly innocuous patriotic song in falsetto harmony. Repeated later, the mild ditty turns slowly into a fanatical hymn of hate. The brilliantly effective framework is (or should be) used to set off the central story of Sally Bowles, the madcap English girl who finds fulfilment in this crazy place. Here, alas, compromise sets in with a vengeance. This isn't Isherwood's Sally, or even John van Druten's. Memories of Dorothy Tutin and Michael Gwynn in *I Am A Camera* are a nagging reminder of what might have been. I was told in New York that the producer of *Cabaret* banished Herr Issyvoo with the remark: 'We gotta put balls on the guy. If he shacks up with the girl, he's gotta sleep with her!' True or false, the fact remains that Isherwood has been turned into an unsuccessful American novelist, Cliff Bradshaw by name, who behaves like Gary Cooper in his early films and is anxious to give Sally's unborn child – *his* child – a name. He departs sulking when Sally uses her white fur coat to pay for an abortion.

It is almost beyond belief that artists of the calibre of Harold Prince (producer) and Joe Masteroff (author) should have seen fit to reduce the fascinating brother-and-sister relationship of Isherwood and Sally to that of a boring and commonplace *affaire*. Contrary to their purpose, they have succeeded in emasculating the story. It would have been more merciful to have rechristened Sally Bowles 'Millie Robinson' and have done with it. It is all the more disappointing (and wasteful) because in Judi Dench they have an actress more than capable of playing the original Sally. Even allowing for the diminished character, she has some fine moments. She sings well; the title-song, in particular, is projected with great feeling. She isn't really the right build for the flapper period – I envisage Sally all saucer-eyes and elbows – and she lacks the frenetic gaiety. Towards the end, she communicates disillusion and pain most movingly. My own feeling is that she should be more, not less, frenetically gay at the end, but that's a question of interpretation. I intend no disparagement by saying that, songs apart, she is best when passive: observing, watching other people and listening to them. This is the iron test of good acting. On the whole, Judi Dench has too much warmth and intelligence for the Sally of *Cabaret*.

The other major innovation – not quite so destructive – concerns the landlady's suitor, Herr Schultz. I don't remember any Jewish greengrocers in Berlin but, anyway, this character is conceived as the equivalent of an owner of a Bagel shop in Brooklyn; in other words, he is a sop to the vast Jewish audience of Broadway. His solo, 'Meeskite', is an excellent but totally irrelevant sortie into the territory of Yiddish humour. Peter Sallis has a good stab at it, and manages to be both squashed and lithe. He partners Lila Kedrova, who plays the landlady, Fräulein Schneider. She is fey rather than tough and seems to be forever exiting. Their inhibited love scenes – including a very silly song about the gift of a pineapple – recall Canon Chasuble and Miss Prism. They are not evocative of Berlin.

There are good performances from Pamela Strong as a whore with a heart of swastikas, and from Richard Owens as a Nazi of an early vintage. Needless to say, Barry Dennen, as the MC, walks away with the show. For the record: he doesn't (and couldn't) equal Joel Grey in New York, who is not only one of the greatest artists I have ever seen but also made the first ten minutes of the show into the kind of experience that leaves one with tears in one's eyes, electric shudders running down one's spine, hair standing on end, and generally limp from shock and incredulity. Nevertheless, he gives a most accomplished and creative performance. For some inexplicable reason, the last line of his gorilla song, '. . . she isn't a meeskite at all' has been turned into 'she doesn't look Jewish at all'. This seems to associate the cabarets with anti-Semitism. It makes nonsense of the basic conception of the show and is a slur not on Jews but on the cabarets of pre-Hitler Berlin. It is extremely offensive and should be changed back at once.

Visually, musically and choreographically, *Cabaret* is superb. Boris Aronson's scenery incorporates tilted mirrors, to reflect the tinsel and glow of the cabaret setting, with lighted windows and an iron spiral staircase to give a sense of environment; Patricia Zipprodt's costumes are high camp at its best; the music (John Kander), brilliantly orchestrated, raises pastiche to the level of art, although some of the songs are perhaps too derivative of Kurt Weill (accentuated in New York by being sung by Lotte Lenya); the lyrics (Fred Ebb) have the authentic mixture of romanticism and disillusion; the dances devised by Ronald Field allow the girls – extremely well contrasted, by the way – to prance about with the appropriate look of deadpan impertinence; lastly, Harold Prince's direction is as impeccable here as in New York. The good things in *Cabaret* are great. The bad ones bring one near to despair. To say that I was in two minds about some of it is the understatement of the year: I left the theatre a manic-depressive. There is, however, no question in my mind that, taken as a whole, *Cabaret* is the most exciting musical I have ever seen. Of course, mine is a special case. *Cabaret* reminded me that, after thirty years, I still carry a spiritual identity card, inscribed 'ich bin ein Berliner'.

Anger, Twelve Years On

Martin Esslin reviews Time Present *at the Royal Court*

It is eery, how history closes the circle: twelve years to the month after Osborne's *Look Back in Anger* opened the new era of British drama, the curtain rises at the self-same spot to reveal his latest play *Time Present*; and what does the curtain reveal? The exact replica of that elegant drawing room set, those elegant uppercrust characters, that creaking exposition, that corny, melodramatic plot that were the birthright and the bane of the kind of dreary play which *Look Back in Anger* was supposed to have finished off once and for all time. And what is more: the angry young man whose wit struck terror into the ranks of the philistines now releases a flood of jokes directed against teenagers, the avant garde, hippies, happenings, action painters, artistic experimenters and appeals to those sectors of his audience who nod approvingly when the characters with whom they identify on the stage hold forth about high taxation and Parliament spending their well-earned money, who bellow with laughter when someone mentions some progressive fool who goes around with coloured gentlemen who are 'very New Statesman', and refers to Italians as 'wogs'. Thus do the angry young men of 1956 turn into the Edwardian high Tories of 1968, the iconoclasts of yesteryear into the satisfied upholders of established values of today. *Time Present* is an interesting play, interesting as a symptom of our return into what might become an era of neo-Victorian values, interesting above all as a milestone in the development of its author who, after daring but unsuccessful forays into foreign parts – the wicked wastes of Central Europe, the torrid passions of Lope de Vega's Spain – has returned to the pastures with which he is most familiar: his own milieu. Only that this milieu is no longer the provincial bed-sitter of *Look Back in Anger*, the seaside landlady's digs of *The Entertainer*, but the world of highly successful actors and actresses who hobnob with junior lady ministers and loll in leather armchairs in Chelsea or Kensington.

After an exposition both highly traditional and clumsy – a mother telling her own daughter about her first and second marriage and the past of her stepsister, with a wealth of names hard to remember and relationships impossible to disentangle – we are introduced to the protagonists: the elder daughter of that self-same mother, Pamela (Jill Bennett) an actress who has left her own house after parting with her man with whom she shared it and is now staying with a lady politician, Constance (Katharine Blake). Constance and Pamela seem to have little in common. Constance is intellectual and left-wing, Pamela is emotional and high-Tory in her views; Constance is active, Pamela contemplative; no wonder they are constantly quarrelling with each other. And yet, and yet . . . on a deeper level there is an attraction, a bond between them. We wonder what it might be . . . Pamela's father, her mother's first husband, is a great actor Knight, Sir Gideon Orme, and he is lying on his death-bed in hospital. The mother and the daughters are taking it in turns to watch by his bedside. This situation creates its own suspense: will the great man survive? It also provides an opportunity for occasional dips into his scrap book with quaint quotations from old plays, which will drive tears of nostalgia up the nostrils of the dowagers in the orchestra stalls, echoes of Henry Ainley and Godfrey Tearle. What used to be the stuff of savage satire in *The Entertainer* has

become a fruitful source of sentiment in *Time Present*. Occasionally as Pamela and Constance bicker, the telephone rings; will it bring news of Sir Gideon? Not yet. But we know the news must surely come as Act One ends. And so it does; so, indeed, it does . . . The great man is no more.

Act Two opens with Pamela's mother and teenage half-sister (who only exist for exposition's sake it seems) acquainting us with the fact that several weeks have passed and that we are on the morning of the Memorial Service for dear Sir Gideon. Pamela has not been there – she loved her father too much to attend an occasion at which knighted actors read the lessons and everyone who is anything in the theatre puts in an appearance. Also, she is worried: for believe it or not, Pamela is pregnant, pregnant by Murray, the television personality and budding playwright of genius, who is Constance's recognised lover and who puts in a brief and colourless appearance towards the end of Act One. Murray overhears Pamela enquiring about the addresses of abortionists, he is ready to break the news to Constance that he loves

Katherine Blake and Jill Bennett in Osborne's *Time Present*

his Pamela, but Pamela will have none of it. She tells Murray that she does not love him. But – are we detecting a slight trembling in her voice, as she makes this declaration, could it be that she wants to prevent her dear friend Constance from being so terribly hurt? Could it be? We shall never know. All we do know is that Pamela arranges with her agent, Jewish and a homosexual to boot, that she will move in with him for the time being, that she suddenly is pretty brusque and rude to Constance, that she even pretends that Murray's play (which we know she *loved*) is bad, no, worse than that, vulgar! and that she departs, leaving Constance alone at the telephone, urging Murray to come and console her, which he apparently promises to do. As the lights dim, we even guess he tells Constance on the phone that he loves *her*. So Pamela's self-sacrifice *has* worked, she has saved Constance from the loss of the man she holds so dear . . .

Where in this moving and worthy melodramatic plot, compared to which the plots of Somerset Maugham and Noël Coward are cynical avant garde stuff, and even Rattigan and Douglas-Home positively modern and 'with it', where in all this are we to find John Osborne? No fear, he is there all right: in the wit of the invective, the restlessness and self-disgust which streams out of Pamela with the same energy and force with which they poured out of Bill Maitland in *Inadmissible Evidence*. The real Osborne can also clearly be seen in the three wickedly well observed show-business characters on the fringe of the action: Abigail, the politically committed fey actress, Edward, the younger star actor who recently had his nose improved and appears in one major film epic per year, and the homosexual actors' agent, Bernard. These portraits may be unfair, but they *are* very diverting.

There is a hint of the true power of Osborne also in the central theme of the play: the latent, supressed, subconscious Lesbian relationship between the two women which they do not want, or do not know how to face, and which drives them to alleviating spasms of hostility and attraction. But, alas, this really fascinating subject for a play is barely developed, as though the author did not quite have the courage to confront it head-on. Melodramatic plot-device like Pamela's pregnancy, militates against such a confrontation, for it is as mechanical and contrived as the traditional mislaid letter in Victorian melodrama. It is this which forces him into the superficial similarity with that genre that is the most surprising feature of the play, as though Pamela's affair with Constance's lover were not, in itself, enough to focus the issue and drive it into the open. There is also the almost total absence of personality in that lover (it is not helped by a colourless performance by the actor in the part, but seems to me inherent in the text) which makes him into a mere cipher. But there is a real theme of great interest and potential tragic force in the situation of homosexuals who simply do not have the courage to face their own nature and are therefore driven into endless shallow and unsatisfactory heterosexual love affairs. Jill Bennett, in the part of Pamela, gives a performance of such depth and virtuosity that she almost succeeds in forcing the play into this area of geniune tragic greatness. But, alas, she is defeated by the contrivance and indecision of the text, as well as by the weakness of some of the other performances.

If you are sitting in the stalls at the Criterion as the curtain rises on Hutchinson Scott's set for *The Real Inspector Hound* you feel suddenly misplaced, almost as if you are being tricked by *trompe l'oeil* mirrors. There you are in your cosy proscenium-style seat but, facing you, as in theatre in the round, are more seats, more shaded lights stringing another circle, surrounding a miniature stage bedecked in mock-baroque decor. It's a witty epigram on the visual tricks the mind can play when fantasy takes over – and on what is to follow. In his new comedy Tom Stoppard has one beady and amused eye trained on the theatrical banalities. The other, half-closed in a wink, is fixed on that subtle relationship between players and spectators. Where is the division between experience and actors? In a memorable display of knockabout fantasy he explores the link to its logical nightmare conclusion. Only those who don't believe in bad dreams (or the theatre) could fail to respond; although – as in *Rosencrantz and Guildenstern* – in trying to prove his point Stoppard gets saddled with a plot which is at times over-convoluted in its cleverness.

In an age of earnest happenings and the cult of the improvised, Stoppard is courageous enough to continue to cultivate the reactionary talents of the craftsman. He is a polisher and a parer in a very English tradition – the unemphatic understatement, the throwaway jokes, the menace in the humdrum – and makes his point cumulatively and with self-deceptive ease. And the fact that he also manages to be very funny indeed has, of course, brought the response that before he can be said to have proved himself, he must tackle more *angst*-ridden territory. I think it would be a great loss to our comedic heritage if he were lured away into 'more serious', psychological fields. He has admitted that it is the ideas for plays which he finds difficult (and nothing is more difficult to hit upon than a ripe idea for comedy); and when he doesn't latch on to a very good one – as in *Enter a Free Man* (a mundane, much worked-over situation) – it seems to affect his whole style.

As in *Rosencrantz and Guildenstern*, *The Real Inspector Hound* is about a couple of outsiders who are, nevertheless, essential to the action. This time they are critics – and, naturally, The Critics have said that they are an extremely unrepresentative duo. But are they? Surely the essence of good parody is to go that hair's-breadth further. Birdboot has affairs with actresses and eats chocolates. Any 'real' actress will swear to critics' passes; and if they don't actually hand out the Black Magic they often suck indigestion tablets and publicly comb their hair. Moon is a fairly typical second-string. (Incidentally what is this thing called Moon for Mr Stoppard? Already he has cropped up in a radio play, 'M is for Moon among other things', and a novel, *Lord Malquist and Mr Moon*.) He has a feeling of depressed doom that Number One will never die ('Stand-ins of the world, stand up,' he wails), and is played with sharp hopelessness and vindictiveness by Richard Briers. Shambling Birdboot (an accurately sweaty performance by Ronnie Barker) joins him as the lights go down: 'Has it started yet?' he whispers loudly staring at the corpse on the floor of the stage. 'Yes,' replies Moon. 'Are you sure?' 'It's a pause,' Moon explains. 'You can't *start* with a pause,' says the old-hand Birdboot.

Critics at Play

Helen Dawson reviews The Real Inspector Hound *at the Criterion*

Harold Hobson believes that critics never discuss the play in the interval. This can only mean that Mr Hobson never goes for a drink in the bar as this is almost all they do talk about, unless it's to repeat what they said about last week's controversial offering. This, again, is neatly parodied by Birdboot, as he shows Moon the slides of the reproduction in neon of one of his notices outside a West End theatre. As the play progresses, the two of them write their reviews aloud. Moon is the one with intellectual aspirations: 'It reminds me of Voltaire's cry – "*Voilà!*"' or 'it has *élan* while avoiding *éclat*.' This too, is exaggerated – but the truth is there: the tendency to treat each new author as though he were Ibsen, each boulevard bauble as though it emanated from the Berliner Ensemble. 'We are entitled to ask,' says Moon, 'Where is God?' Birdboot scans the programme to see if he can find out.

On the stage itself a quite appalling thriller is frolicking along merrily. Stoppard has a field-day in turning the familiar who-dunnit components into pure zany. As well as the long-ignored corpse, there's the beautiful widow. Lady Cynthia (for whom Birdboot instantly conceives a passion), her tennis-racket-armed friend Felicity (the previous object of Birdboot's lust), her crippled half-brother Major Muldoon, a depleted home-help and – on the run – a mad and handsome murderer. They all give quite terrible performances. Every time the radio is switched on there is news of fresh disasters: 'The police are combing the swamps with loud hailers shouting "Don't be mad, give yourself up . . ."' The phone rings endlessly: the first time the char helpfully replies, 'This is Lady Muldoon's drawing room, one morning in early spring'; later Birdboot mesmerically rises from his aisle seat to answer it – at the other end is his wife, anxiously checking up on him. From this moment fantasy takes over. Birdboot, finding himself on stage, accordingly pursues his new-found affection for Lady Cynthia. The play repeats itself, with the lines taking on a different meaning as critic says to actress, publicly, in mid-scene, 'We can't go on meeting like this.' In the stalls Moon blenches with embarrassment. Soon he, too, is on stage and involved. The plot takes over. As the curtain falls they are both dead. The nightmare has triumphed and it is the hour of the third-stringers. *The Real Inspector Hound* is an almost magically simple success. Where it does become over-involved and over-pointed (the thriller the first time around goes on too long), director Robert Chetwyn does a great deal to disguise the fact. For the rest, he has paced the whole production with much skill and accommodated the assortment of comedic styles into a single running strand. And, as any expert director would, he has responded fully to Stoppard's rare and fantastical ear for dialogue.

As an added bonus there is a first-class curtain-raiser, *The Audition*. First seen at the Arts in 1966 this is a well-calculated musical satire by Sean Patrick Vincent (*not,* it turns out, one and the same as the accomplished, stuttering leading actor David Baxter). Another simple idea – a threesome, responsible for a grossly ambitious musical, trying it out in miniature in front of a lethargic and money-minded impresario. 'Just tell it in your own natural way,' he dictates from the front row of the circle, as they tie themselves up in anguished knots on stage. The music and the songs are (intentionally) derivative; the pathos of the joke is not.

1968 Awards

voted for by the London Theatre critics

Best new play: *The Hotel in Amsterdam* by John Osborne
Best new musical: *Cabaret* by John Kander, Fred Ebb and Joe Masteroff
Best performance by an actor: Alec McCowen as Hadrian VII
Best performance by an actress: Jill Bennett in *Time Present*
Most promising actor: Barrie Rutter
Most promising actress: Angela Pleasence
Best Production: Peter Gill's D. H. Lawrence plays
Best designer: Boris Aronson for *Cabaret*

Two vote winners: above Osborne's *The Hotel in Amsterdam* with Paul Scofield, David Burke and Judy Parfitt; left, John Gielgud and Irene Worth in Peter Brook's National Theatre *Oedipus*

Because of a changed publication date Plays and Players took its last look at 1968 before it was quite over. This has meant that polling had to close before the London opening of *Soldiers* – though it has received one vote on the strength of a reading of the script and will be open to receive more in next year's poll. Generally the critics found it a depressing year, but came out strongly in favour of John Osborne's *The Hotel in Amsterdam* as the best play of the year with six of the potential 16 votes going to the play premièred at the Royal Court and now playing at the Duke of York's. An equal number of votes went to Alec McCowen's performance in the title-role of *Hadrian the Seventh* at the Mermaid, making it, in the critics' estimation, the best performance of the year by an actor. Best performance by an actress was considered to be that of Jill Bennett in *Time Present*, which received five votes. In the 'most promising' category the votes were most widely cast and no less than 17 names were put up by the 16 critics voting. Since one critic voted twice in this category, Barrie Rutter's performance in the National Youth Theatre's production of *The Apprentices* at the Jeannetta Cochrane Theatre emerged as the Most Promising Actor with two votes. There were also 17 votes cast in the Most Promising Actress category but with Angela Pleasence collecting six of them for her performance in *The Ha-Ha* at the Hampstead Theatre Club she firmly picked up this award. Voting was close on the year's best production with four votes going to Peter Brook's *Oedipus* for the National Theatre and six to Peter Gill for his *D. H. Lawrence* productions at the Royal Court, giving him the award for the year's best director. Boris Aronson's set for *Cabaret* which, with five votes was voted the best of the year, and the production itself was voted Best Musical.

PLAYS

Index

PLAYERS

253